Y0-GAA-172

MUSICIANS INSTITUTE™

ESSENTIAL CONCEPTS

Soloing for BASS

A Contemporary Approach to Improvising in Any Style

by Dominik Hauser

ISBN 978-1-4234-7643-6

HAL•LEONARD® CORPORATION
7777 W. BLUEMOUND RD. P.O. BOX 13819 MILWAUKEE, WI 53213

In Australia Contact:
Hal Leonard Australia Pty. Ltd.
4 Lentara Court
Cheltenham, Victoria, 3192 Australia
Email: ausadmin@halleonard.com.au

Copyright © 2010 by HAL LEONARD CORPORATION
International Copyright Secured All Rights Reserved

No part of this publication may be reproduced in any form or by any means without the prior written permission of the Publisher.

Visit Hal Leonard Online at
www.halleonard.com

Introduction

For every bassist, sooner or later the need arises for a short fill or a solo break. Until now, you've probably managed to get through these situations by playing a line that's based on a chord arpeggio or pentatonic scale. But what if your solo lasts eight measures or even longer? You'll notice that you will run out of ideas pretty fast unless you have a deeper understanding of harmony.

This book shows you all the common scale and key-center approaches that musicians use today in styles as different as rock, jazz, funk, and blues, with specific examples applied to the bass guitar. It explains the theoretical relationship between chords and scales, and demonstrates how scale substitutions and superimpositions are applied. Even though this book deals with soloing, the information you learn here can easily be applied to groove playing, and will help you become stronger and more aware as an all-around bass player. Each chapter includes backing tracks for you to play along with.

Dedication and Acknowledgments

I would like to dedicate this book to my brother Markus; keep fighting.

I would like to express my thanks to Tim Kobza, John Rosenberg, and Kurt Walther for their great playing, and Mike Aarvold for the awesome mix.

Thanks to Barrett Tagliarino for helping me with this manuscript.

All music written, arranged, and produced by Dominik Hauser.

Bass—Dominik Hauser
Guitar—Tim Kobza
Piano—John Rosenberg
Drums—Kurt Walther
Mixing Engineer—Mike Aarvold

About the Author

Born in Switzerland, Dominik Hauser was educated at Jazz School St. Gallen, where he received his master's degree in music. As composer, arranger, and bass player for the jazz-funk group the Ruleless, he was awarded the prestigious Prix Walo and performed at the Montreaux Jazz Festival. After moving to Los Angeles in 1996, he studied film scoring at UCLA and began working in the film industry. Dominik is a sought-after bass instructor at the Musicians Institute, where he teaches arranging and theory in the MI degree program, along with jazz studies and fretboard improvisation for bass. Listen to some of Dominik's compositions and find out about his latest projects at *www.hausermusic.com.*

Also Available from Dominik Hauser:

Chords for Bass (HL00695934)
Bass Blueprints (HL00696026)
Beginning Jazz Bass (HL00696191)

1 Seven Modes of the Major Scale

When you hear musicians solo over a tune, you might think that they make every note up on the spot; this is not really true. There are a lot of rules that most good improvisers follow, whether they learned them formally or by trial and error.

The most important part of soloing is knowing which notes sound good and which ones you should avoid. Understanding what key you're in is the first step in learning which notes to play. A *key* is created by the feeling that one particular note is at the center of the music; this is the note you would most likely stop on at the end of a song.

The *octave* divides into 12 steps, giving 12 possible key-center tones: C, C♯/D♭, D, D♯/E♭, E, F, F♯/G♭, G, G♯/A♭, A, A♯/B♭, and B. (C♯ is the *enharmonic* equivalent of D♭—it's the same note on your bass. There are many enharmonic equivalents.) Keys in today's music may be either *major* or *minor*, now giving us a total of 24 possibilities: C major/minor, C♯ major/minor, D major/minor, etc.

For most songs, it is fairly easy to figure out what key you're in. The key most often has the same root and quality as the chord you usually play to finish a tune. The chord will sound resolved (at rest), as if it does not need to be followed by another one. For example, if you hear an F major chord at the end of the song and it sounds final, then you're in the key of F major.

The most common and simple tunes use chords and scales from their respective key. This type of music is *diatonic*: ultimately derived from a single scale. Ninety percent of all music that you hear is diatonic, except for some jazz and fusion. First, we'll look at all the diatonic chords and *modes* (different scales derived from a parent scale) within a major key.

A major scale consists of seven unique notes. It can be started on any of those notes, giving us seven modes. For example, we may play a C major scale from C to C (C–D–E–F–G–A–B–C), from D to D (D–E–F–G–A–B–C–D), from E to E, and so on. Each unique note in the key of C is considered a *degree*; there are seven degrees in any key. Each scale degree corresponds to a mode. We'll look at each of these modes separately.

Degree: I
Chord: Cma7
Scale: Ionian

Degree: II
Chord: Dmi7
Scale: Dorian

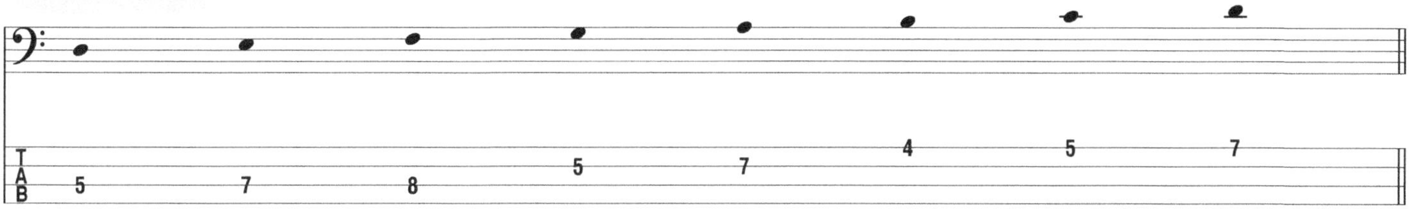

Degree: III
Chord: Emi7
Scale: Phrygian

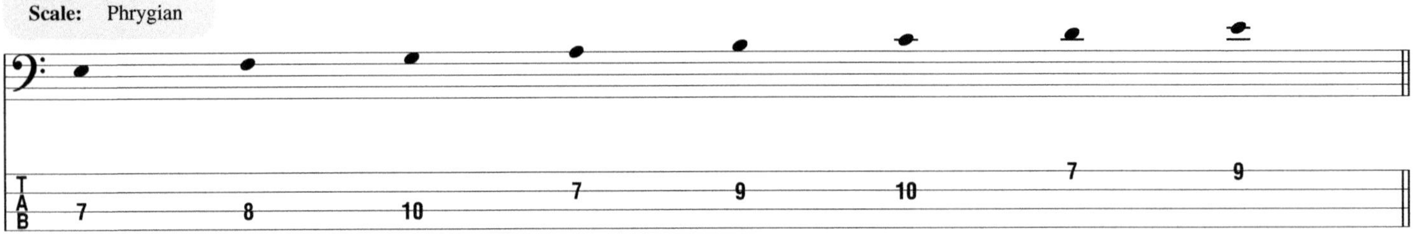

Degree: IV
Chord: Fma7
Scale: Lydian

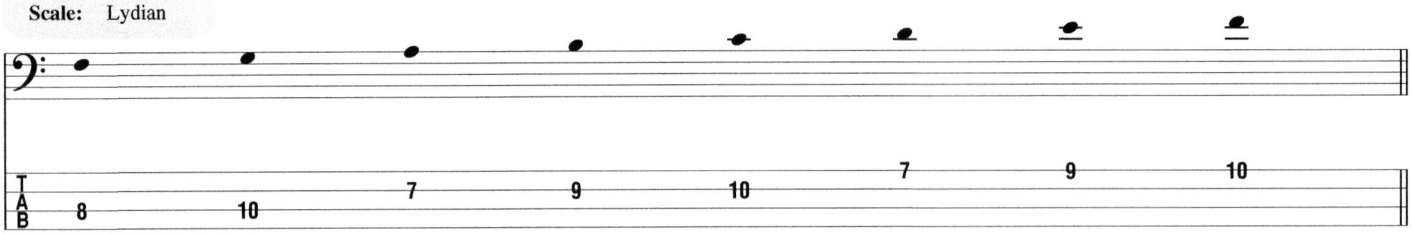

Degree: V
Chord: G7
Scale: Mixolydian

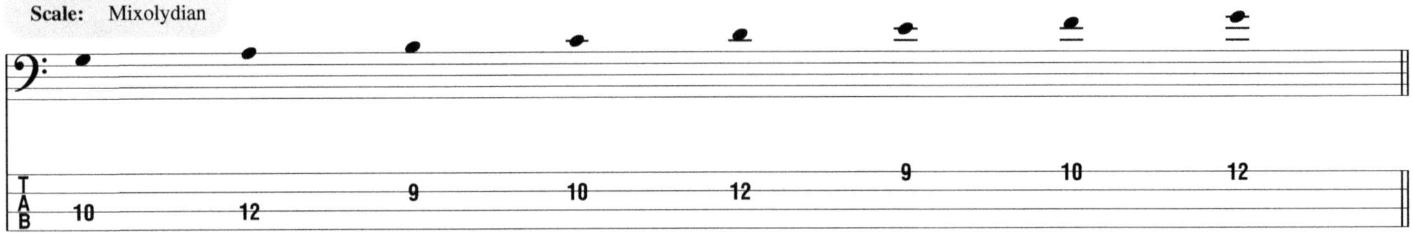

Degree: VI
Chord: Ami7
Scale: Aeolian

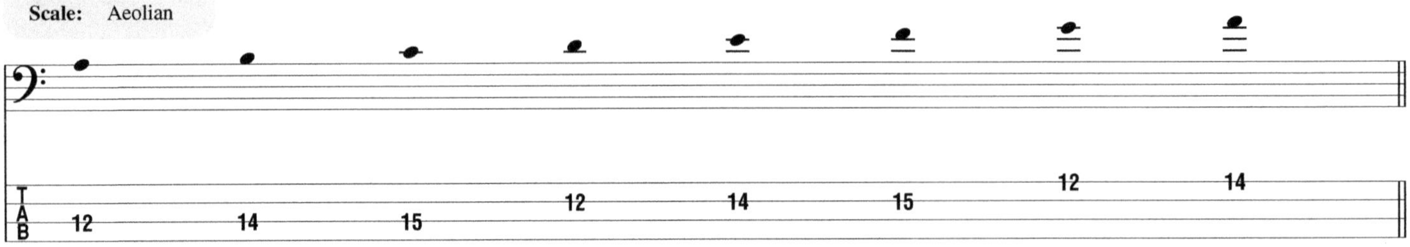

Degree: VII
Chord: Bmi7♭5
Scale: Locrian

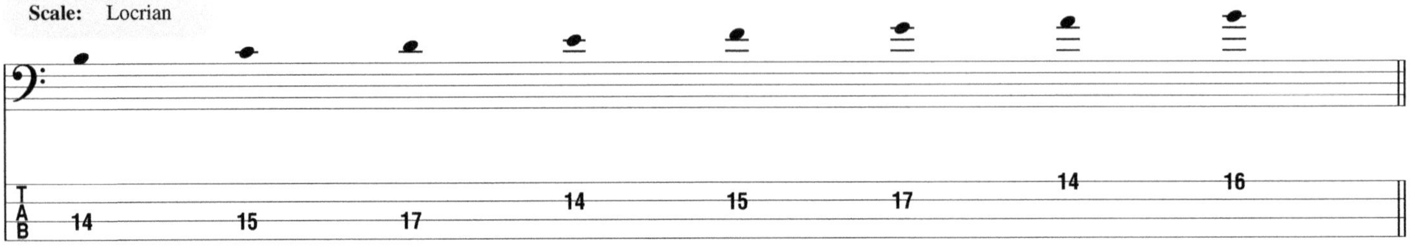

Ionian

Theory and Application

The *Ionian* mode has the same starting note and is actually the same as the major scale. This is the most common scale. Music in a major key can always resolve back to this scale.

Track 1

Degree: I
Chord: Cma7(9/13)
Scale: Ionian

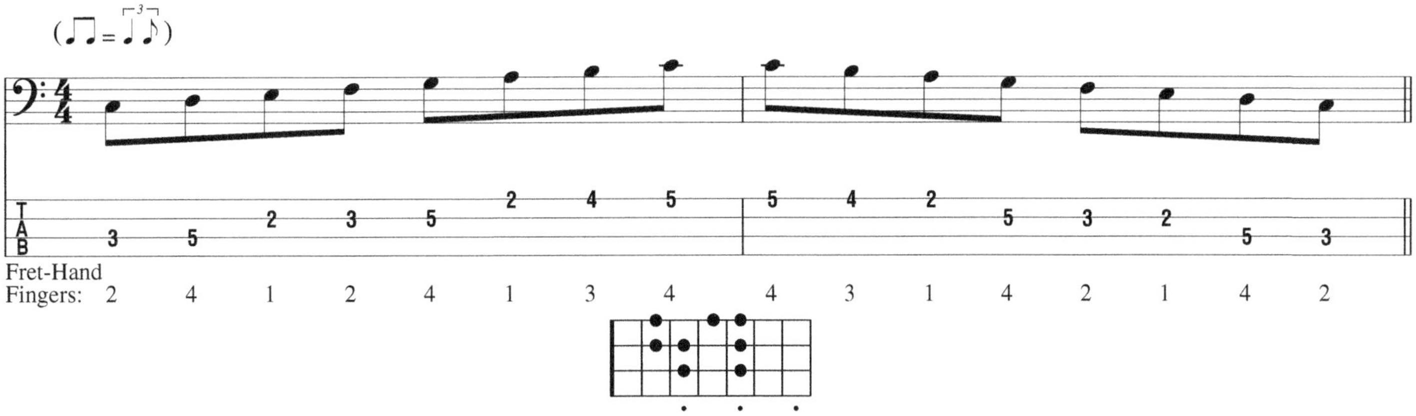

When soloing with scales, there are three different levels in terms of note importance: *chord tones*, *extensions*, and *passing tones*.

1. The most familiar-sounding, or “inside” notes, are *chord tones*. These are the notes in the scale that make up a chord or arpeggio. They always consist of the *root* (1), *third* (3), and *fifth* (5). The *seventh* (7) is also considered a chord tone for styles like jazz, R&B, and funk. In this book, we will always consider the seventh a chord tone. You can never go wrong by playing any of these four notes over their respective chords since they are always supported by a guitar or piano, and therefore, don’t clash.
2. The *extensions* (also known as *tension notes*) are notes that are not supported by the chord, but still work. These are usually the “interesting” notes since you’re introducing a new sound. The usable extensions vary depending on the scale that you’re playing. They can be the *second* (2), *fourth* (4), or *sixth* (6).

Extensions may be named seven steps higher than where they stand in the scale (2+7=*9*, 4+7=*11*, 6+7=*13*). This is because if you build an extended chord, you stack the notes in thirds; for example, 1–3–5–7–9. For soloing purposes, this does not matter; the second and ninth are the same. You can play any note wherever you like on the fretboard.

Scale

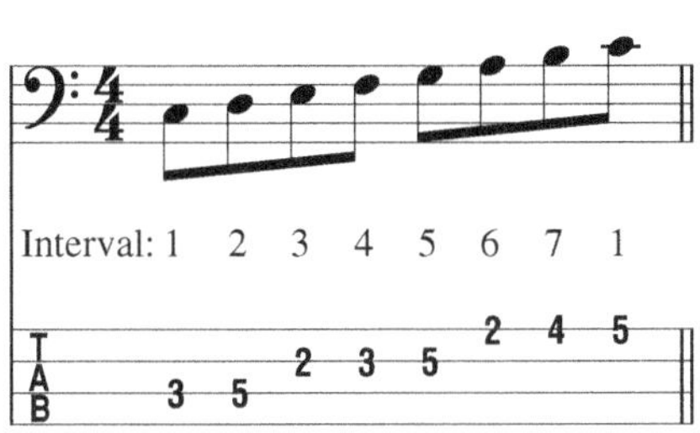

Scale with Extensions

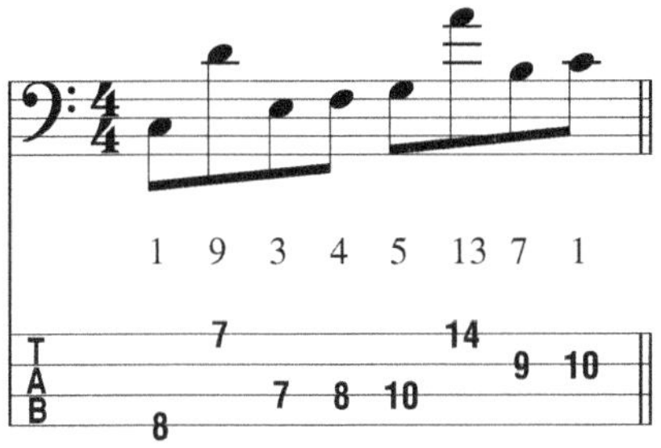

Arpeggiated Scale

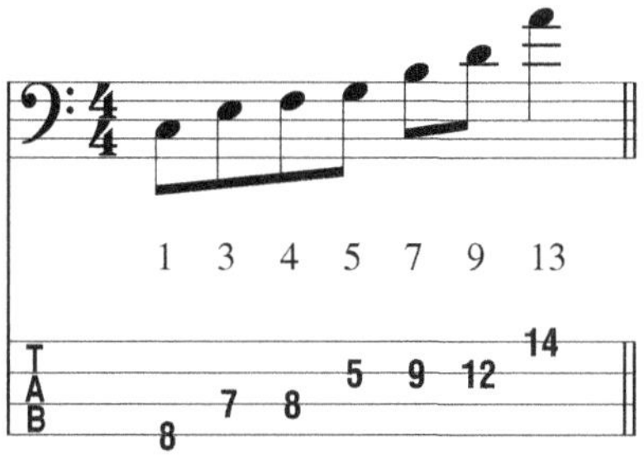

3. *Passing tones* are the last category. These notes cannot be sustained since they clash with the supporting chord. Depending on the scale, they too stand on the second (2), fourth (4), or sixth (6) degree. Passing tones are only used to connect chord tones and extensions; never end a phrase on these notes.

To sum this up, we have:

(C) Chord Tones: good, inside, clear
(Ex) Extensions: good, interesting, new
(P) Passing Tones: dissonant, unsettled, vague

Let's apply this to our major scale now.

Degree: I
Chord: ma7
Scale: Ionian

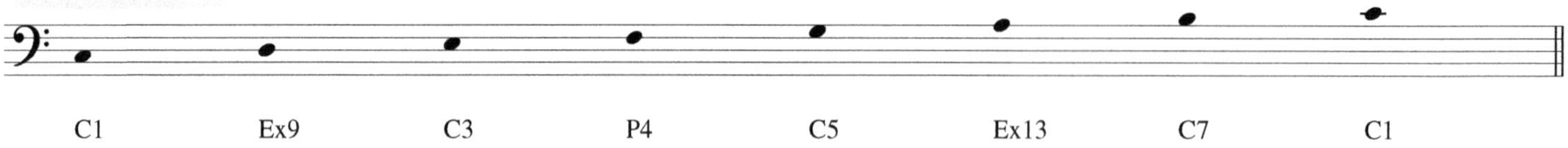

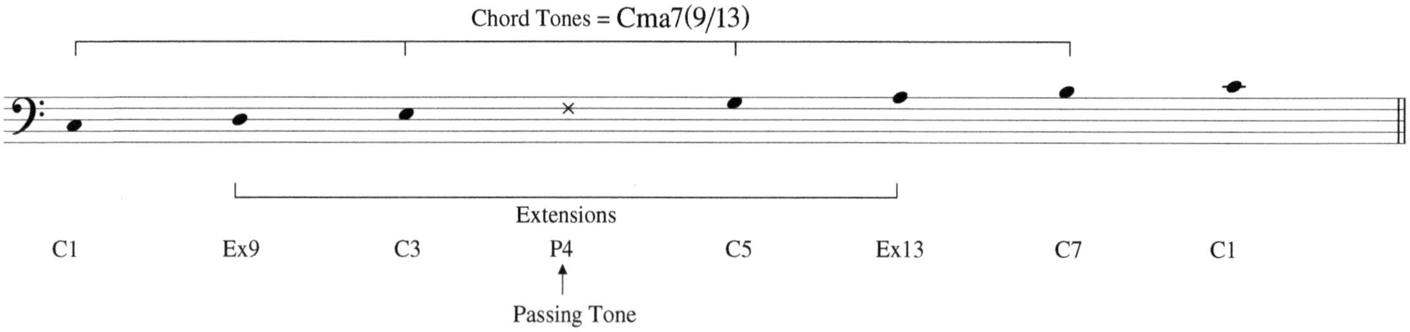

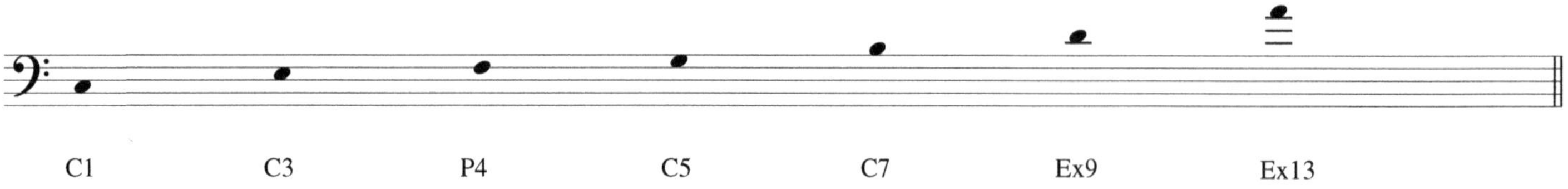

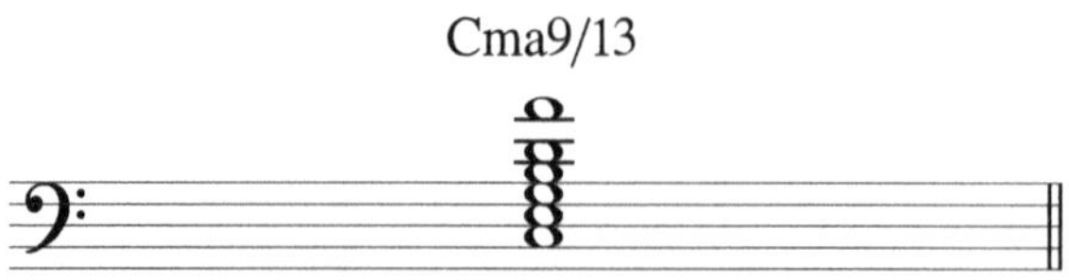

Here is the piano playing the scale in thirds so you can get used to the major seventh chord sound with and without extensions.

Track 2

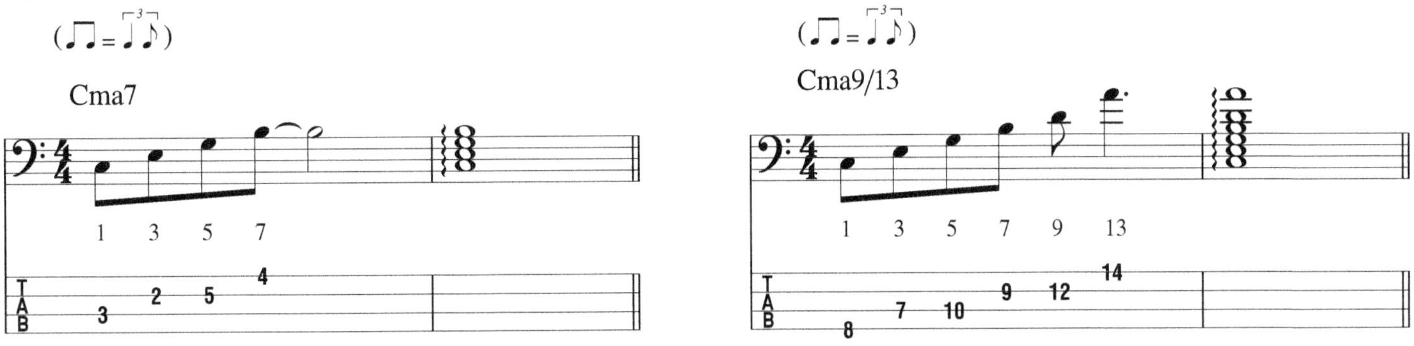

Now let's visualize and play this scale across two octaves on your bass. Try to be aware of what degree (1, 9, 3, etc.) you play at any time.

Track 3

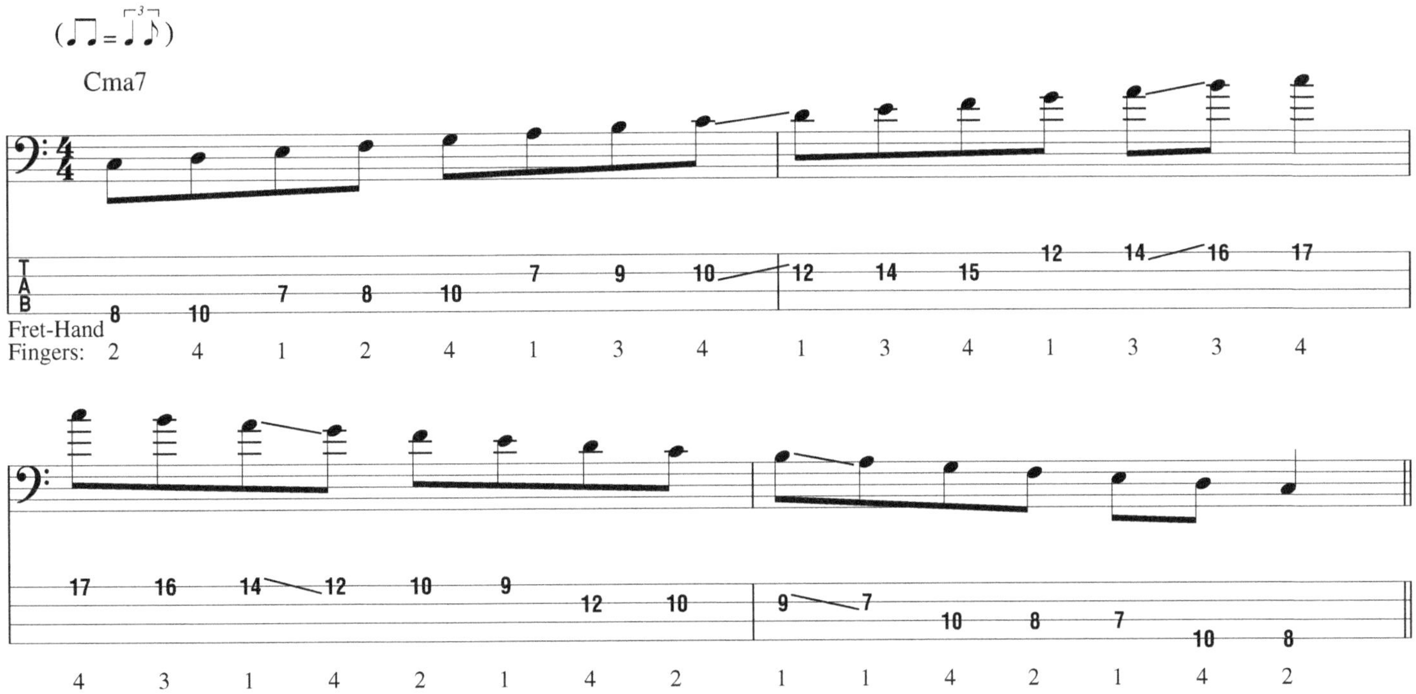

The suggested fingering is only one of many with which you can execute the position shifts; I encourage you to find alternate fingerings. The more ways of visualizing the scale you have, the easier it will be to solo.

The Ionian mode stands on the first degree of a major key, and therefore, is the best choice for soloing over the one (I) or *tonic* major chord: the chord that determines the key center. If you encounter a major seventh chord that lasts four measures or longer, it becomes *modal*. Since it doesn't move on, this means that the chord loses its sense of direction. When that happens to any major seventh chord (even if it is not a I chord), Ionian works well. The Ionian mode is also used over the ♭III chord in a minor key. In A minor, the ♭III degree is Cma7, and Ionian would be the correct scale to play. In another key, C minor, the ♭III is the E♭ma7 chord, and E♭ Ionian would be the scale choice.

> To recap, Ionian can be used for the:
> - I chord in major
> - ♭III chord in minor
> - Whenever a major seventh chord lasts four measures or longer (becomes modal)

Scale Exercises

It is very important to practice the scales in this book in every key so you're prepared for any possibility. The following exercises are some of many (and I will vary them throughout the book) to keep you on your toes. The intent is to get really comfortable with each scale and be able to visualize it all over the neck.

Being able to play a scale in thirds is one of the most common ways of practicing a new mode. It's very melodic and works well for later use in solos. Let's try this with the A major scale in a one-octave range.

Track 4

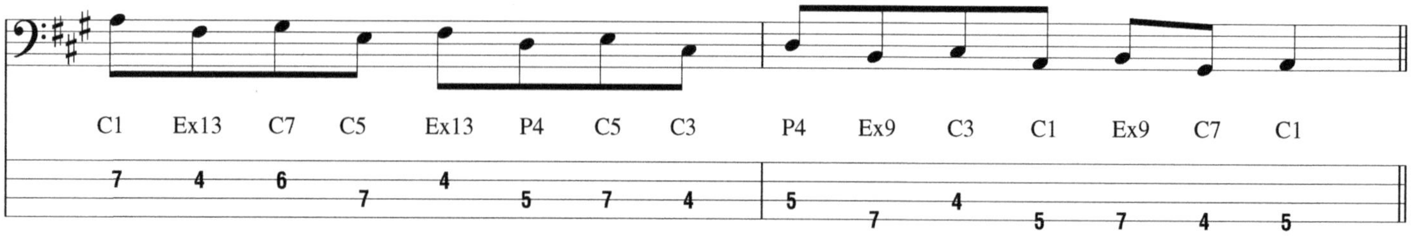

Here is the same exercise in B major (two octaves).

Track 5

A good way of visualizing the scale on your fretboard is to play all of its notes on only one string. The following D major scale is executed on the D string.

Track 6

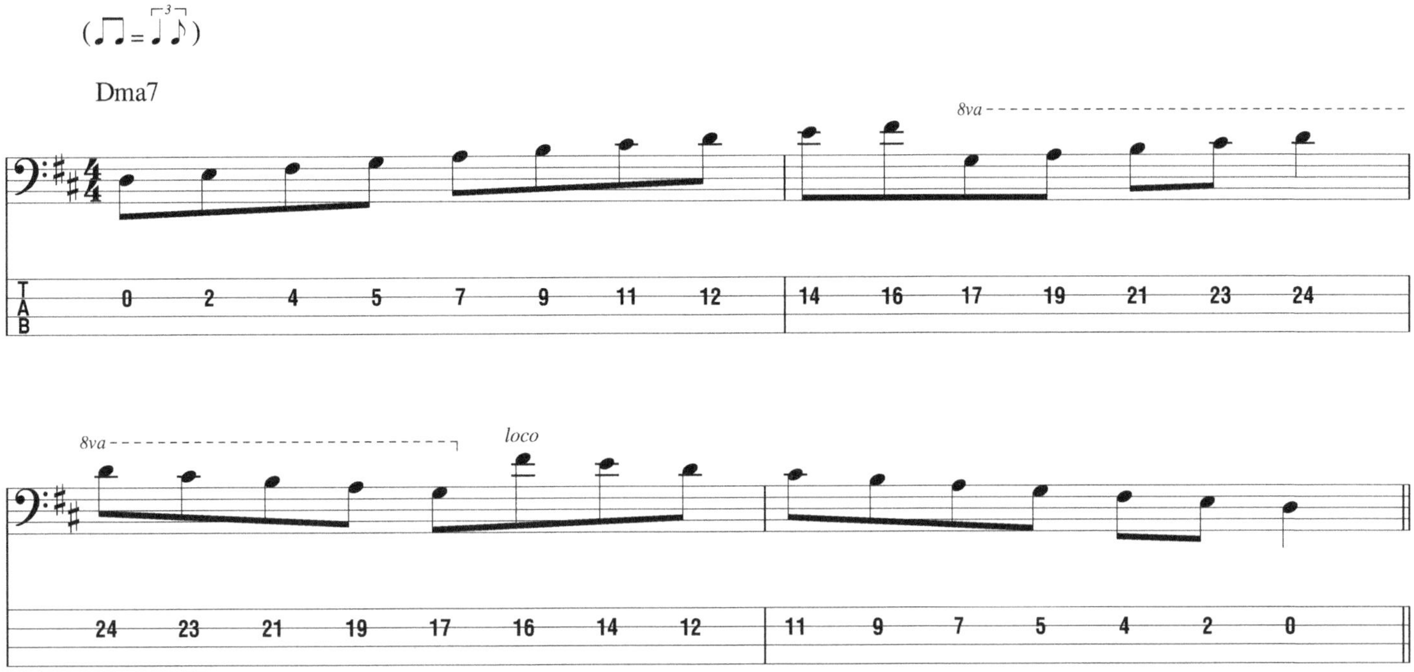

If we play an E♭ major scale on the G string, the lowest possible note will be the third degree of the scale.

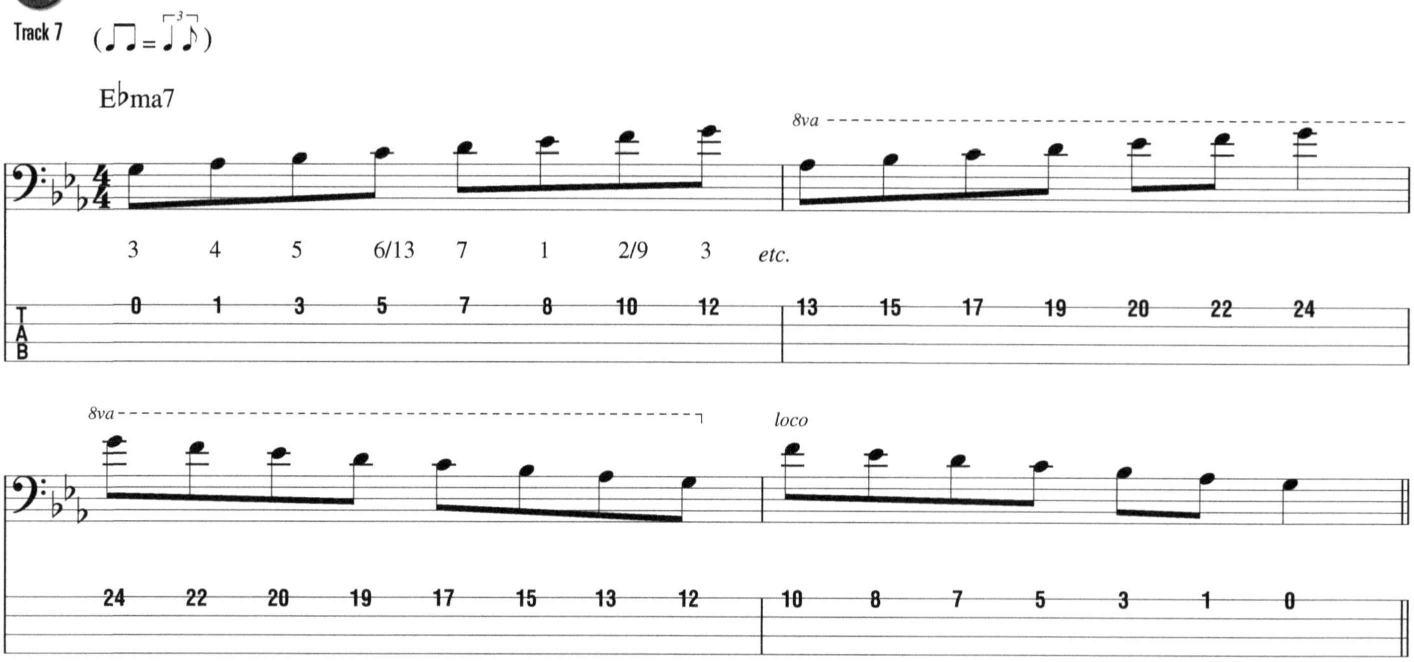

Solo Exercises

The following tune uses two different major chords: Cma7 and E♭ma7. Each chord lasts for four measures, so the progression becomes modal. This means that you'll improvise using the C major scale for four measures and then E♭ major for four measures. Try to come up with some simple melodies using only these two major scales, each over its respective chord. Just a tip, a melodic bass solo tends to sound better if you stay in the higher range (above the 12th fret).

Track 8 provides an example of how you might approach such a solo. The top staff uses only *slash rhythm* marks with chord symbols above. Slash rhythms indicate that you can play whatever you like that is appropriate to the song's style. In this instance, it's a solo, but it could also mean to play a groove. The second staff shows you the scales in a one-octave range. If you're inexperienced, it's a good idea to use a single-scale fingering and just move it up for the new chord to avoid confusion. Later, you'll want to stay in one position and change fingering patterns to navigate through different keys.

Track 9 gives you the opportunity to solo over the same progression by yourself. Make sure you allow for little pauses in your solo. Think of it like a conversation—where the pauses give a listener time to think about what you have just "said." Don't bury the audience by overplaying. Good luck and have fun!

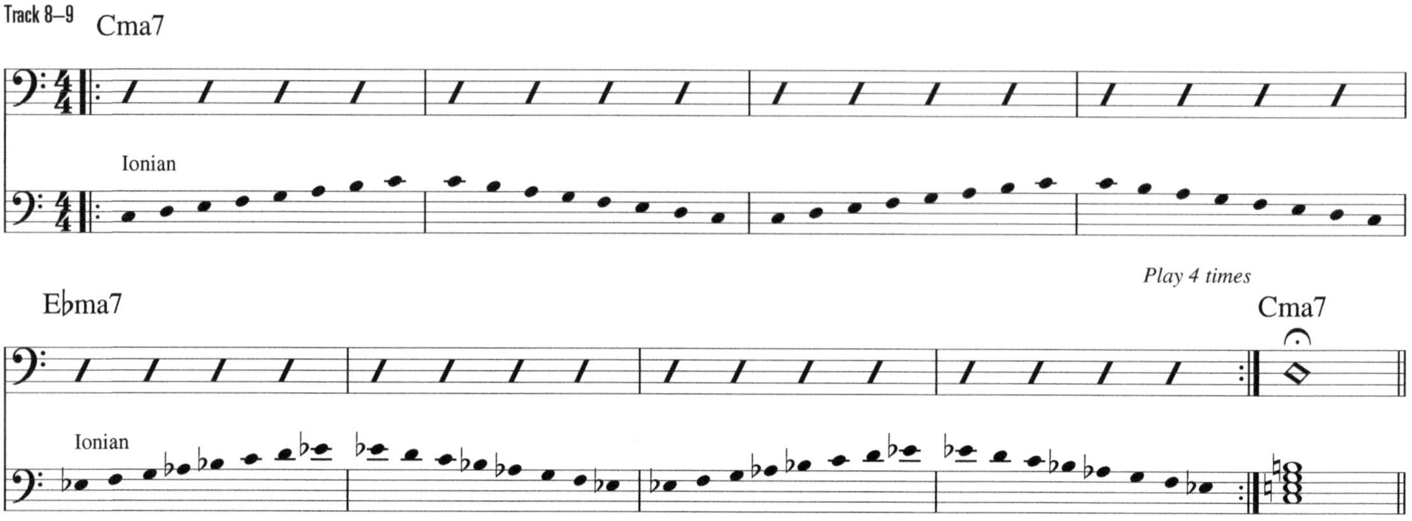

Here is a similar exercise, but with four different major seventh chords. Each chord uses the Ionian scale from its respective root.

Track 10

Dorian

Theory and Application

The *Dorian* mode comes from the second degree of the major scale. It is probably the most commonly used minor scale for soloing. It is used more often than the *natural minor* scale for reasons we will discuss in this chapter.

Track 11

Degree: II
Chord: Dmi7(9/11)
Scale: Dorian

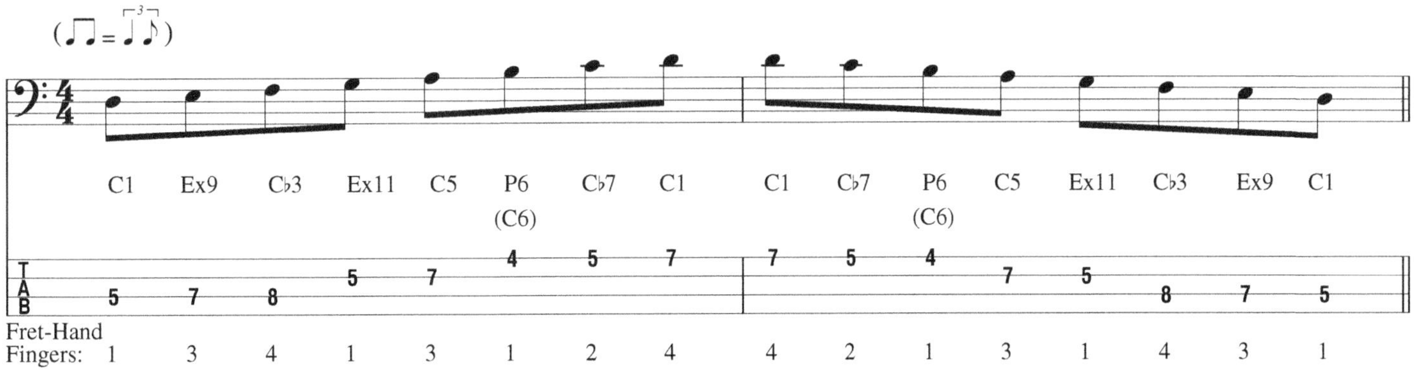

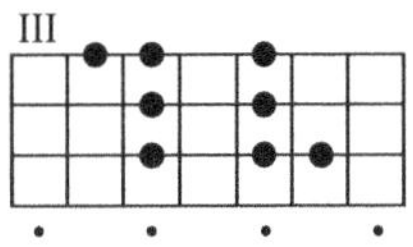

The Dorian mode outlines a minor seventh chord, and uses the second and fourth notes as extensions (9 and 11, respectively). If Dorian is played over a IImi7 chord in a major key (for example, Dmi7 in the key of C major), then its sixth or thirteenth (B) is used only in passing. The sixth creates a *tritone* interval with the third of the minor chord (from F to B), which is the same tritone contained in the V7 chord that often follows the IImi7. The tense tritone sound should be saved for the V7 chord (G7 in this key) in this situation. On the other hand, if the Dorian mode is used over a Imi7 chord in a minor key or a modal minor chord (one lasting more than four measures, which serves the same function as a I chord), the sixth can be used to great effect as an extension.

The places to use the Dorian mode are:
- the IImi7 chord in major
- the IVmi7 chord in minor
- any modal minor seventh chord lasting four measures or longer
- a substitute scale for Imi7 in a minor key

Scale Exercises

Here is a two-octave D Dorian mode. Remember that the fingering shown here is only one of many.

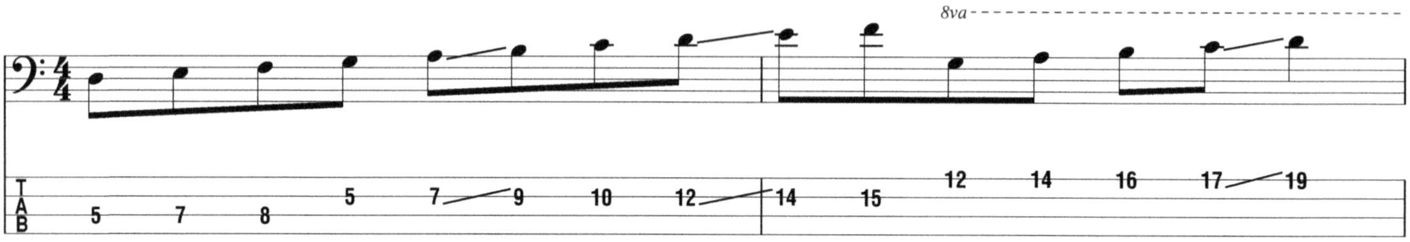

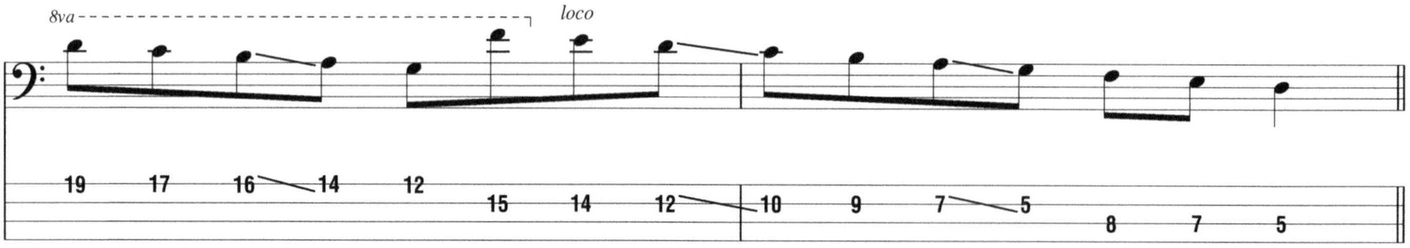

Staying in only one position (with little or no shifting) is another great way of practicing scales. Here we play E♭ Dorian in the *VI position.* This means that you use your 1st finger on the 5th and 6th frets, the 2nd finger on the 7th fret, the 3rd finger on fret 8, and the 4th finger on frets 9 and 10—one finger per fret, except for the 1st and 4th finger. The lowest possible note you can play will be the B♭, which is the fifth of the mode.

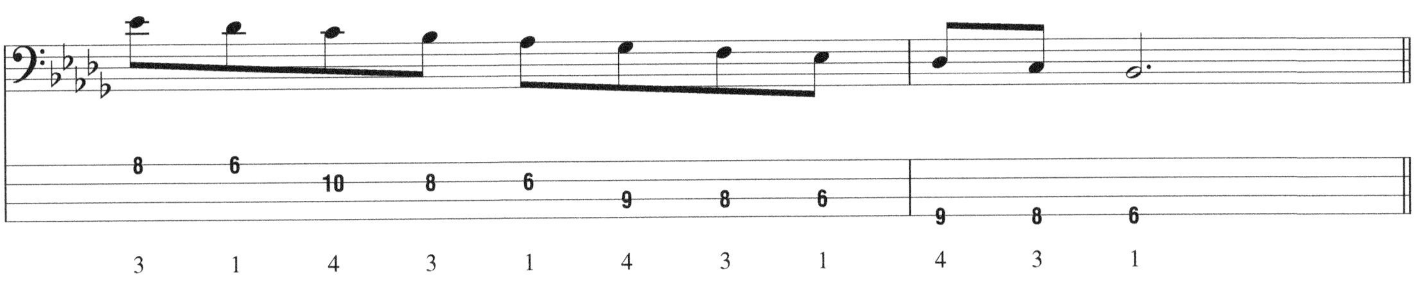

Let's play a two-octave A♭ Dorian mode.

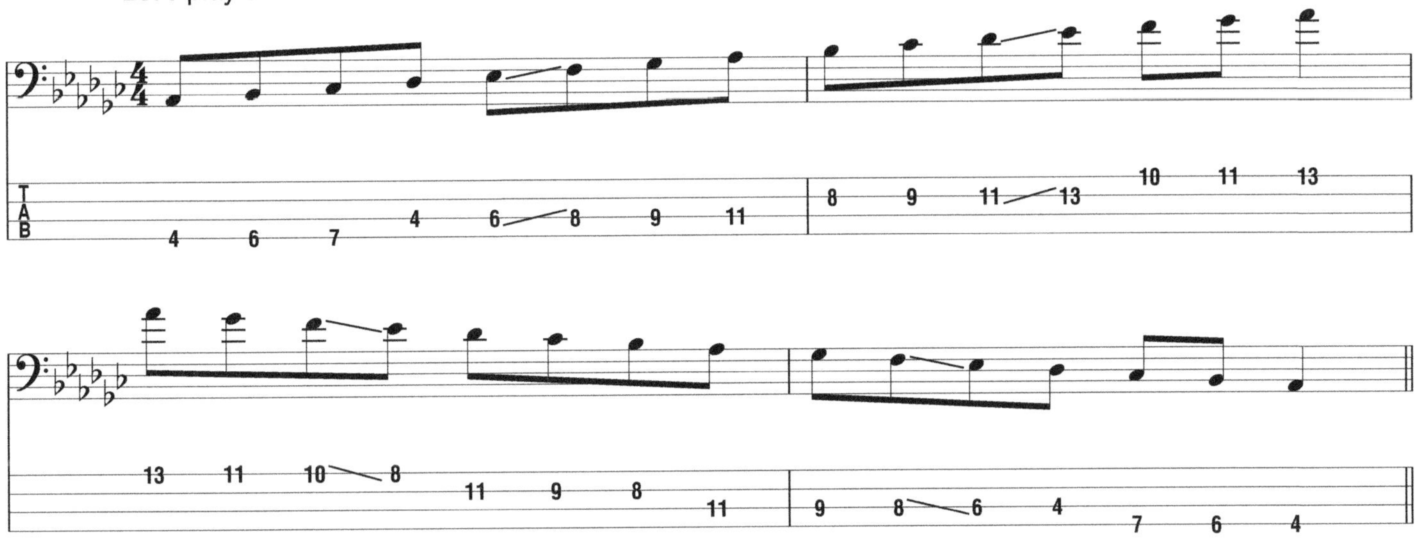

This is A Dorian in thirds.

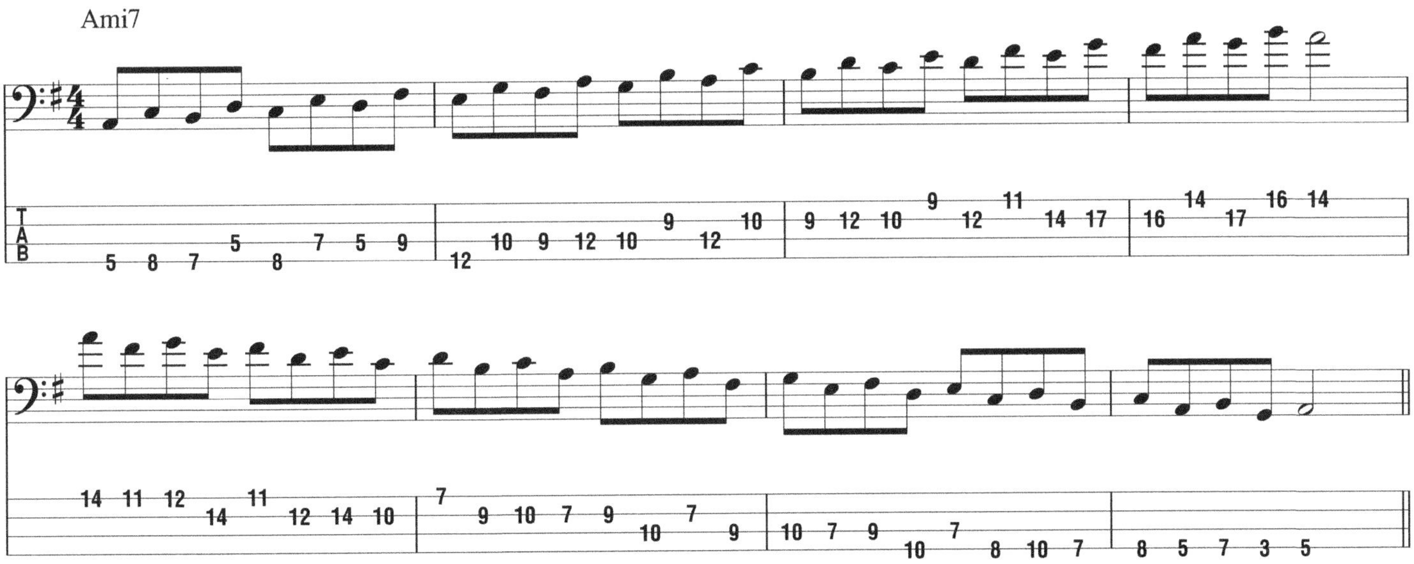

Playing in fourths is another great way of studying a scale. Here, we have B Dorian in fourths.

Solo Exercises

The following tune uses two different minor seventh chords: Gmi7 and Emi7. Each chord lasts four measures, and therefore, becomes modal. This means that you're in G Dorian for four measures and then E Dorian. Here, the sixth note of the scale is usable. The tritone interval (three whole steps from ♭3rd to 6th) sounds cool over minor chords in this modal context.

Track 12 gives you an example of how you might approach a solo over these chord changes. Track 13 gives you the opportunity to solo over the same progression by yourself. Good luck!

Track 12–13

Here's a similar exercise, but with *three* minor seventh chords. Each chord uses Dorian from its respective root.

Track 14

Mixolydian

Theory and Application

The *Mixolydian* mode comes from the fifth degree of the major scale. This means that D Mixolydian is the fifth mode of G major and is equivalent to a G major scale played from D to D. Mixolydian is used to solo over dominant seventh chords.

Track 15

Degree: V
Chord: G7(9/13)
Scale: Mixolydian

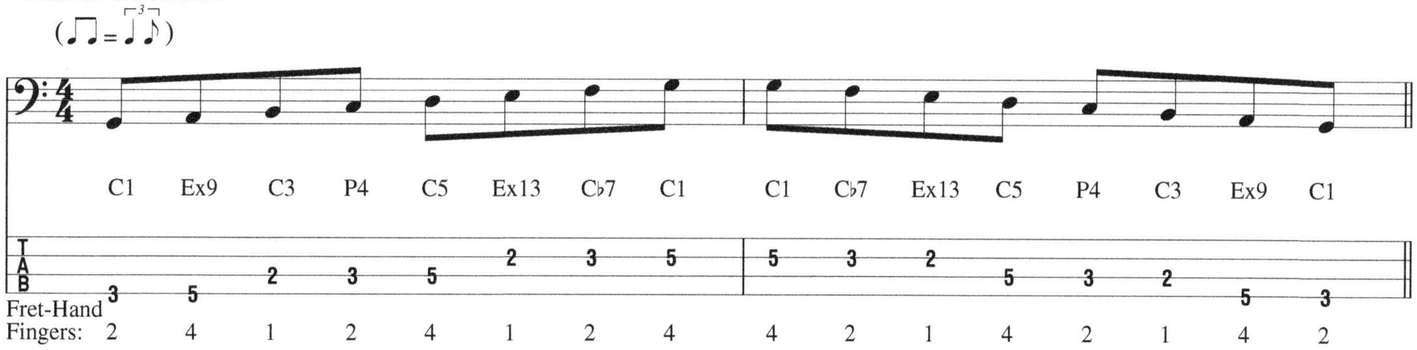

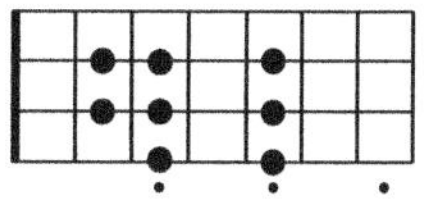

Mixolydian outlines a dominant seventh chord and uses the second and sixth notes as extensions (9 and 13). The fourth is used only in passing.

The Mixolydian mode also outlines a *seventh suspended fourth* chord (7sus4). In this case, the fourth replaces the third as a chord tone. Now, the third should be used only in passing.

G7sus4(9/13)

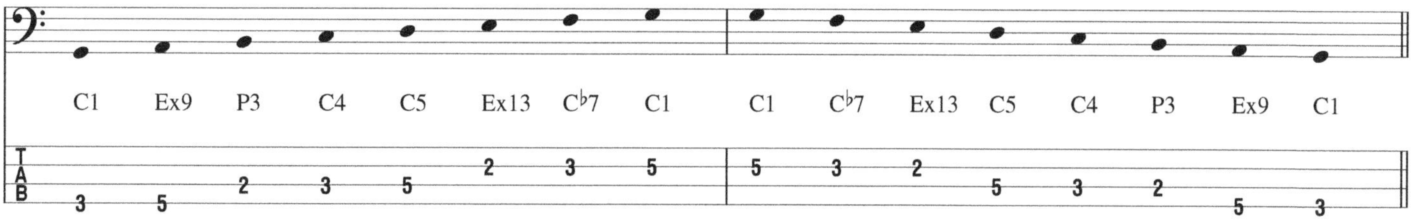

Even though Mixolydian is a dominant scale, it should not be used for the fifth chord in a minor key (for example, G7 going to Cmi).

The places to use a Mixolydian scale are:
- the V7 or V7sus4 chord in major or modal contexts
- the ♭VII7 chord in minor
- the I, IV, and V chord in blues

Scale Exercises

Here is a two-octave F♯ Mixolydian mode.

Here's C Mixolydian in fifth position with the sixth being the lowest available note in the pattern.

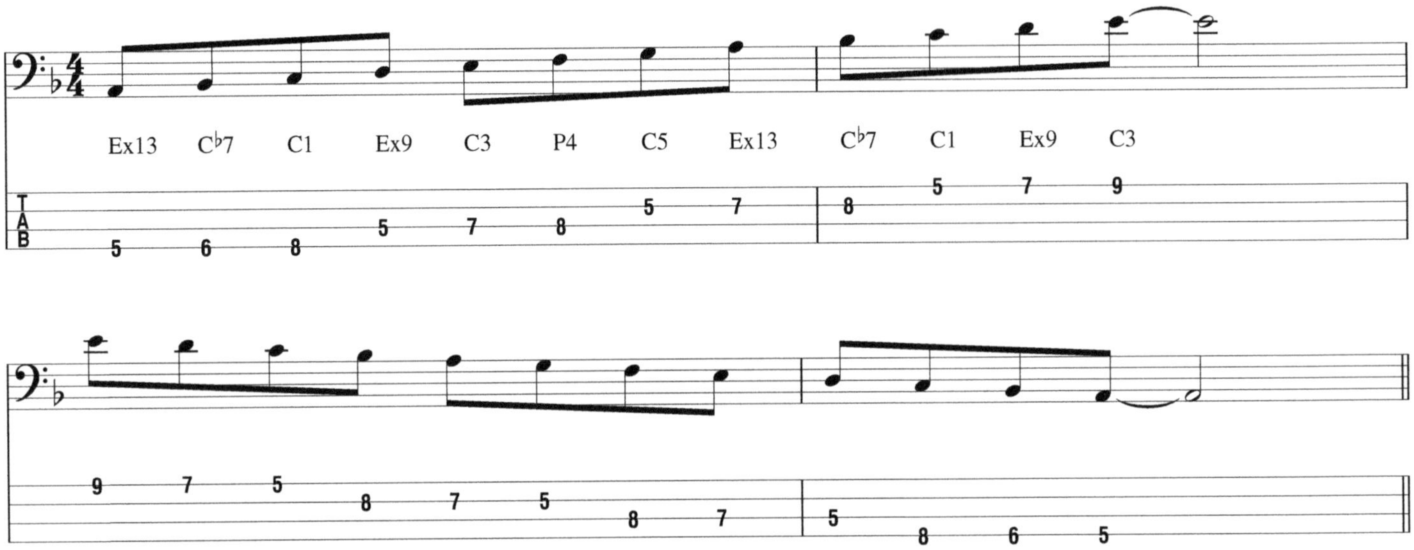

Let's play a two-octave B♭ Mixolydian scale in fourths.

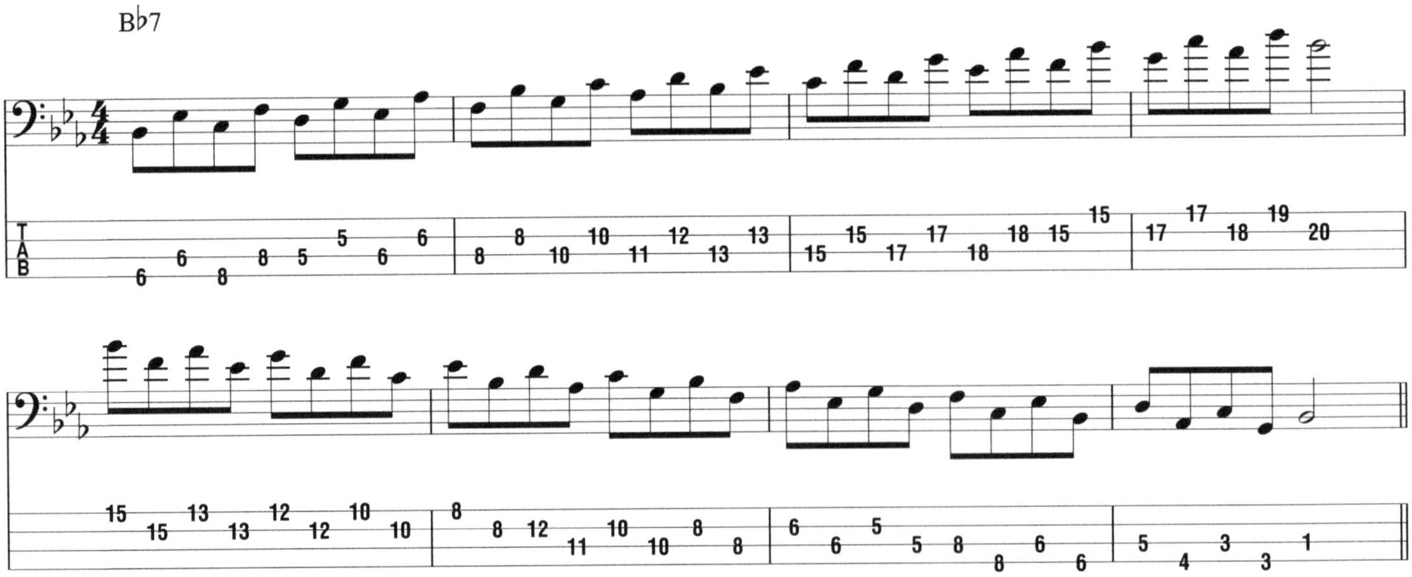

Here's the G Mixolydian scale on the G string only.

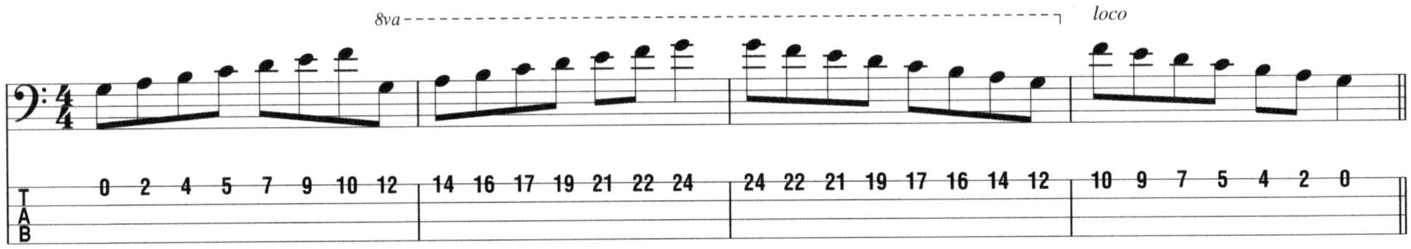

Solo Exercises

The following tune uses two different dominant seventh chords: A7 and C7. Play their respective Mixolydian scales on each chord. Remember to only use the fourth note of the scale in passing. Track 16 is an example of how this solo could sound using only the seven notes of the mode. Track 17 gives you the opportunity to solo over the same progression by yourself.

Track 16–17

Here, we have a blues in F. Each chord uses Mixolydian for soloing.

Track 18

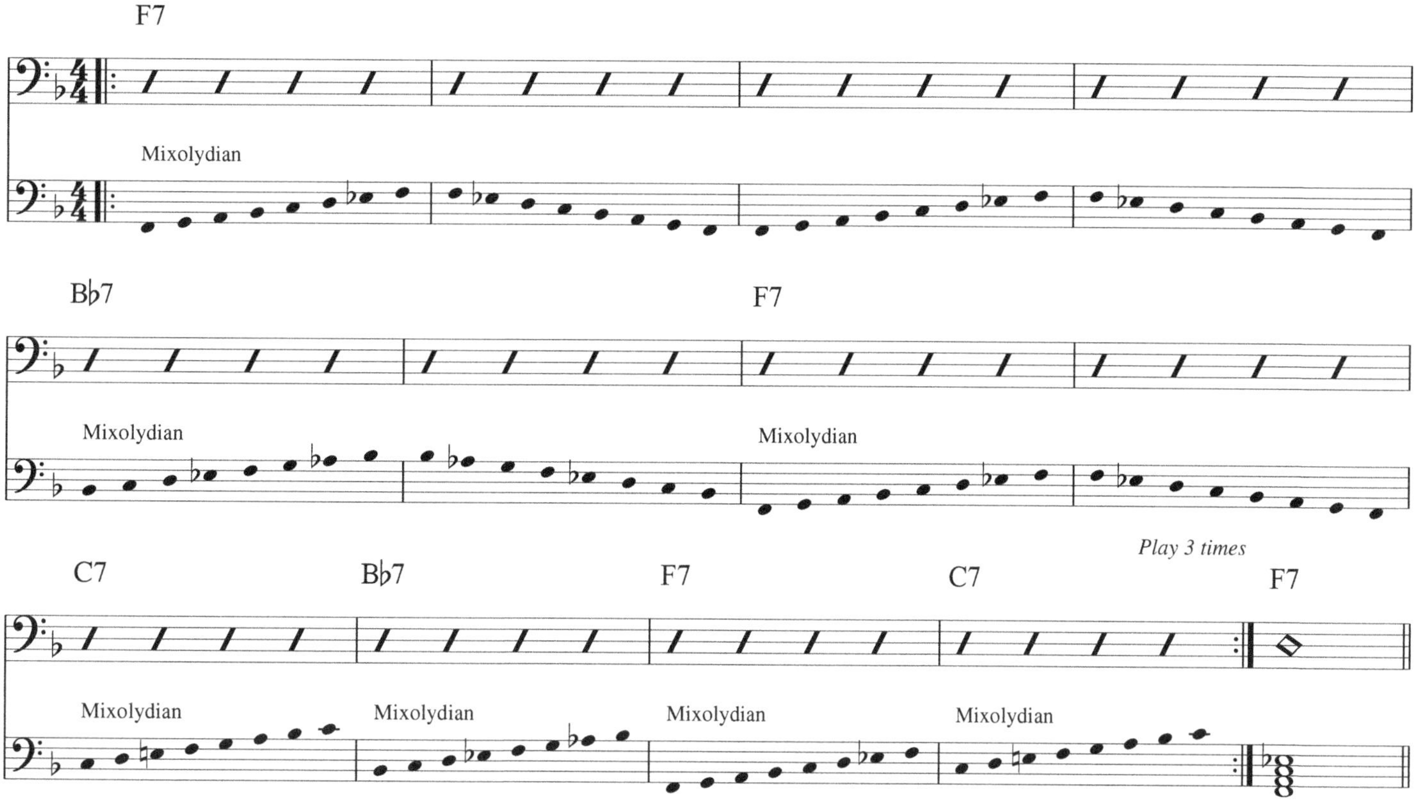

Combined Scales: Solo Exercises

So far, we have only used one particular mode for each exercise. Now, we're going to use all three that we have learned so far, applying them to a chord progression.

This example uses the I, IImi7, and V7 chords in C major (Cma7, Dmi7, and G7). The I chord, Cma7, uses the C Ionian scale. On Dmi7, you will use D Dorian, and on G7, you'll use G Mixolydian.

Try targeting the chord tones of each scale before you go too crazy with all seven notes. You may notice that the notes of C Ionian are the same as D Dorian and G Mixolydian; the difference lies in the weight distribution. While you're on Cma7, the B is a chord tone (7); on Dmi7, however, the B becomes the sixth and can only be used in passing; over the G7, the B becomes a chord tone again—the third. This is why it's important to be aware of what each note's function is in relation to the chord of the moment.

Track 19

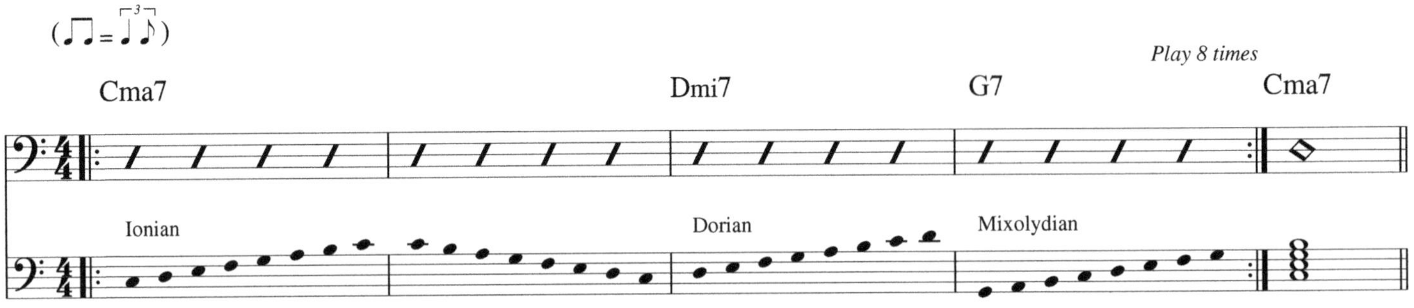

Here's one more example where every major seventh chord uses Ionian, every minor seventh chord uses Dorian, and every dominant chord uses Mixolydian.

Track 20

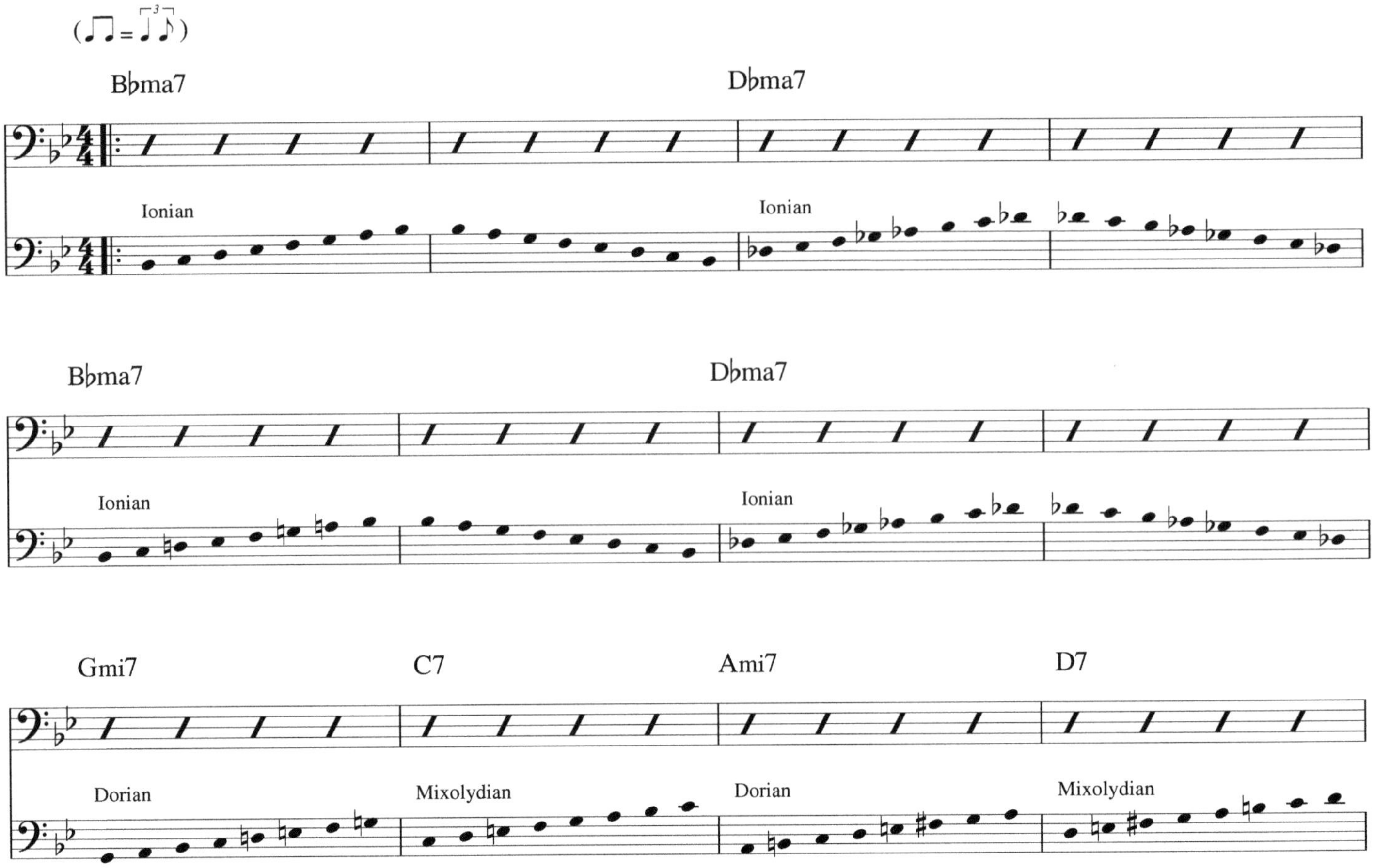

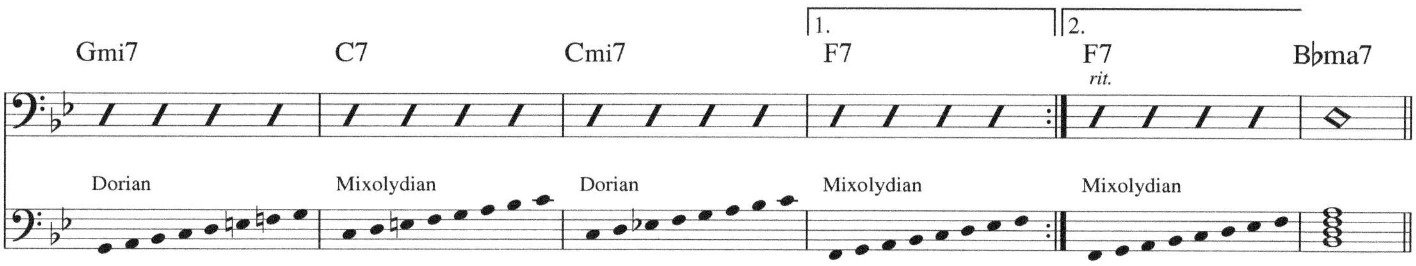

Aeolian

Theory and Application

The *Aeolian* mode comes from the sixth degree of the major scale. It is used to solo over minor seventh chords. Aeolian is also known as the *natural minor* scale. If a tune is in a minor key, Aeolian is the scale that is used for the Imi7 chord.

Track 21

Degree: VI
Chord: Ami7(9/11)
Scale: Aeolian

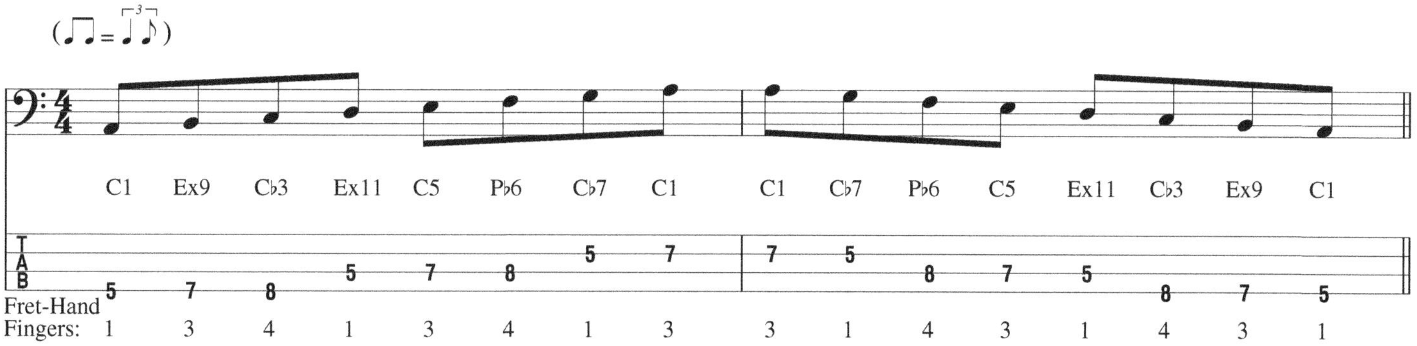

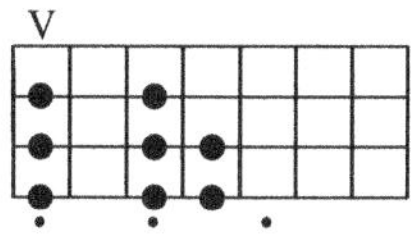

In similar fashion to Dorian, Aeolian is used over minor seventh chords. The difference lies with the sixth note of the scale; Aeolian has a minor sixth and Dorian has a major sixth. The sixth of Aeolian is only used as a passing note and should never be sustained. As in Dorian, the second and fourth notes of the scale are very pretty and make great extensions.

Aeolian is the preferred scale choice over a:
- Imi7 chord in minor
- VImi7 chord in major
- modal minor seventh chord

If a minor seventh chord is modal, it is much more common to use the Dorian mode rather than Aeolian, since the sixth note is not sustainable in the Aeolian mode.

Scale Exercises

Let's try F♯ Aeolian in two octaves.

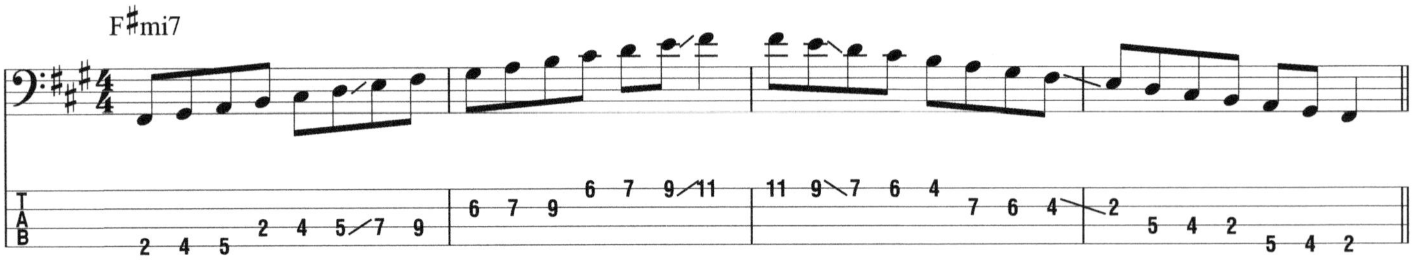

Here's E Aeolian in three octaves.

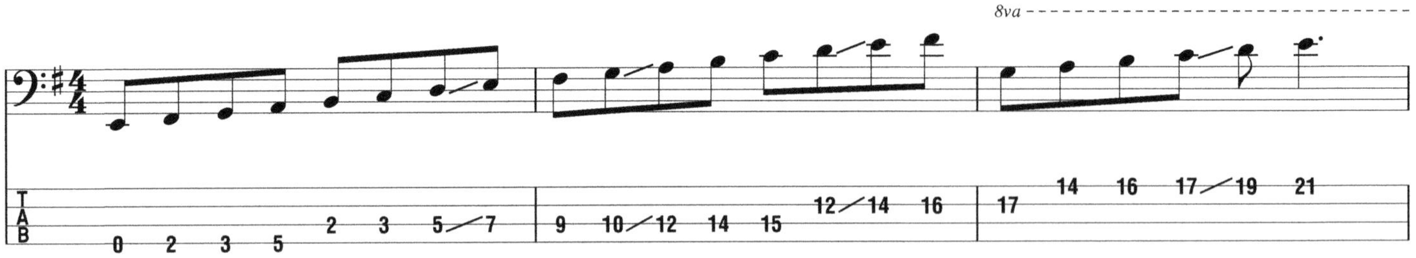

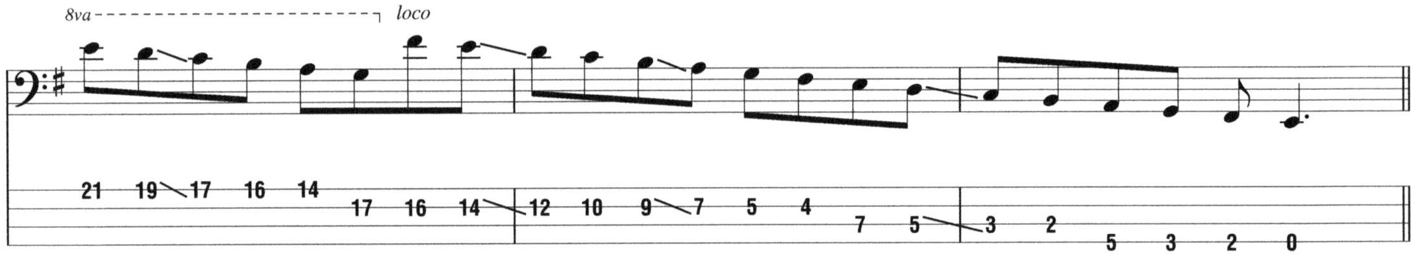

Now play the D Aeolian scale in fifths.

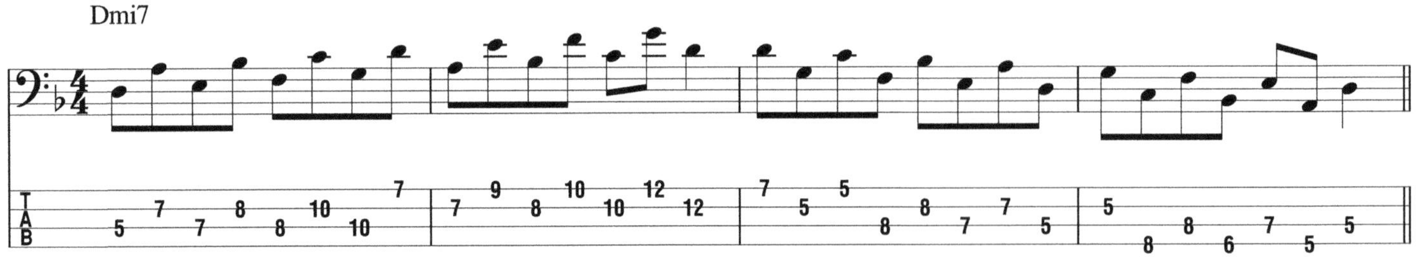

This is G Aeolian on the D string only; the lowest note is the fifth of the scale.

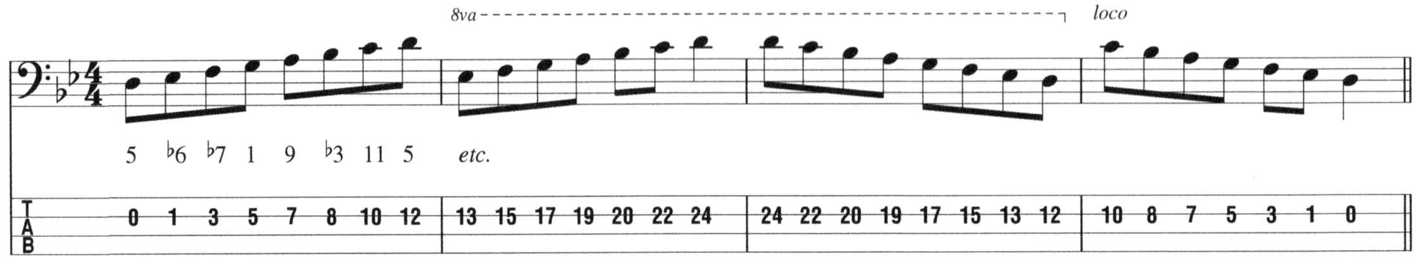

Solo Exercises

The following tune uses two different chords: E♭ma7 and Cmi7. Play Ionian over E♭ and Aeolian over Cmi7. Remember to only use the sixth note of Aeolian in passing.

Track 22

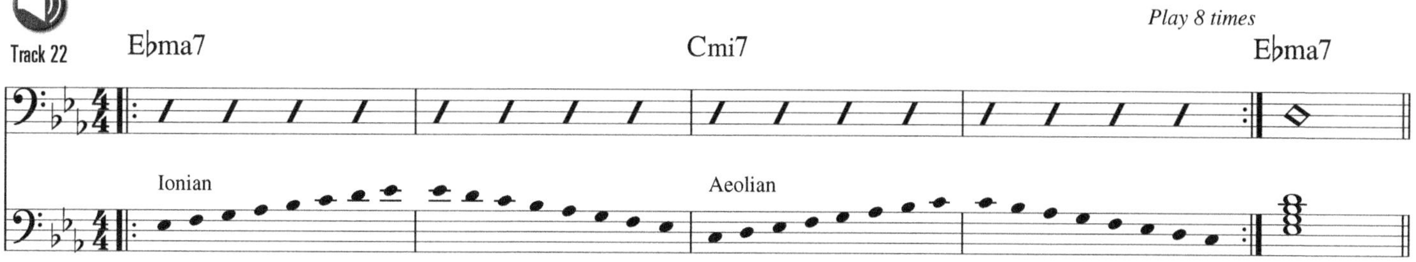

This exercise only uses minor seventh chords. Play the Aeolian scale from each respective root.

Track 23

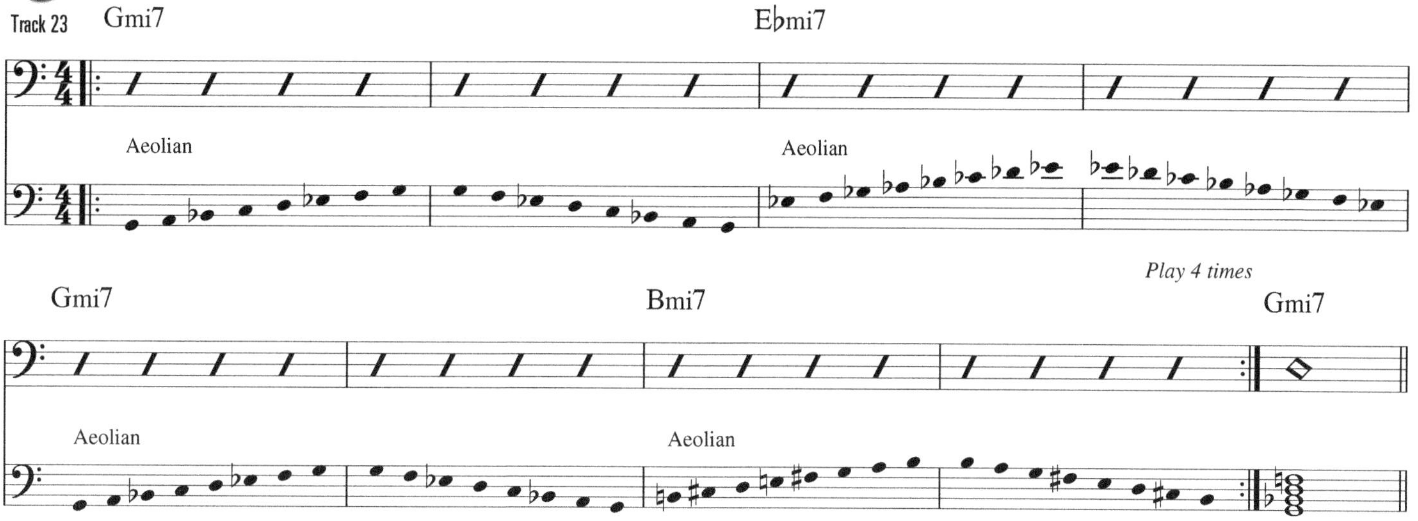

Locrian

Theory and Application

The *Locrian* scale comes from the seventh degree of the major scale. It is used to solo over minor seventh (flat five) chords.

Track 24

Degree: VII
Chord: Bmi7(♭5)(11/♭13)
Scale: Locrian

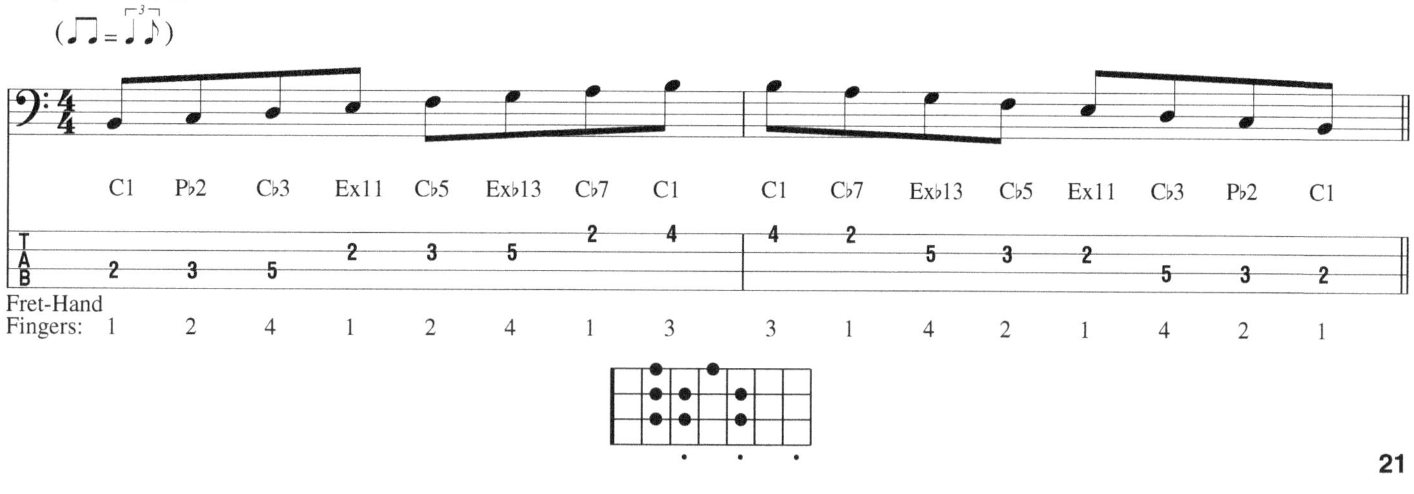

Locrian is the first mode that we have encountered with a *diminished fifth*, which is the defining interval of that scale. The minor second can only be used in passing, and the fourth and minor sixth make nice extensions. Locrian will work over any mi7(♭5) chord that you encounter, even if it is not the VIImi7(♭5) or IImi7(♭5) chord. Locrian is the preferred scale choice for any minor seventh (flat five) chord.

Scale Exercises

Here is a two-octave G Locrian mode.

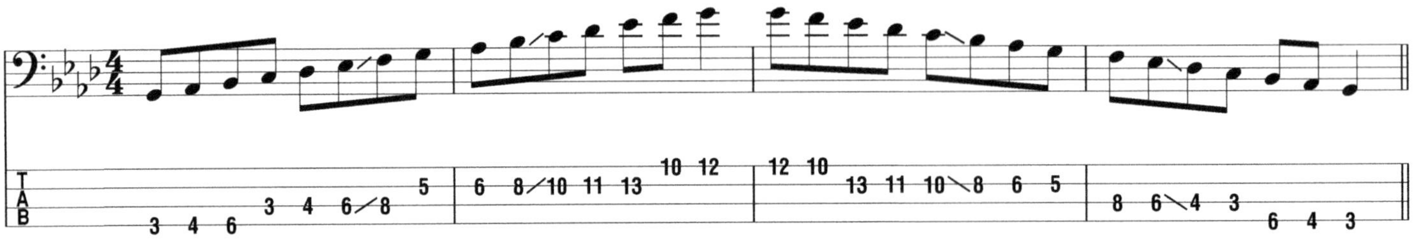

Playing any scale in sixths is very melodious. Here's C Locrian played using this pattern.

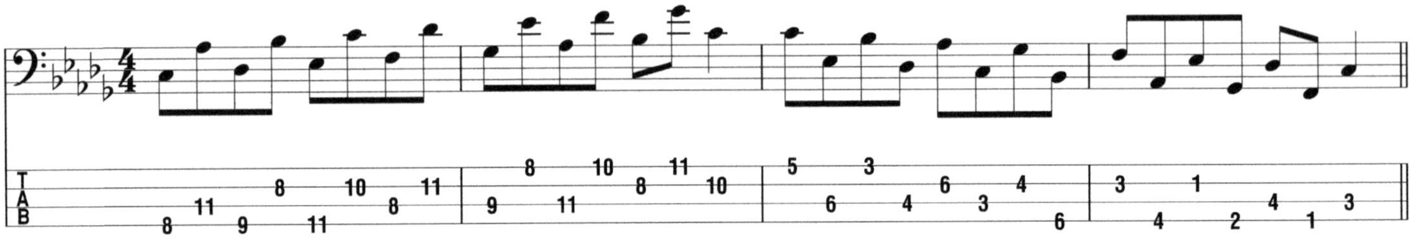

Here's B Locrian in seventh position.

D♯ Locrian on the G string only.

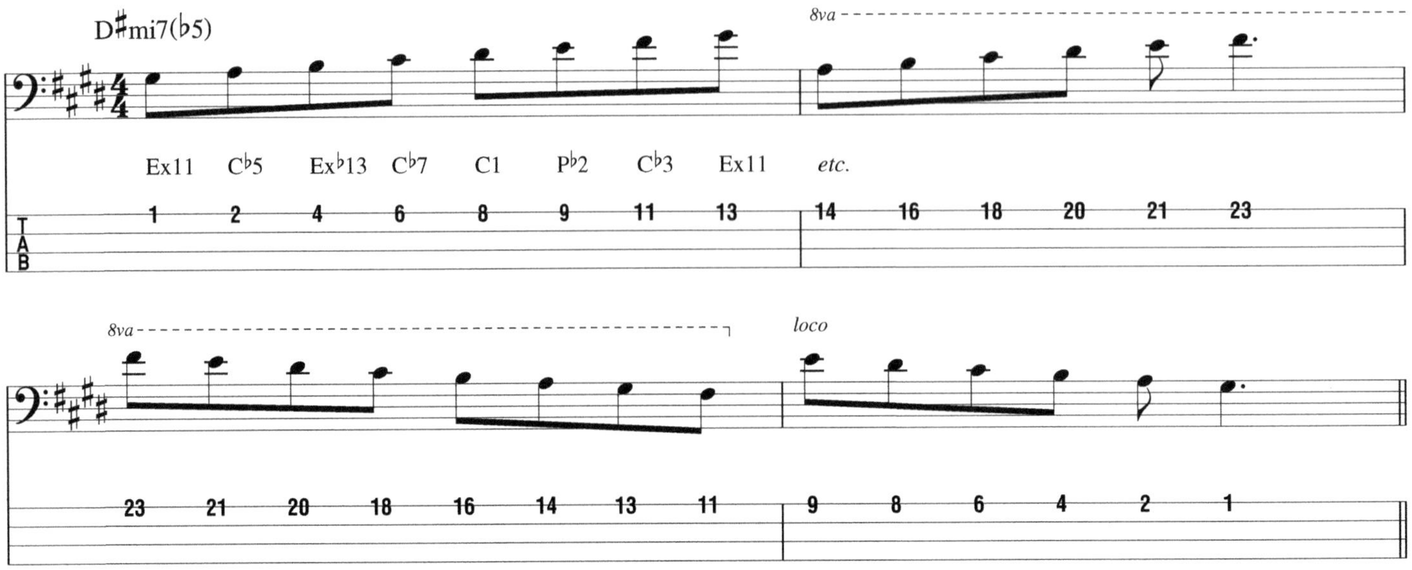

Solo Exercises

This exercise uses only two mi7(♭5) chords, and you will be playing Locrian for both of them.

Track 25

Here we have a VImi7(♭5)–IImi7(♭5)–V7–Ima7 progression that is diatonic with the exception of the II and VI chords, which are mi7(♭5) instead of minor seventh chords. Play Locrian on Ami7(♭5) and Dmi7(♭5), Mixolydian on G7, and Ionian on Cma7.

Track 26

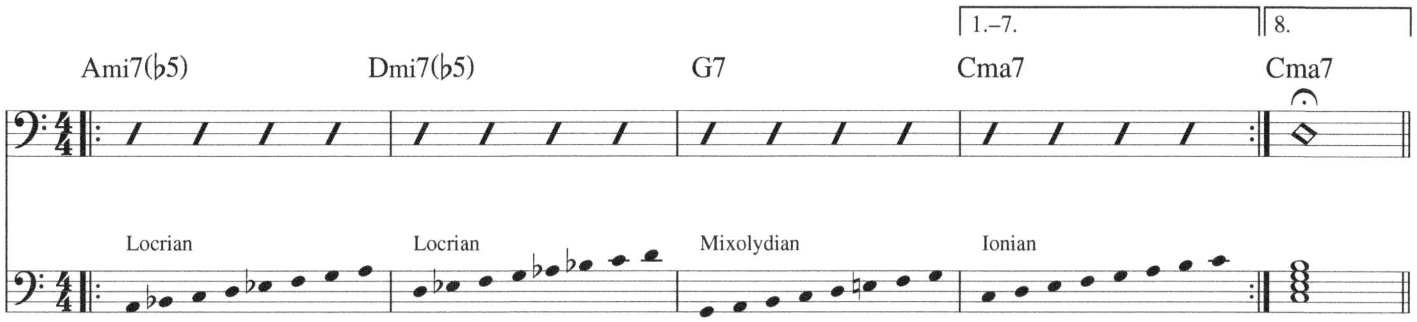

Phrygian

Theory and Application

The *Phrygian* mode comes from the third degree of the major scale. It is used to solo over minor seventh chords.

Track 27

Degree: III
Chord: Emi7(11)
Scale: Phrygian

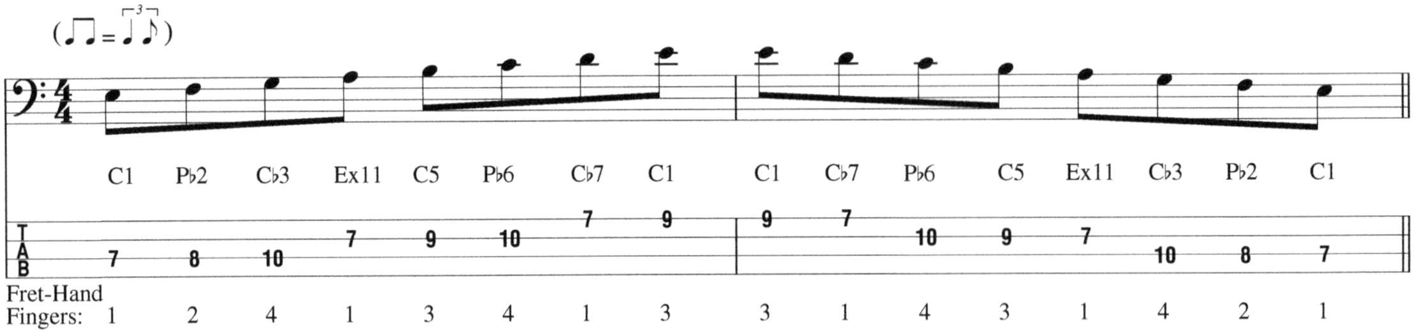

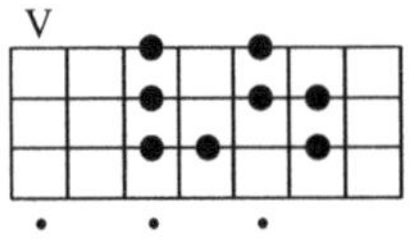

Since two of the scale notes can only be used in passing (♭2nd and ♭6th), Phrygian is the least useful scale to use when soloing over minor seventh chords. Except for when a "Spanish" flavor is desired it is not very common to use this scale for modal playing. If such a situation arises, the word "Phrygian" would be written next to the chord symbol to indicate the appropriate scale.

Phrygian is the preferred scale choice over a:

- IIImi7 chord in major
- Vmi7 chord in minor (quite rare)

Scale Exercises

A two-octave Phrygian scale.

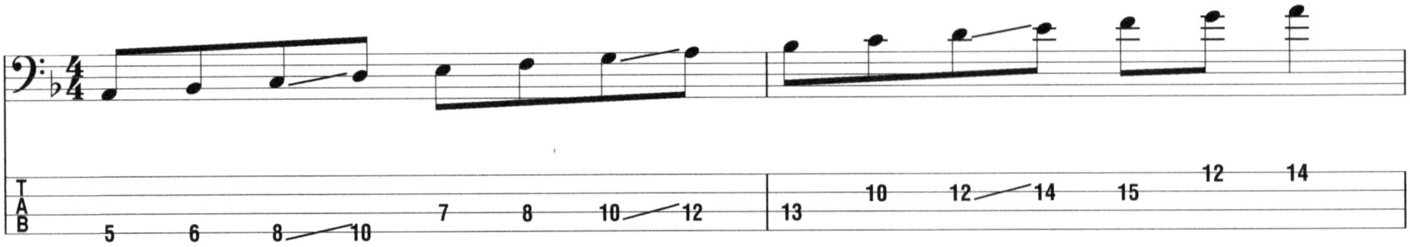

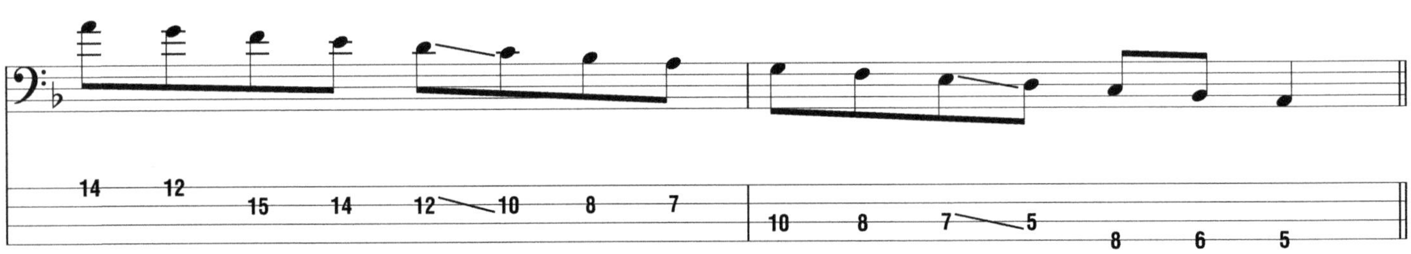

If you play any scale in sevenths, you'll get quite a workout. Here is D Phrygian.

It's always helpful to visualize a scale across the whole neck. Let's try E Phrygian over three octaves.

This exercise groups the G Phrygian scale in three-note figures.

Solo Exercises

This is a modal progression. Use only Phrygian, and be cautious of the ♭2nd and ♭6th.

Track 28

This Ima7–IIImi7–IImi7–V7 progression uses Ionian over Fma7, Phrygian over Ami7, Dorian over Gmi7, and Mixolydian over the C7 chord.

Track 29

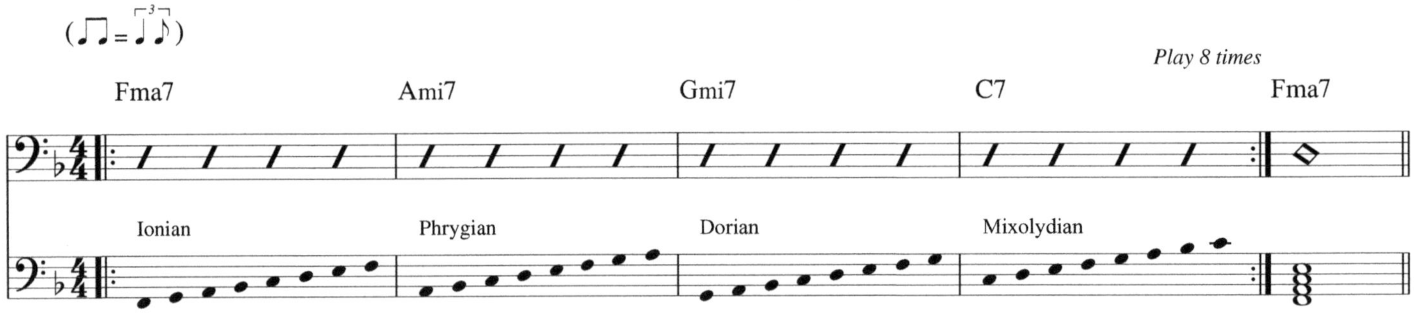

Lydian

Theory and Application

The *Lydian* mode comes from the fourth degree of the major scale. It is used to solo over major seventh chords.

Track 30

Degree: IV
Chord: Fma7(9/♯11/13)
Scale: Lydian

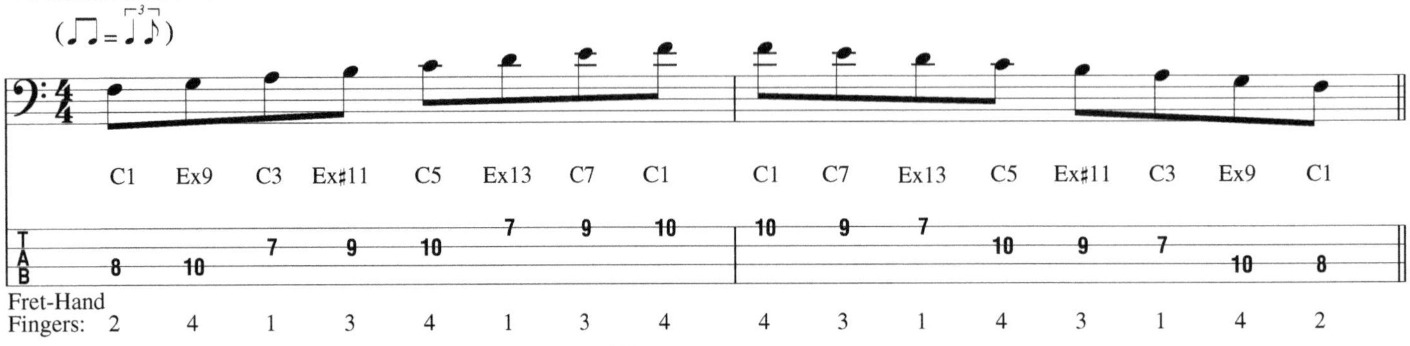

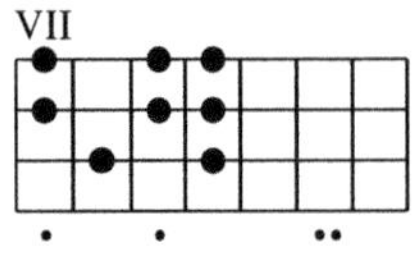

Lydian is one of the best scales for soloing because it is comprised only of chord tones and extensions—every note can be sustained.

Lydian is the preferred scale choice over a:

- IVma7 chord in major
- ♭VIma7 chord in minor
- modal ma7 chords
- Ima7 in a major key—as a substitute scale

The extensions of the Lydian scale form a major triad; a chord symbol like $\frac{\text{G}}{\text{Fma7}}$ is sometimes used instead of the more cumbersome Fma13(♯11). This symbol is called a *polychord* since it consists of a G triad against an Fma7 (*poly* = many).

Scale Exercises

G Lydian over two octaves.

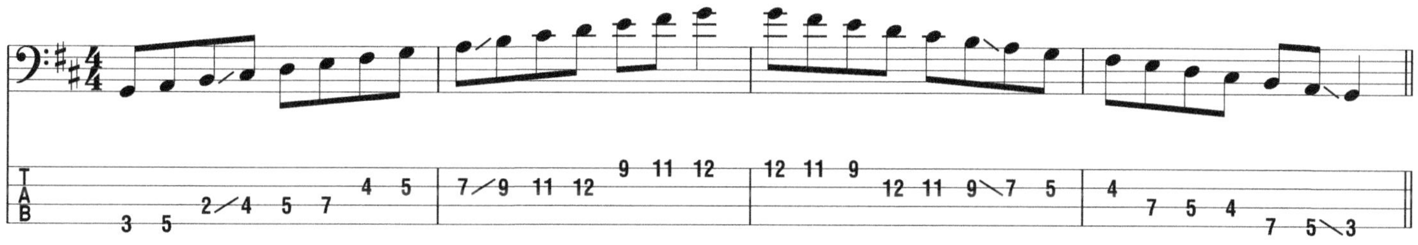

A two-octave B♭ Lydian mode in thirds.

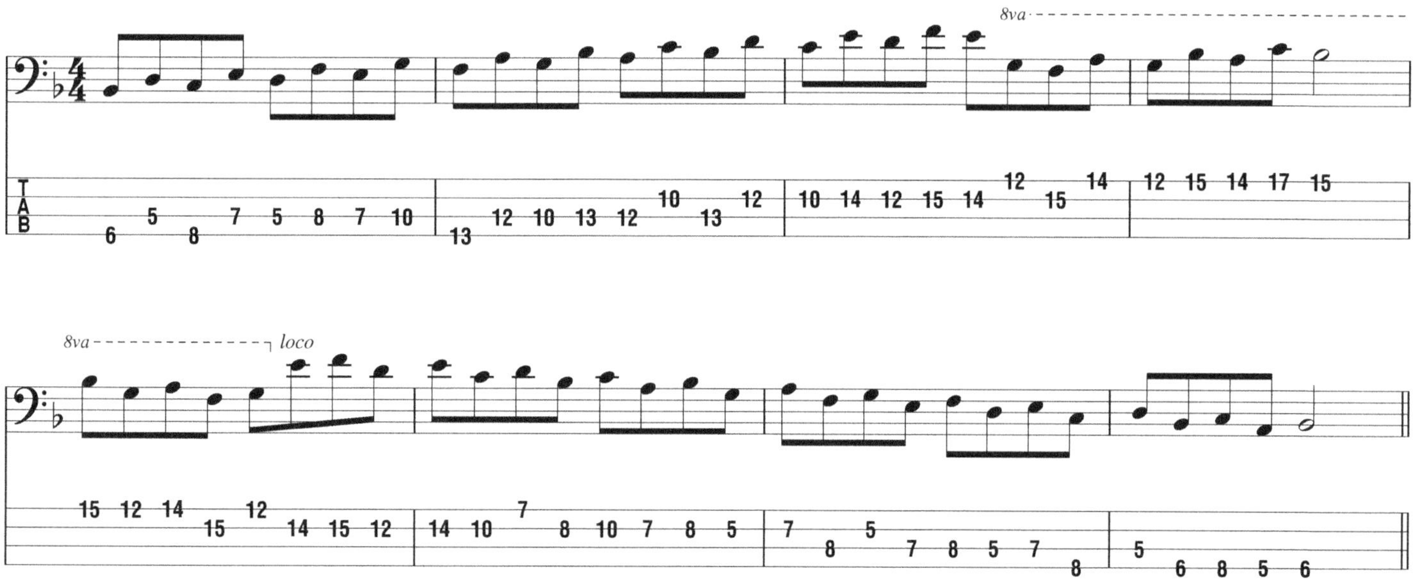

A♭ Lydian in fourths.

A Lydian in four-note groupings.

Solo Exercises

This is a modal chord progression using only major seventh chords. Use the Lydian mode on every chord.

Track 31

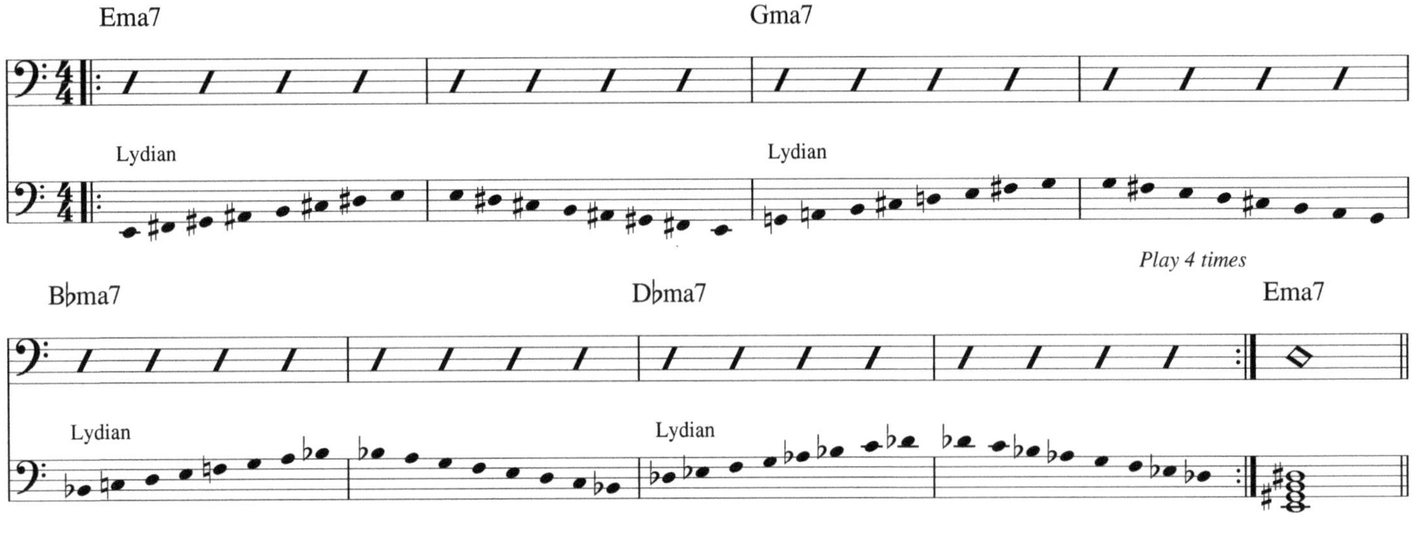

Here we have a Ima7–IVma7–IImi7–V7 progression. For the I chord, we will substitute the Lydian scale, which sounds very jazzy. Play Lydian modes on Gma7 and Cma7, Dorian over Ami7, and Mixolydian over D7.

Track 32

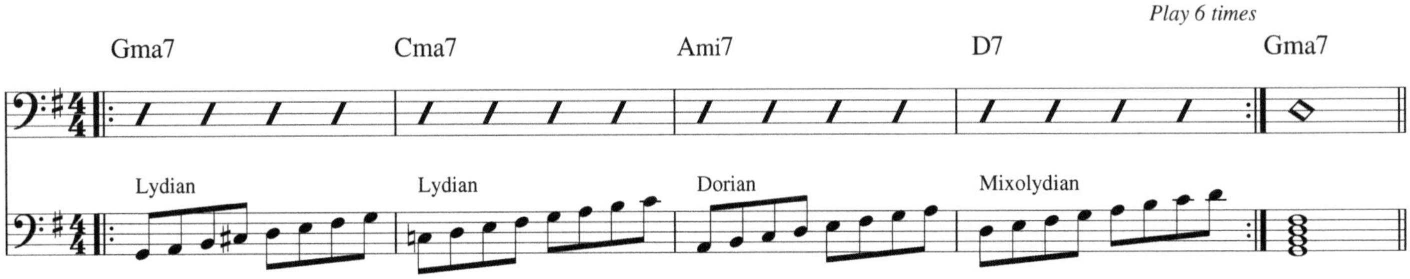

Combined Scale Exercises

Ionian and Aeolian System

Up to this point, we only studied the modes of major and natural minor scales (which are the same). Here is an overview of all the modes in C major and C minor. It is imperative to understand the relationship of the scales within a key so you can choose the correct scale when soloing. Try to memorize the scales and be aware of the intervals that make every scale unique.

Seven Modes of C Major

Degree: I
Chord: Cma7 Ex 9&13
Scale: Ionian

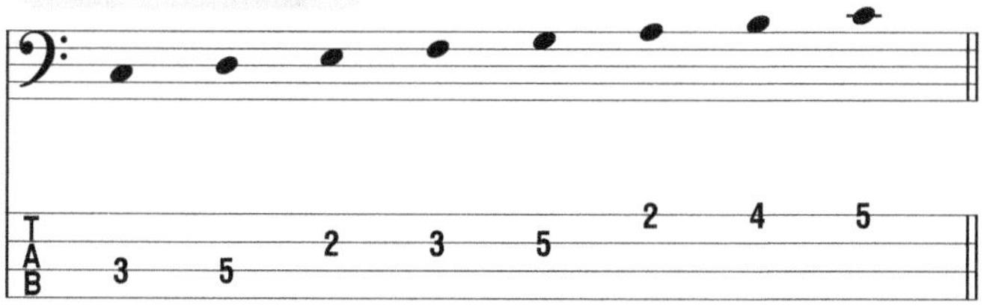

Degree: II
Chord: Dmi7 Ex 9&11
Scale: Dorian

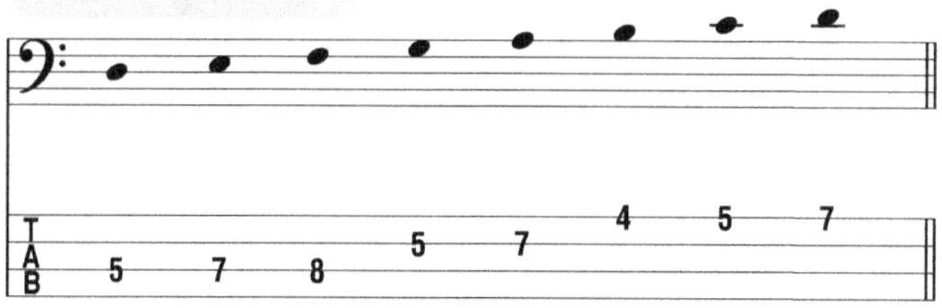

Degree: III
Chord: Emi7 Ex 11
Scale: Phrygian

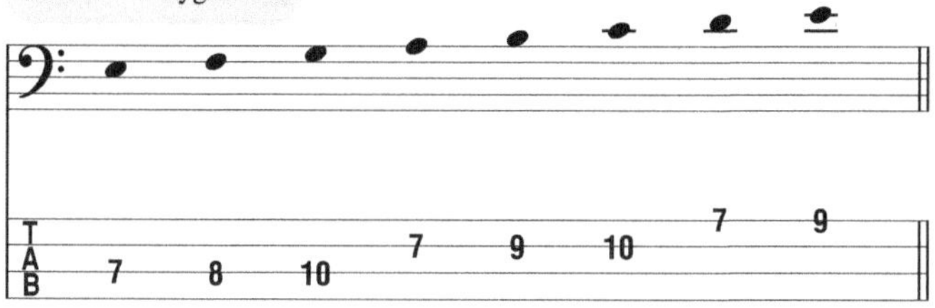

Degree: IV
Chord: Fma7 Ex 9,♯11,13
Scale: Lydian

Degree: V
Chord: G7 Ex 9&13
Scale: Mixolydian

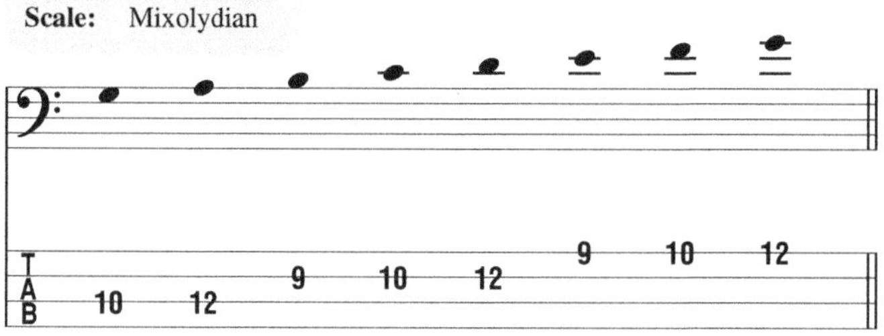

Degree: VI
Chord: Ami7 Ex 9&11
Scale: Aeolian

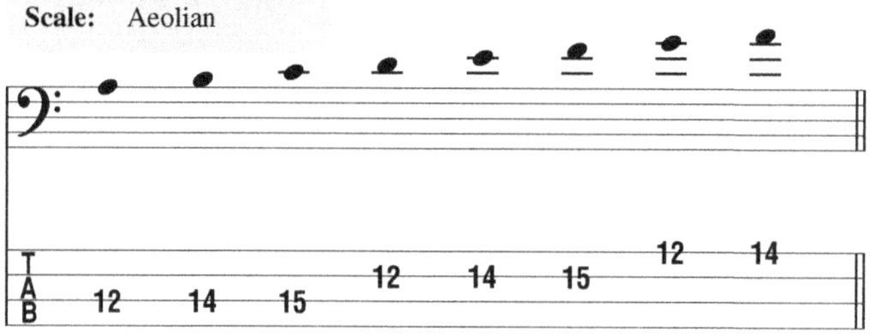

Degree: VII
Chord: Bmi7(♭5) Ex 11&♭13
Scale: Locrian

Seven Modes of C Minor

Degree: I
Chord: Cmi7 Ex 9&11
Scale: Aeolian

Degree: II
Chord: Dmi7(♭5) Ex 11&♭13
Scale: Locrian

Degree: ♭III
Chord: E♭ma7 Ex 9&13
Scale: Ionian

Degree: IV
Chord: Fmi7 Ex 9&11
Scale: Dorian

Degree: V
Chord: Gmi7 Ex 11
Scale: Phrygian

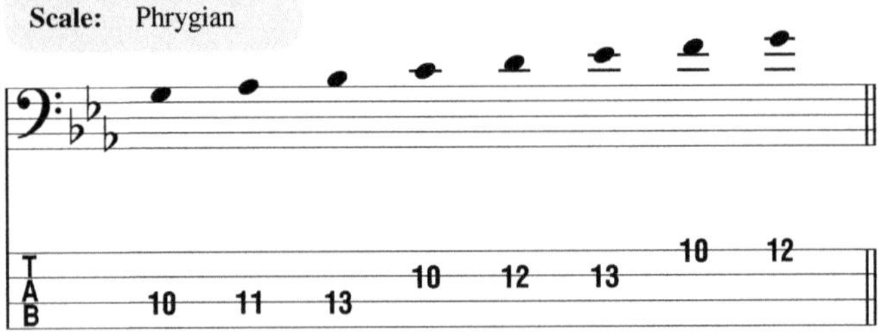

Degree: ♭VI
Chord: A♭ma7 Ex 9,♯11,13
Scale: Lydian

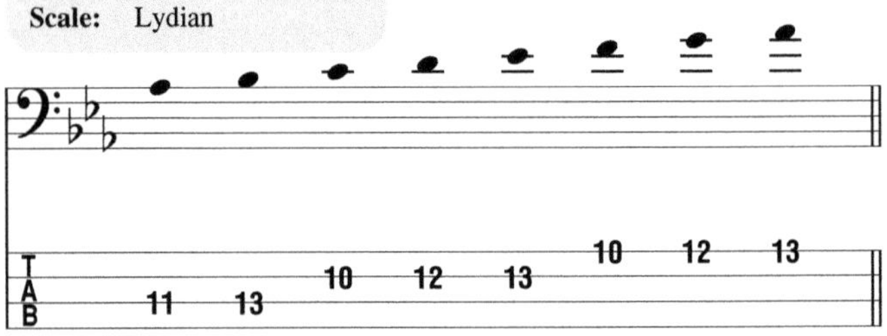

Degree: ♭VII
Chord: B♭7 Ex 9&13
Scale: Mixolydian

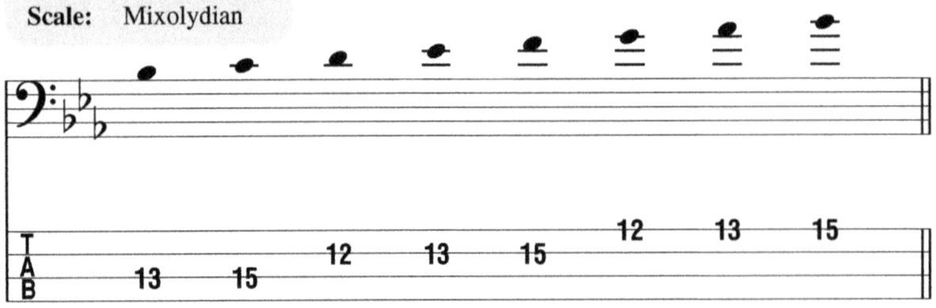

Let's try soloing over a tune that changes chords many times. The first thing to do is figure out what key we are in. In a basic major key, the dominant chord (root letter followed by just the number 7, 9, or 13) is always the V chord. Knowing this can help you locate the key. Find the dominant chord, then count down a major scale from V to I to find the key. The key signature on the music staff can also help, but many times the tune might go through key changes while the signature doesn't change. This happens quite frequently in jazz tunes.

Key Signatures

Here is a list of all the key signatures; take your time and memorize them all.

C major or A minor

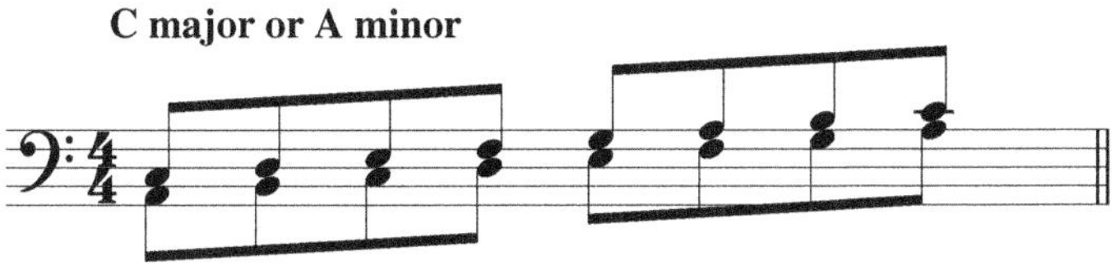

G major or E minor

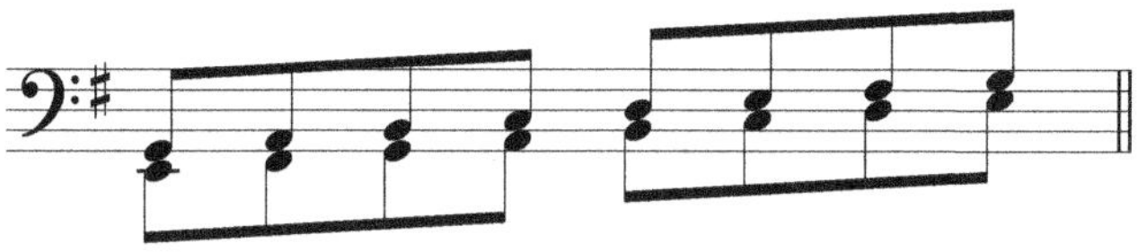

D major or B minor

A major or F♯ minor

E major or C♯ minor

B major or G♯ minor

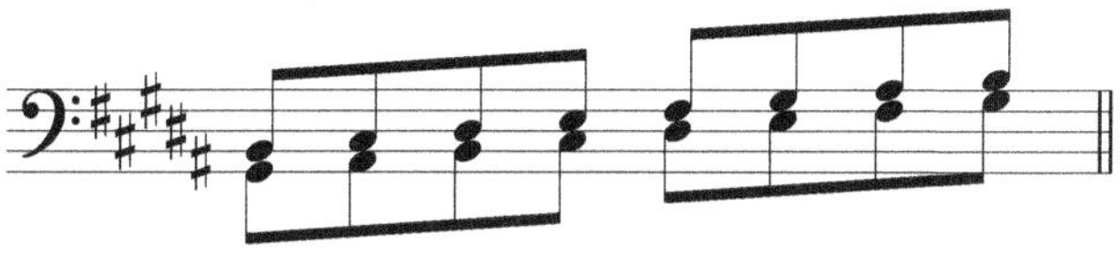

F♯ major or D♯ minor

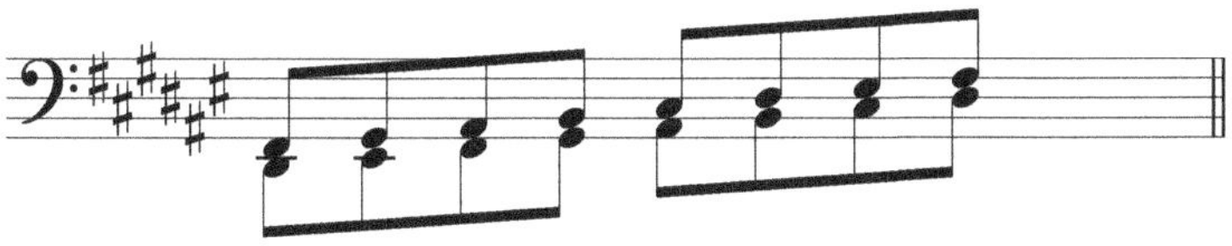

G♭ major or E♭ minor

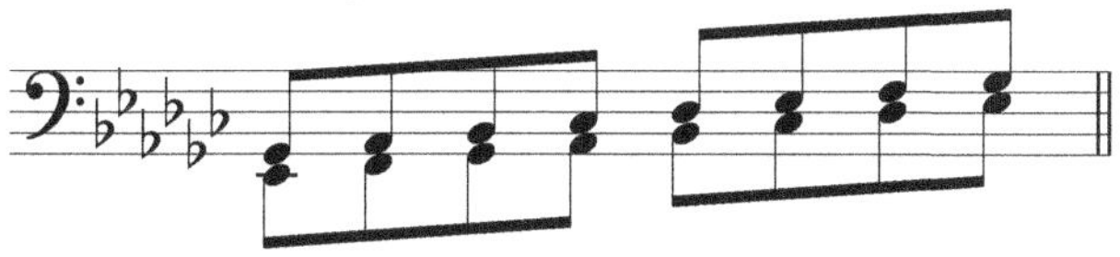

D♭ major or B♭ minor

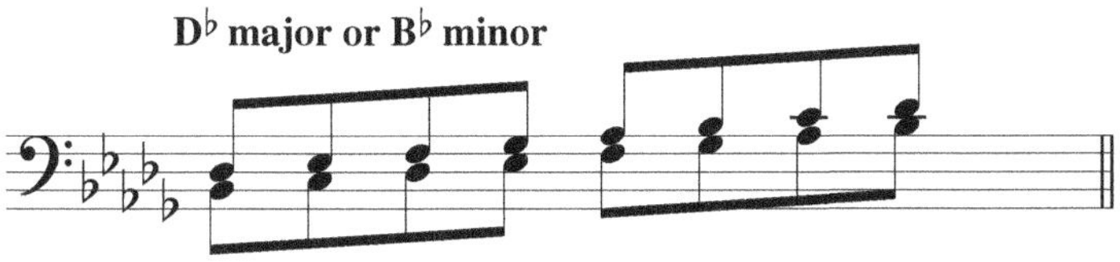

A♭ major or F minor

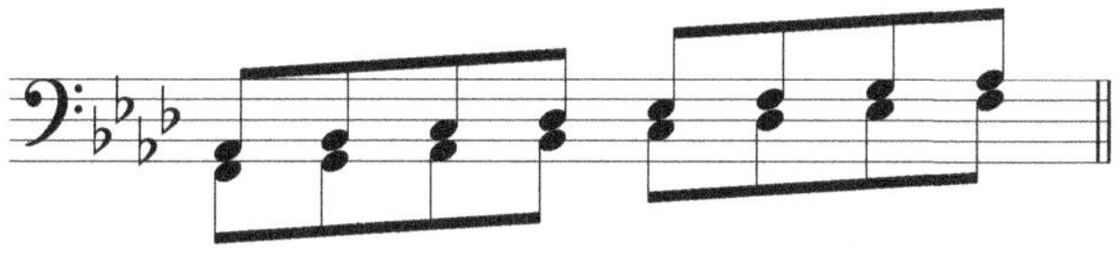

E♭ major or C minor

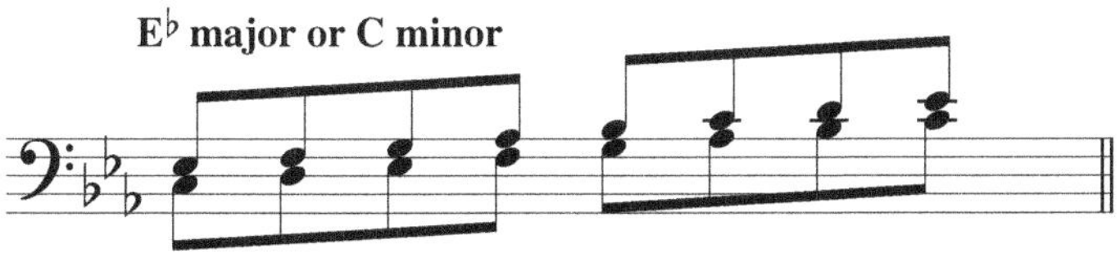

B♭ major or G minor

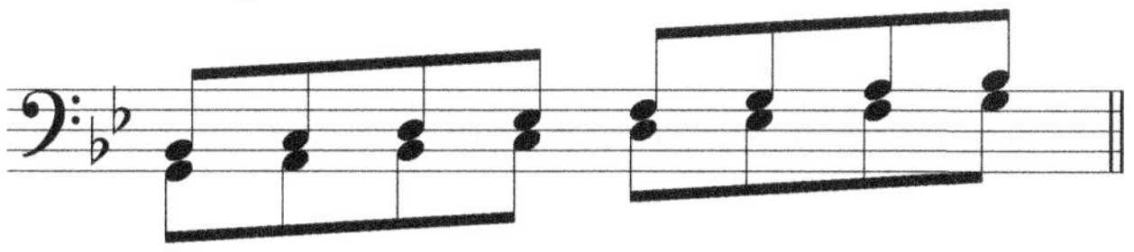

F major or D minor

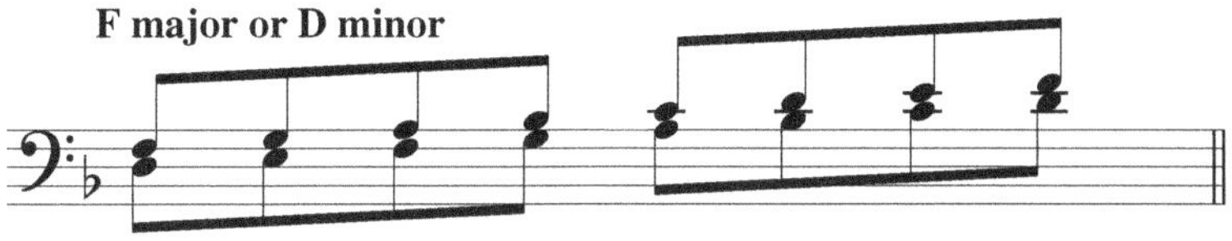

Scale	Notes	Key Signature
C major/A minor	C–D–E–F–G–A–B	No flats (♭) or sharps (♯)
G major/E minor	G–A–B–C–D–E–F♯	1 sharp
D major/B minor	D–E–F♯–G–A–B–C♯	2 sharps
A major/F♯ minor	A–B–C♯–D–E–F♯–G♯	3 sharps
E major/C♯ minor	E–F♯–G♯–A–B–C♯–D♯	4 sharps
B major/G♯ minor	B–C♯–D♯–E–F♯–G♯–A♯	5 sharps
F♯ major/D♯ minor	F♯–G♯–A♯–B–C♯–D♯–E♯	6 sharps
G♭ major/E♭ minor	G♭–A♭–B♭–C♭–D♭–E♭–F	6 flats
D♭ major/B♭ minor	D♭–E♭–F–G♭–A♭–B♭–C	5 flats
A♭ major/F minor	A♭–B♭–C–D♭–E♭–F–G	4 flats
E♭ major/C minor	E♭–F–G–A♭–B♭–C–D	3 flats
B♭ major/G minor	B♭–C–D–E♭–F–G–A	2 flats
F major/D minor	F–G–A–B♭–C–D–E	1 flat

Solo Exercise

The key signature in the following example has three sharps; this means that you are either in A major or F♯ minor.

Notice that the Bmi7, E7, and Ama7 chords form a IImi7–V7–Ima7 progression in the key of A major. This means that over the Bmi7 chord you will play Dorian, E7 gets Mixolydian, and Ama7, of course, uses the Ionian scale. The following F♯mi7 is the VImi7 chord of A, so the Aeolian scale is used.

At measure 9, the tune *modulates* (changes key) and we have a II–V–I progression in D major. Now, you have to play E Dorian, A Mixolydian, and D Ionian. At measure 13, the tune returns to the key of A.

At measure 17, we have a cycle of four dominant chords which leads back to the key of A (measure 25). Each chord is its own fifth degree (without resolution) and uses the Mixolydian scale. The last eight measures are in A major again, and use the same scales as the first eight measures.

Track 33

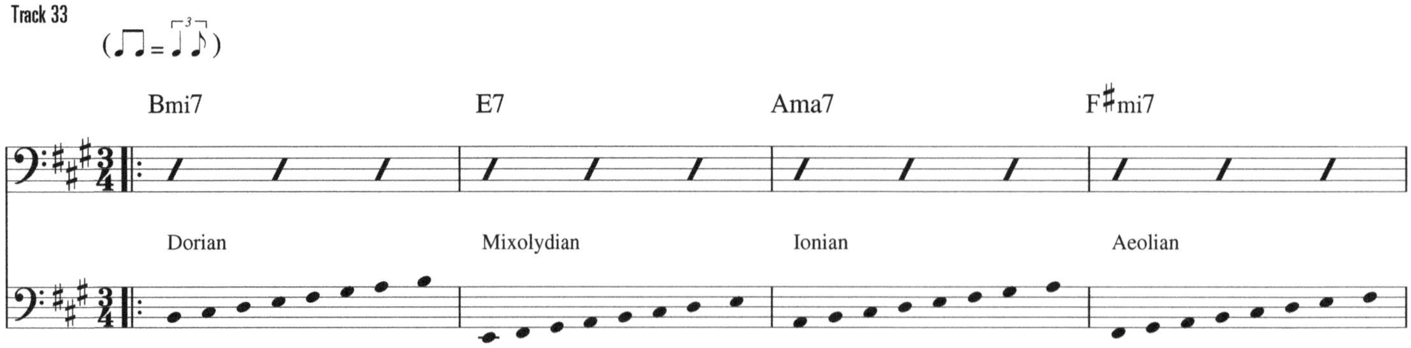

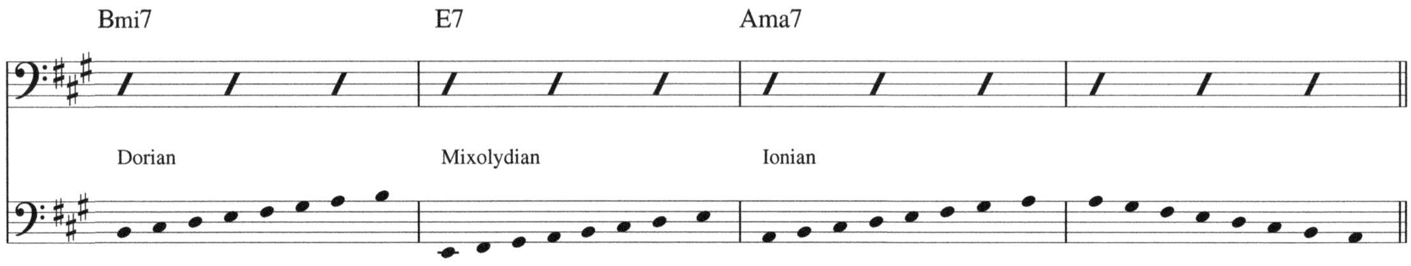

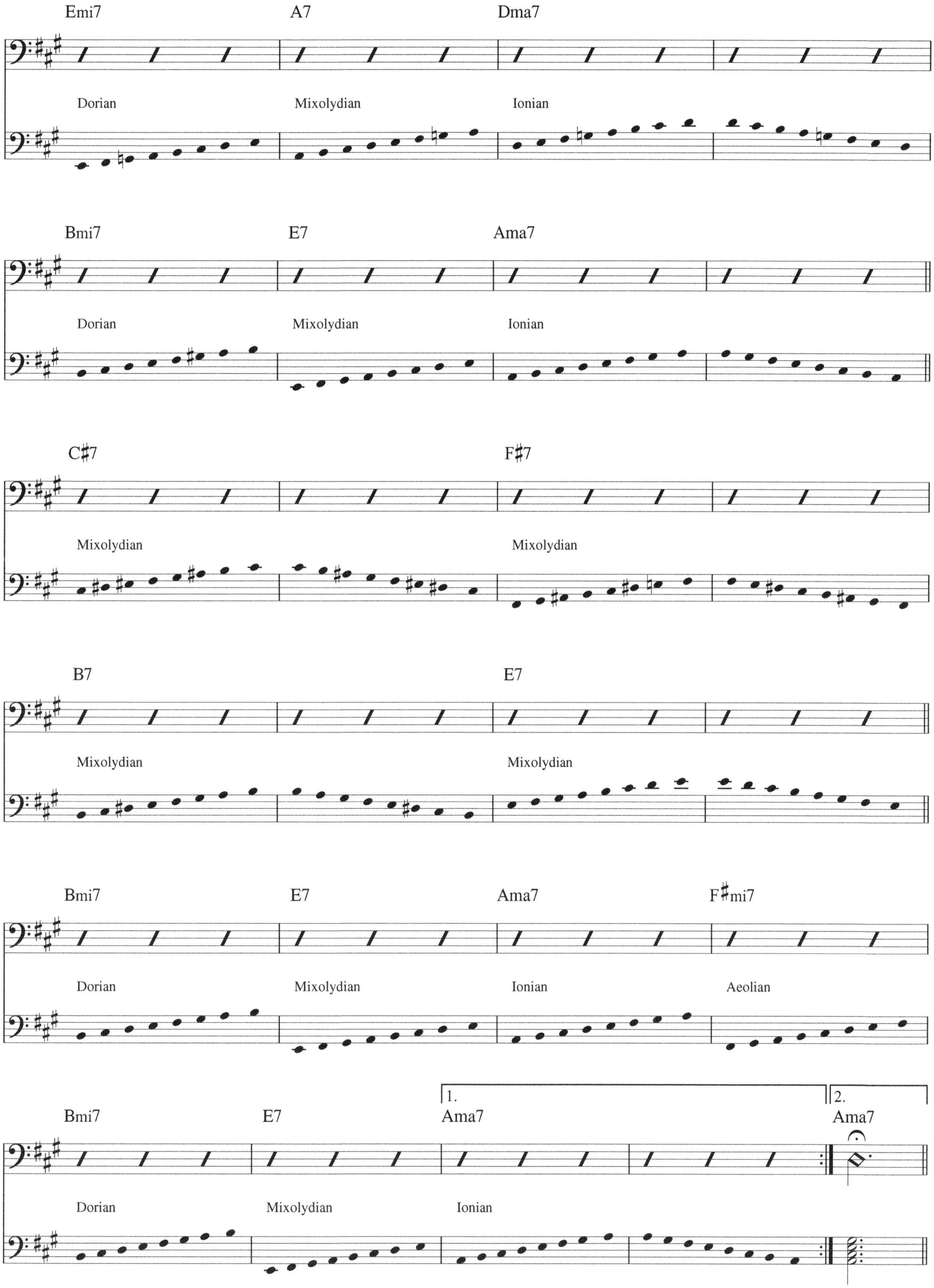
Emi7
A7
Dma7
Dorian
Mixolydian
Ionian
Bmi7
E7
Ama7
Dorian
Mixolydian
Ionian
C♯7
F♯7
Mixolydian
Mixolydian
B7
E7
Mixolydian
Mixolydian
Bmi7
E7
Ama7
F♯mi7
Dorian
Mixolydian
Ionian
Aeolian
1.
2.
Bmi7
E7
Ama7
Ama7
Dorian
Mixolydian
Ionian

2 Melodic Minor Modes

The *melodic minor* scale consists of a new set of seven modes. There is no special name for the first mode of melodic minor as there is with major—we just call the first mode melodic minor.

Seven Modes of Melodic Minor

Degree: I
Chord: Cmi(ma7)
Scale: Melodic Minor

Degree: II
Chord: Dmi7
Scale: Dorian♭2

Degree: ♭III
Chord: E♭ma7(♯5)
Scale: Lydian♯5

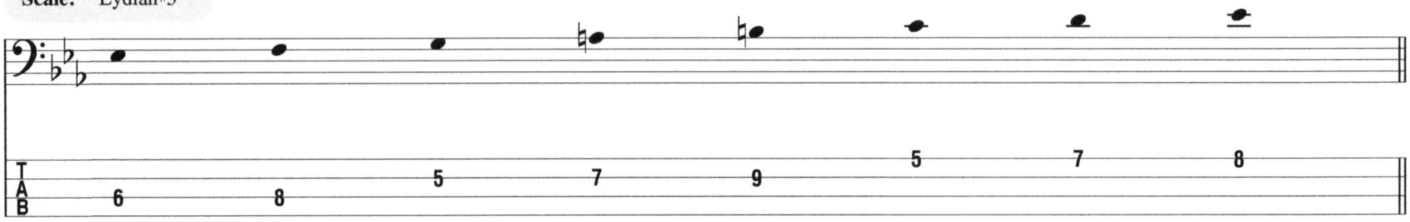

Degree: IV
Chord: F7
Scale: Lydian♭7

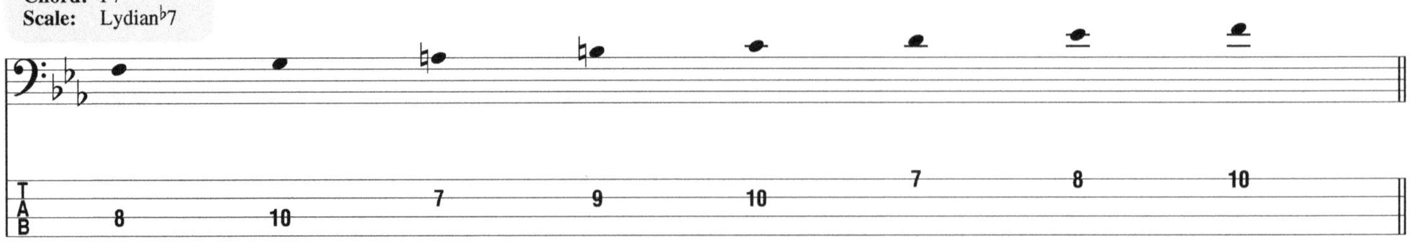

Degree: V
Chord: G7
Scale: Mixolydian♭13

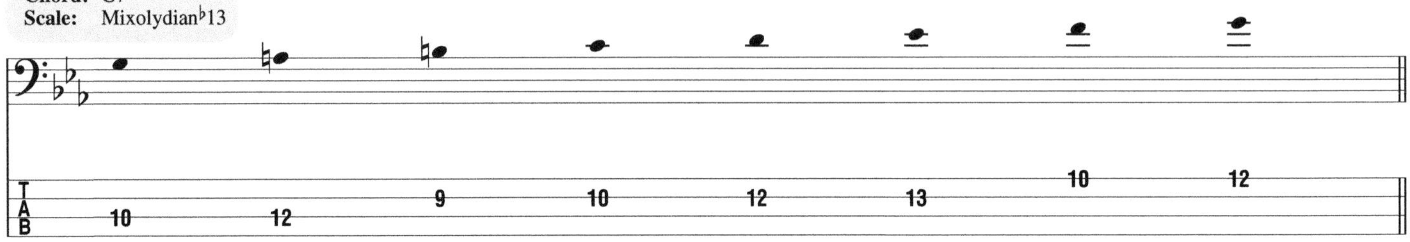

Degree: VI
Chord: Ami7(♭5)
Scale: Locrian♮2

Degree: VII
Chord: Bmi7(♭5)
Scale: Locrian♭4

Melodic Minor

The melodic minor (and *harmonic minor*) sounds have traditionally been used over dominant chords in minor keys. The fifth degree of a minor key is diatonically a minor seventh chord, but composers tend to substitute the V chord of Aeolian (Vmi7, Phrygian) with a dominant seventh chord to achieve a more interesting musical flow of tension and resolution. This is achieved by raising the seventh note of the minor scale, effectively making a *harmonic minor* sound.

In contemporary improvisation, the various melodic minor sounds are used as substitute scales over specific chords in many temporary situations. It is not common that a tune would be written completely in melodic or harmonic minor, but it is common practice (especially in jazz) to add the colors of melodic and harmonic minor to the vocabulary of an improviser.

Theory and Application

You can think of the melodic minor scale as an Aeolian scale with a raised sixth and seventh, or as an Ionian scale with a minor third. There are no passing notes in this scale, which makes it great for soloing; every note can be sustained.

Degree: I
Chord: Cmi(ma7)(9/11/13)
Cmi6(9/11)
Scale: Melodic Minor

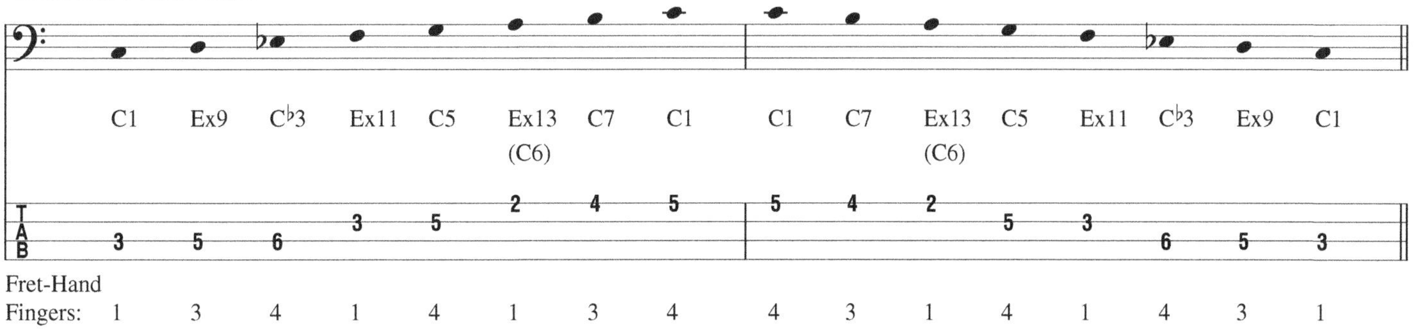

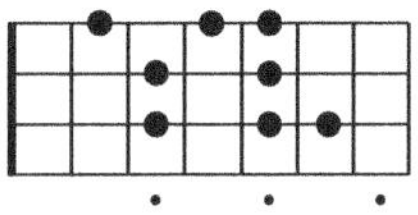

Melodic minor is used to improvise over *minor (major seventh)* (mi[ma7]) and *minor sixth* chords. The minor (major seventh) chord is very tense and mainly seen in jazz. The scale itself, though, is frequently used as a substitute over a Imi7 chord.

Melodic minor is the preferred scale choice over:

- Imi(ma7) and Imi6 chords in minor
- as a substitute scale for Aeolian and Dorian, especially if used over the Imi7 chord
- modal minor (major seventh) and minor sixth chords

Scale Exercises

Here is a two-octave C melodic minor scale.

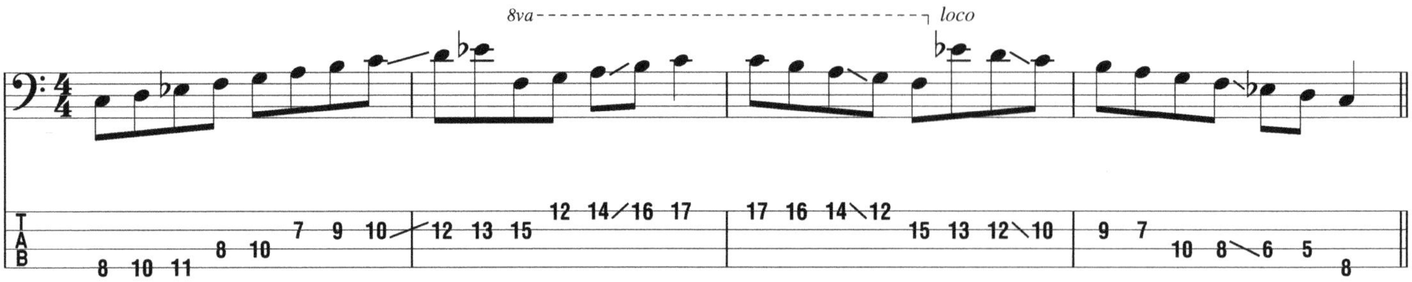

If you play the B melodic minor scale in four-note groupings, you'll get a nice sequence.

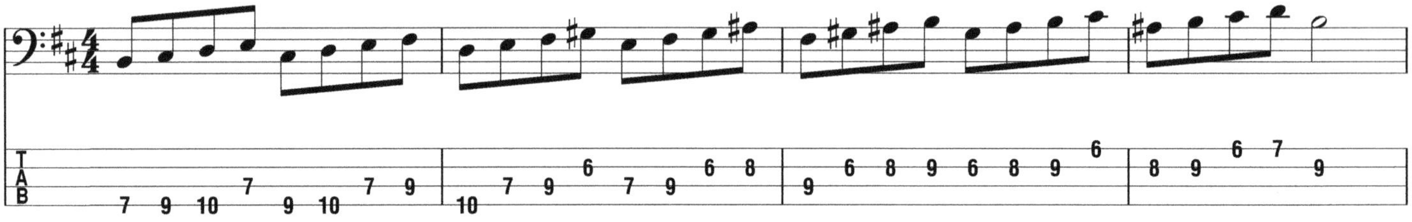

This exercise navigates the scale in alternating ascending and descending fifths over a two-octave range.

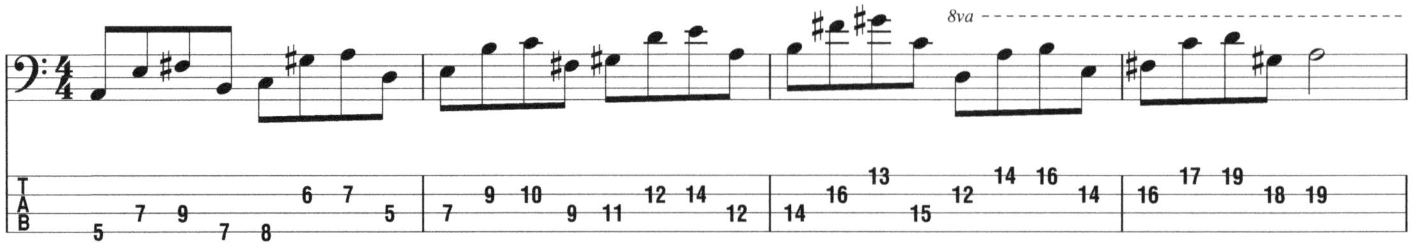

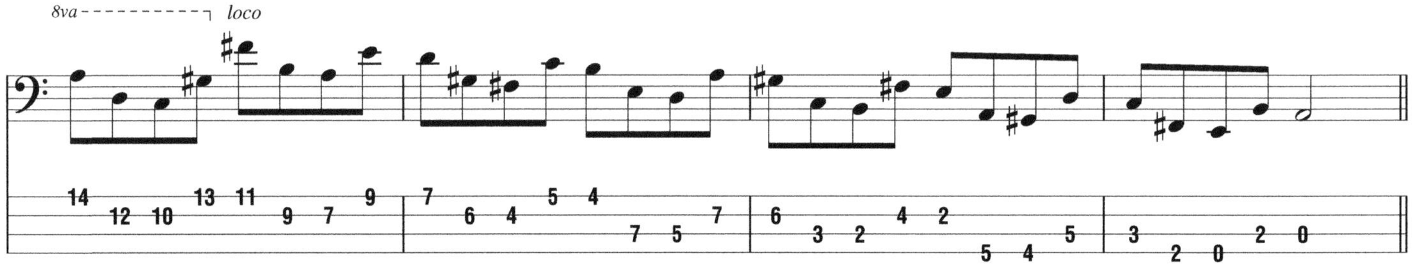

This is F♯ melodic minor on the A string only.

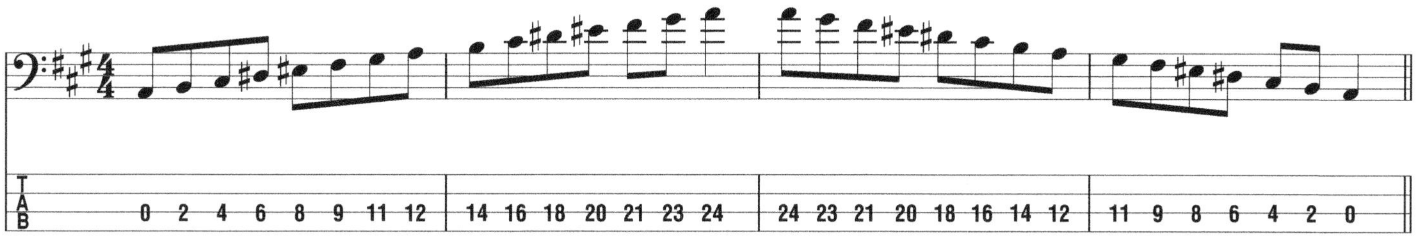

Solo Exercises

This is a modal chord progression using only minor (major seventh) chords. Use the melodic minor scale for every chord. Track 34 gives you an example of how to approach this solo. It might take you a while to get used to the sound of these chords. Track 35 is only accompaniment for your solo.

Track 34–35

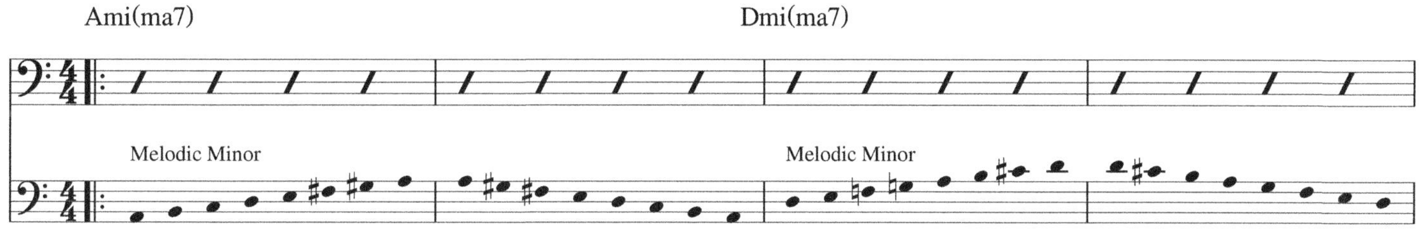

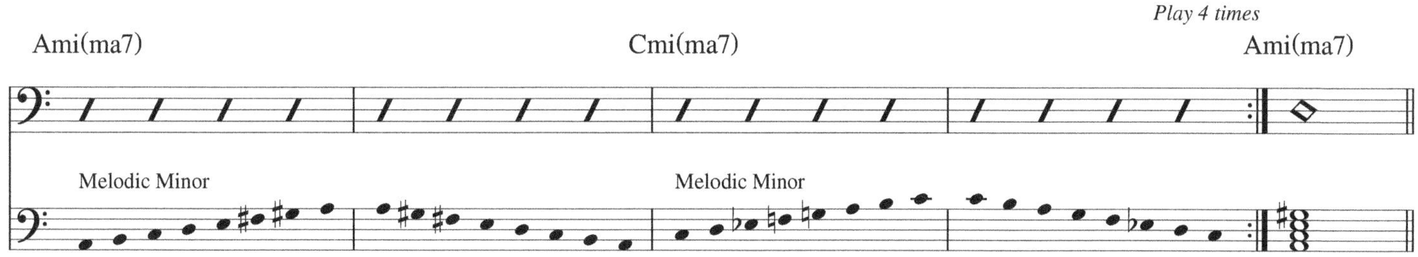

If you analyze this next progression, you'll find that D is the I chord and Bmi is the VImi chord. The I chord uses Ionian for its regular scale, but Lydian is a common substitute—giving you two possible scales for Dma7. Since we only know one scale that fits the minor (major seventh) chord, the only choice over B is melodic minor.

Track 36

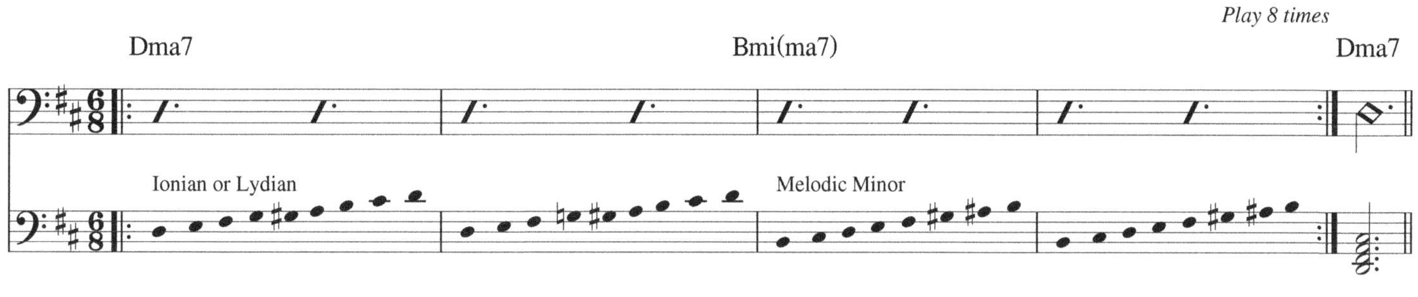

Lydian♭7

Theory and Application

The *Lydian♭7* mode (also known as *Lydian Dominant*) comes from the fourth degree of melodic minor. In Europe, this scale is known as *Mixolydian♯11*; it's the same as the regular Lydian mode with the seventh note lowered a half step, hence the name Lydian♭7. This scale forms a dominant seventh chord with the extensions 9, ♯11, and 13. The extensions of the Lydian♭7 scale form a major triad, and the polychord symbol $\frac{D}{C7}$ is sometimes used instead of the more cumbersome C13(♯11).

Degree: IV
Chord: C9(♯11/13) $\frac{D}{C7}$
Scale: Lydian♭7

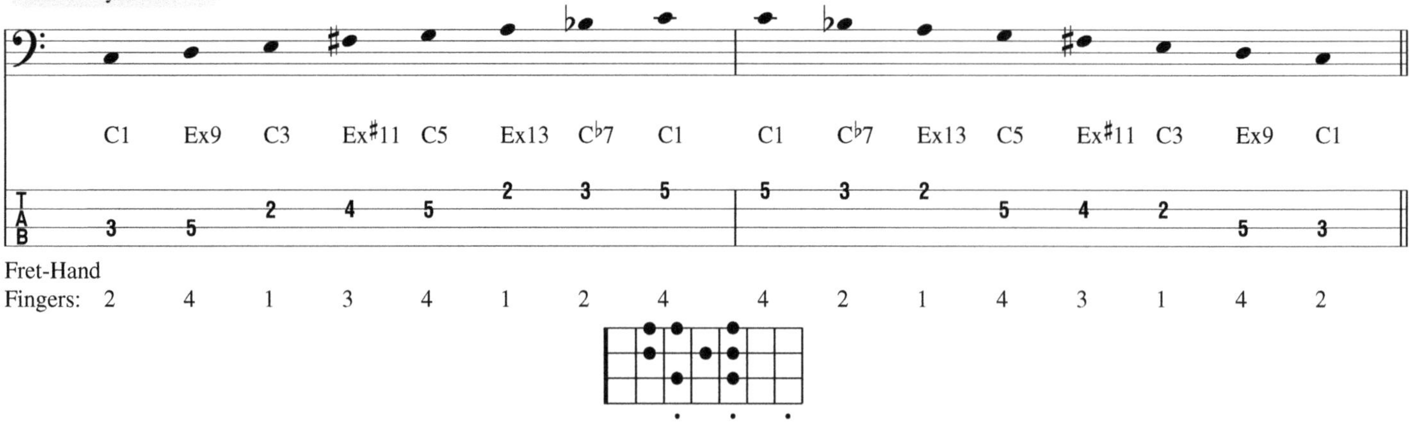

This scale is traditionally used over a *non-functioning dominant chord*, which is any dominant seventh chord that does not resolve up by a fourth (or down a fifth).

Lydian♭7 is the preferred scale choice over:

- IV7 chords
- all dominant chords that resolve down by a half step (C7 resolving to Bma7 or Bmi)
- non-functioning dominant chords

Scale Exercises

G Lydian♭7 over two octaves.

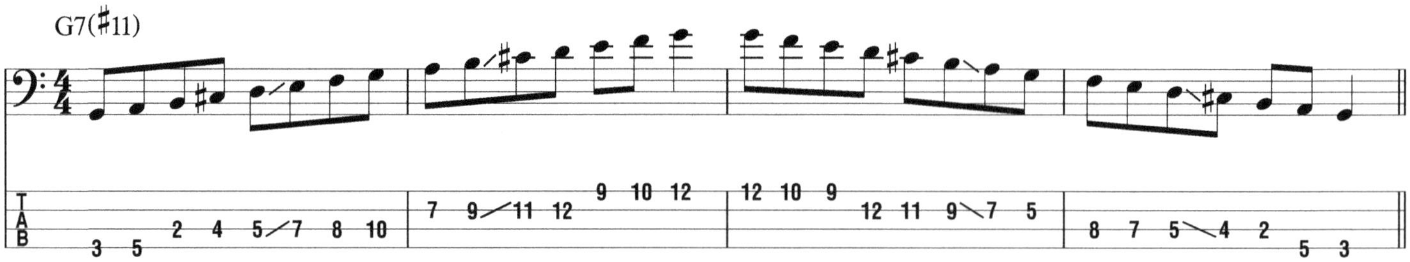

B♭ Lydian♭7 in sixths.

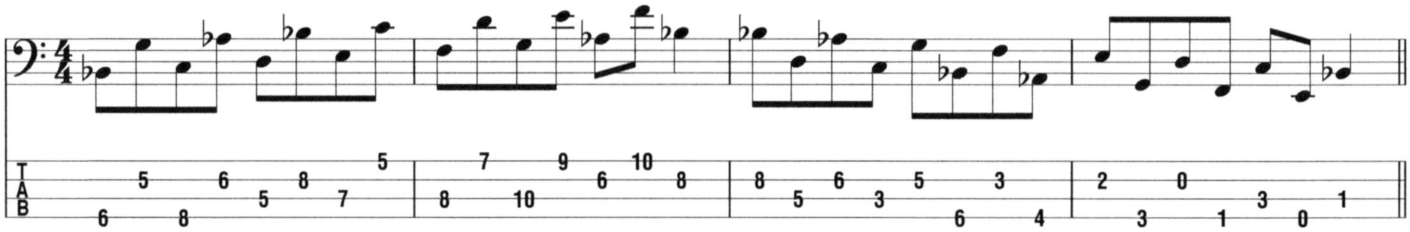

D♭ Lydian♭7 in eighth position.

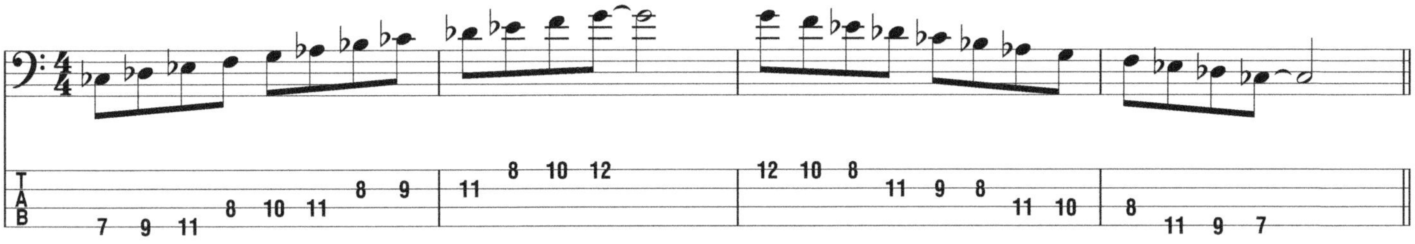

This exercise utilizes the scale in alternating ascending and descending thirds over a two-octave range.

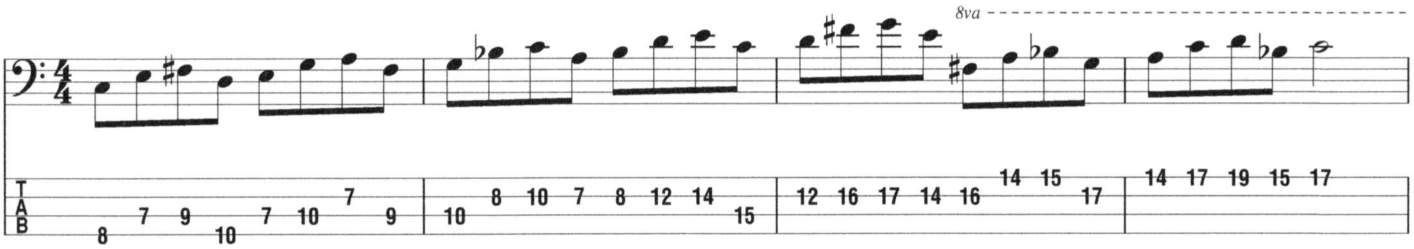

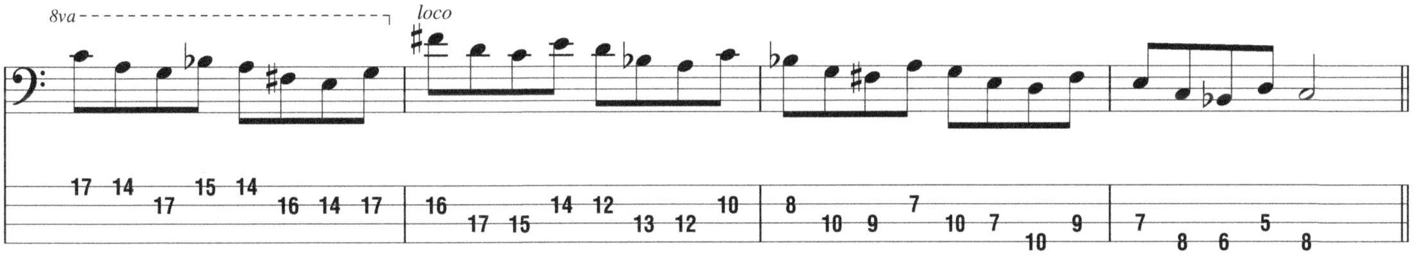

Solo Exercises

This first progression is in C minor; Cmi7 is obviously the Imi7 chord. This means you can play Aeolian, Dorian, or the more tense melodic minor over it. The two dominant chords are both non-functioning, so Lydian♭7 would be the best choice.

Track 37

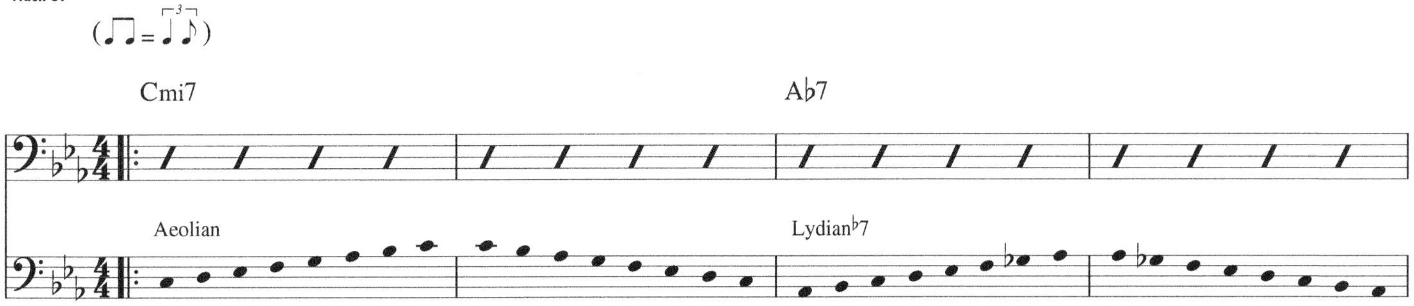

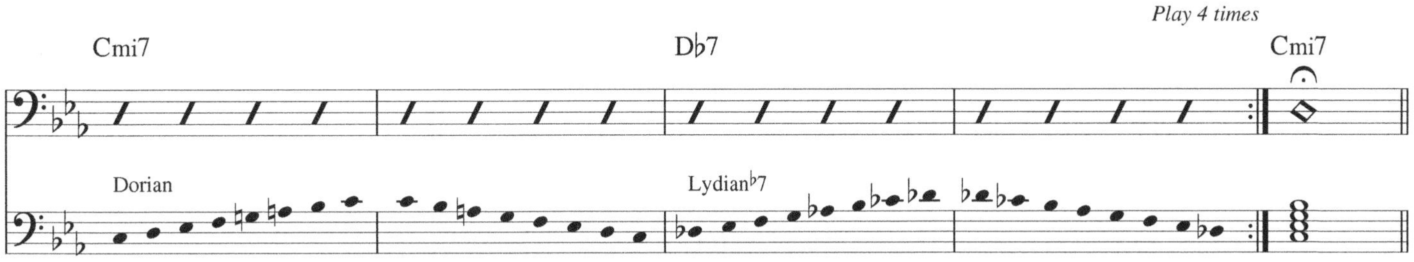

In this example, A is the I chord, and although Lydian might be a great substitute, Ionian should be your first choice. Since D7 is a non-diatonic IV7, Lydian♭7 would be your only choice. Notice that the only difference between A Ionian and D Lydian♭7 is the C♯ changing to C.

Track 38

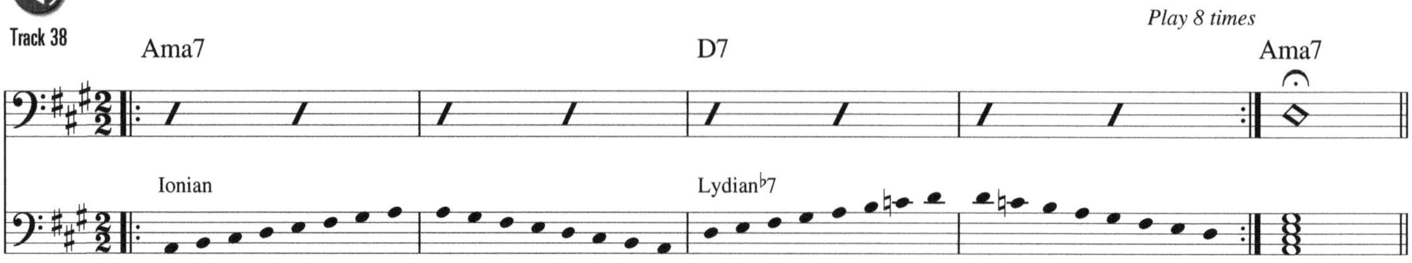

Locrian♮2

Theory and Application

The *Locrian♮2* (also known somewhat confusingly as *Locrian♯2*) comes from the sixth degree of melodic minor. It's almost the same as Locrian, except the second note of the scale is a major second instead of a minor second. This scale spells out a minor seventh (flat five) chord (mi7[♭5]) with the extensions 9, 11, and ♭13.

Degree: VI
Chord: Cmi7(♭5)(9/11/♭13)
Scale: Locrian♮2

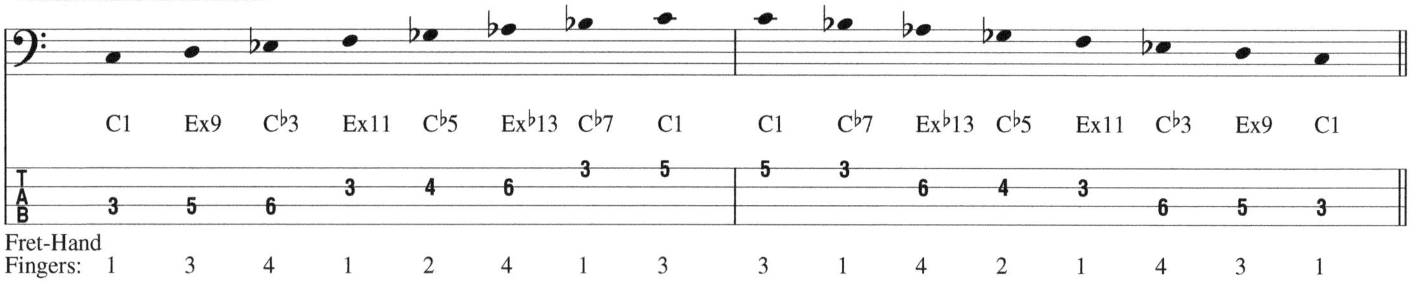

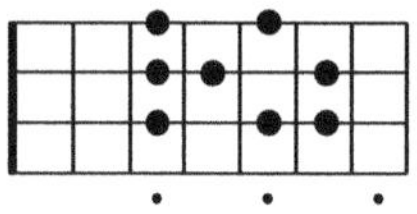

This scale is traditionally used as a substitute for the Locrian scale—most commonly for the IImi7(♭5) chord in a minor IImi7(♭5)–V7–Imi7 progression. It's also a great choice for the rare VImi7(♭5) chord.

Locrian♮2 is the preferred scale choice over:
- VImi7(♭5) and IVmi7(♭5) chords
- as a substitute for mi7(♭5) chords

Scale Exercises

F♯ Locrian♮2 over two octaves.

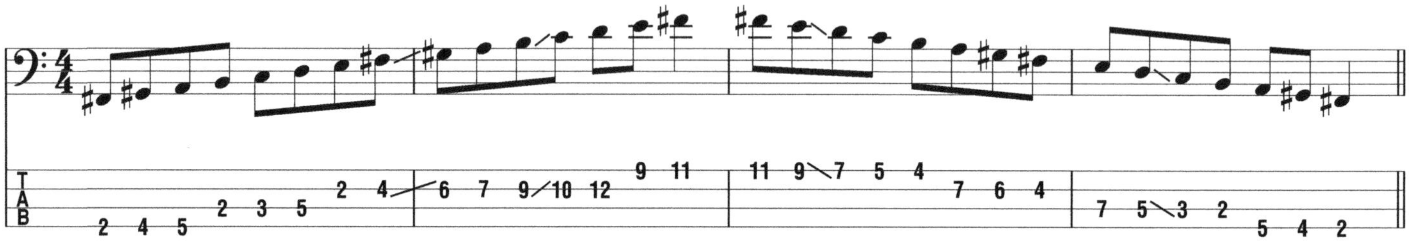

This is the scale from D in sevenths.

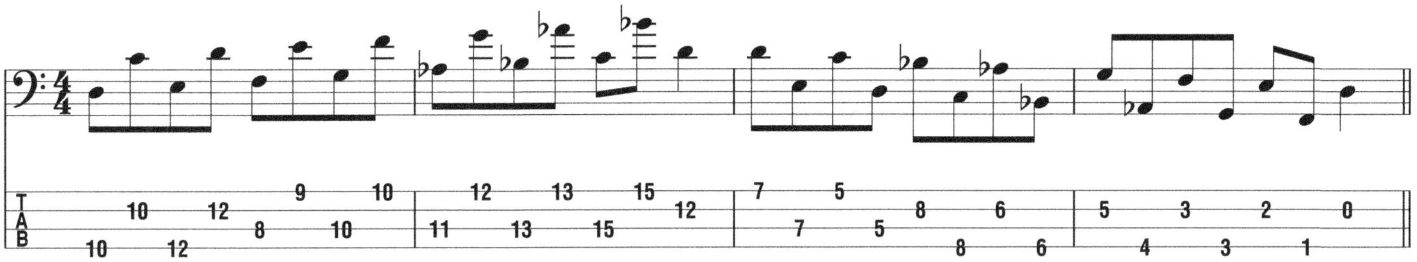

Here are alternating ascending and descending thirds starting on G over two octaves.

Now we have E Locrian♮2 over three octaves.

Solo Exercises

This exercise is in G minor, and the IV and VI degrees both use the Locrian♮2 scale.

Track 39

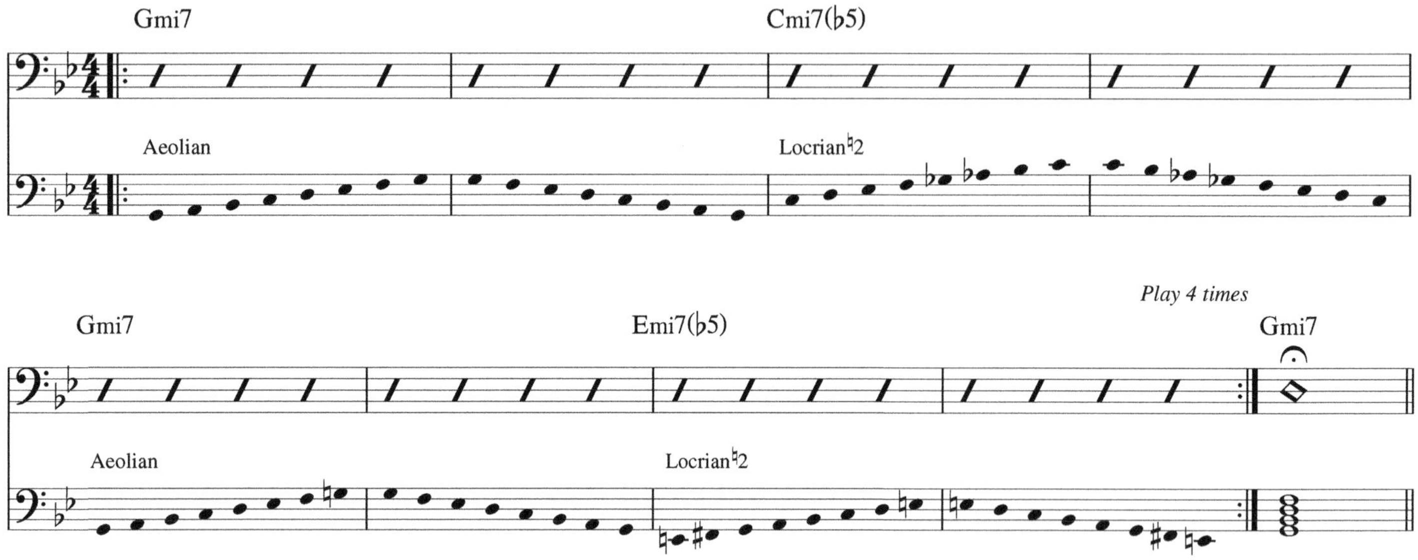

This is a IImi7(♭5)–V7–Ima7 progression (diatonic to B major), except that the II chord is a mi7(♭5) instead of a mi7, so for that chord, Locrian♮2 or Locrian would be the appropriate choices.

Track 40

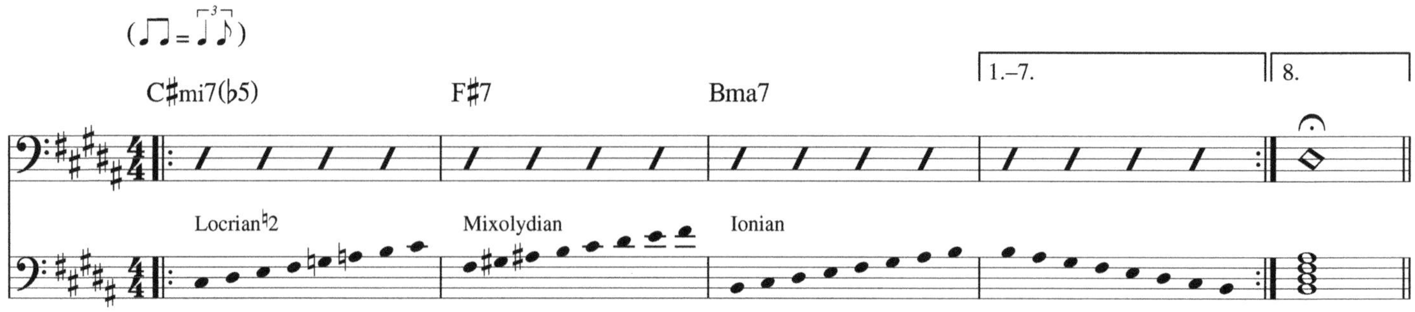

Altered

Theory and Application

The *Altered* scale, also known as *Super Locrian*, is a dominant scale in which every extension has been altered in relation to Mixolydian. It has the same notes as the VII degree of melodic minor, but the spelling has been enharmonically changed to fit a dominant chord.

This scale can be spelled in a few different ways. I like to spell it with the extensions ♭9, ♯9, ♯11, and ♭13. It is not unusual to see ♭5 instead of ♯11, and ♯5 for ♭13.

VII Degree of Melodic Minor

Enharmonic spelling of melodic minor results in the Altered scale.

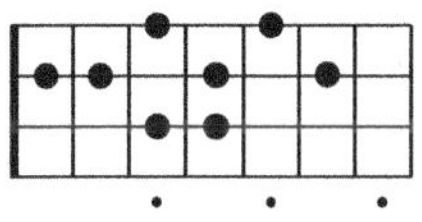

This scale is used for *functioning dominant chords* (resolving up a fourth or down a fifth, as C7 to Fma7 or Fmi7). It is quite "out" and creates a lot of tension. This makes the resolution to the tonic chord that much more satisfying.

Scale Exercises

Here's the G Altered scale over two octaves.

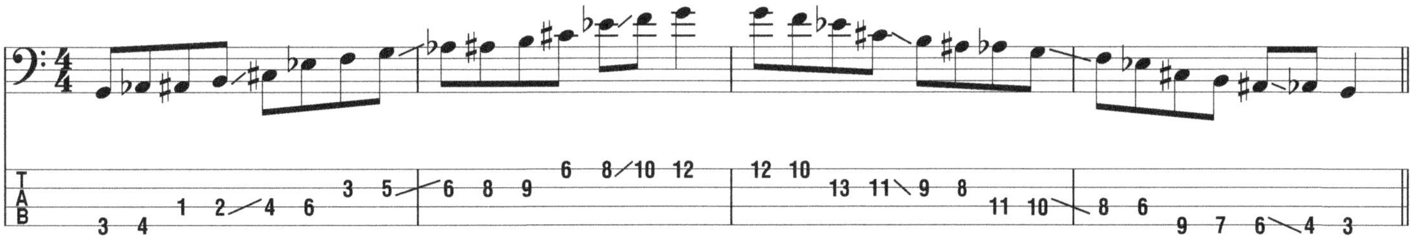

This is the scale from A♯ in fifths (spelled enharmonically so it's easier to read).

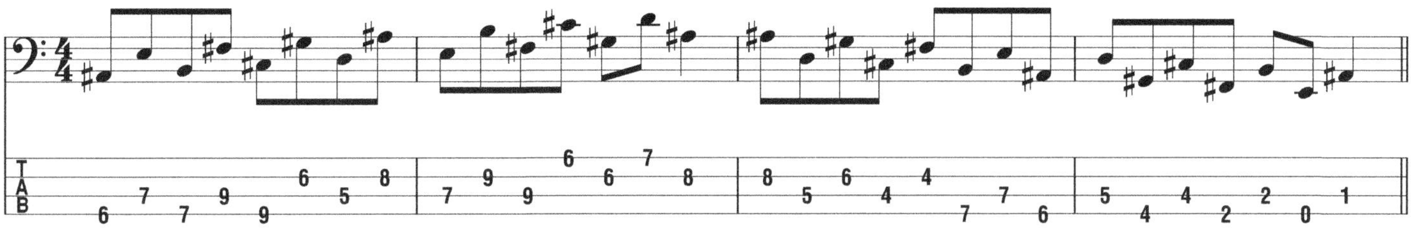

This is E Altered in tenth position (again, spelled enharmonically). The lowest note is the ♭7th (D).

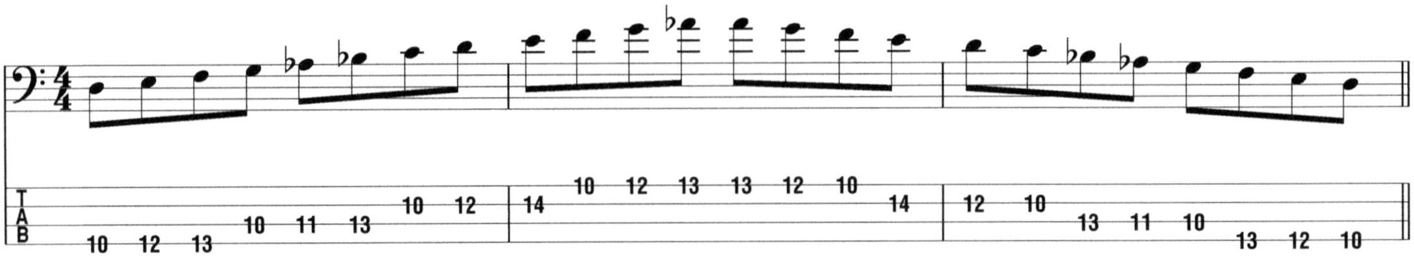

This is A Altered only on the D string (spelled enharmonically).

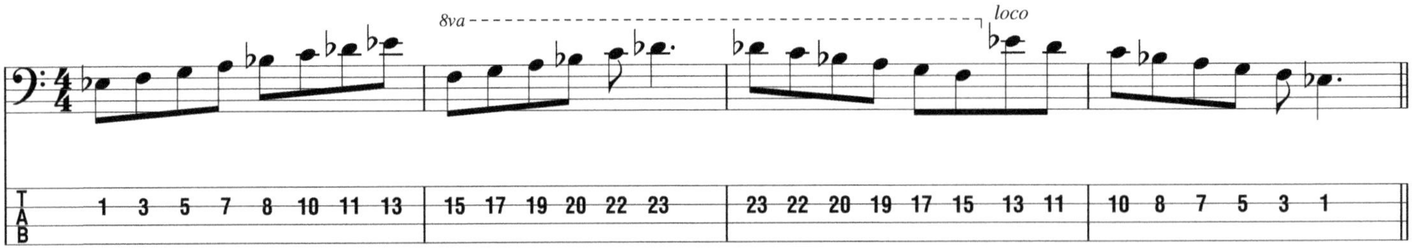

Solo Exercises

As mentioned previously, the Altered scale is the best choice for a functioning dominant chord. In this simple V–I progression, Altered and Ionian work best.

Track 41

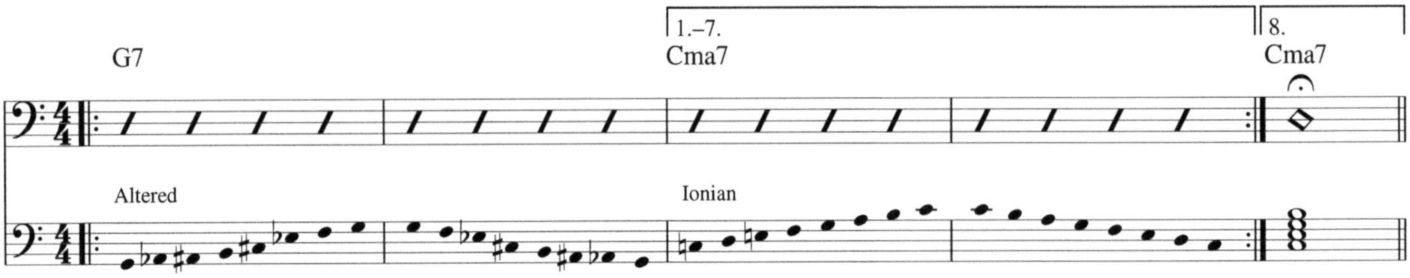

The following example is a Imi6–IImi7(♭5)–V7 progression in F minor. Since the first chord is Fmi6 we have two possible scale choices: Dorian or melodic minor. For the IImi7(♭5) chord, we can use Locrian or Locrian♮2. The C7 is going to use the Altered scale again.

Track 42

Mixolydian♭13

Theory and Application

Mixolydian♭13 is another dominant scale used over functioning dominant chords. It stands on degree V of melodic minor, and adds the extensions 9 and ♭13 to the dominant seventh chord. It can be used to resolve to either a major or minor chord.

Degree: V
Chord: C7(9/♭13)
Scale: Mixolydian♭13

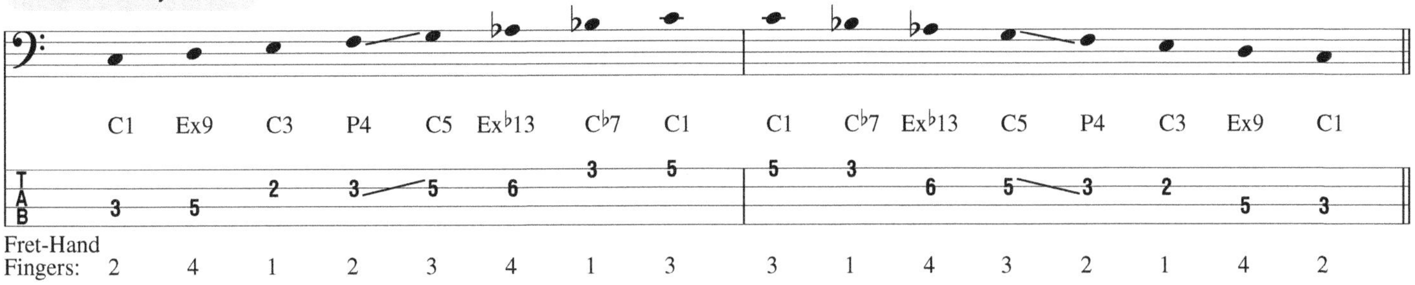

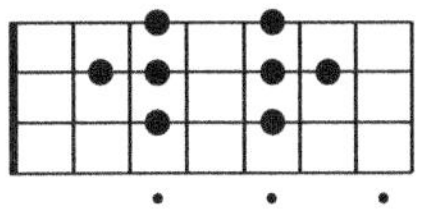

Scale Exercises

This is B Mixolydian♭13 over two octaves.

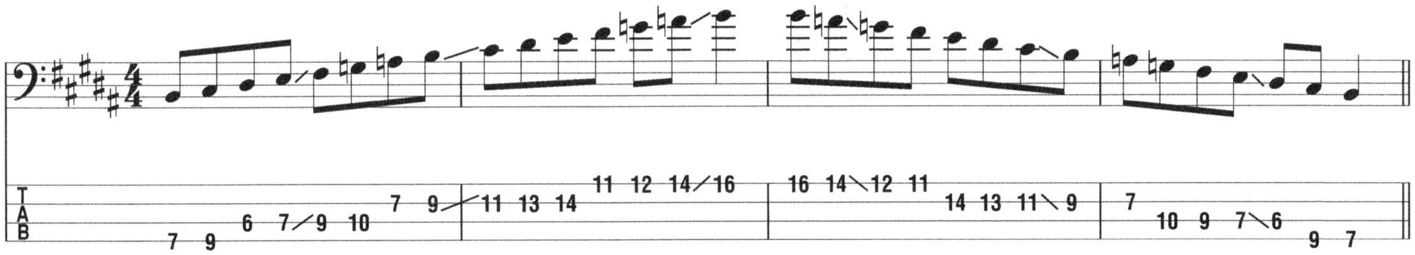

Here's a two-octave A Mixolydian♭13 scale in fourths.

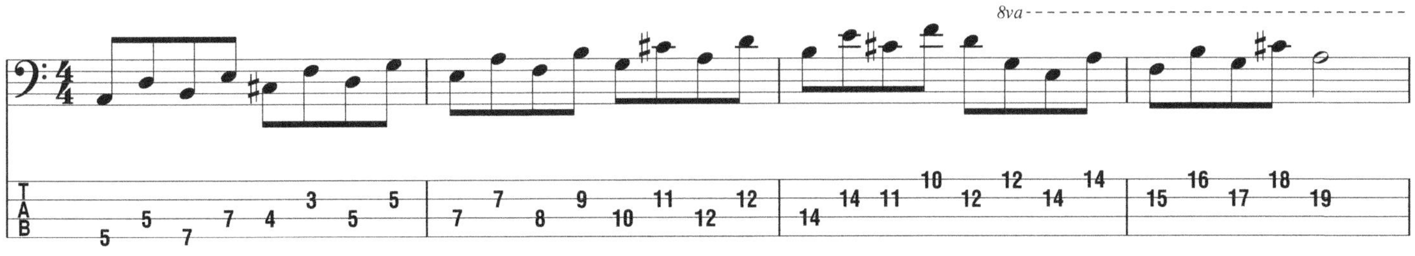

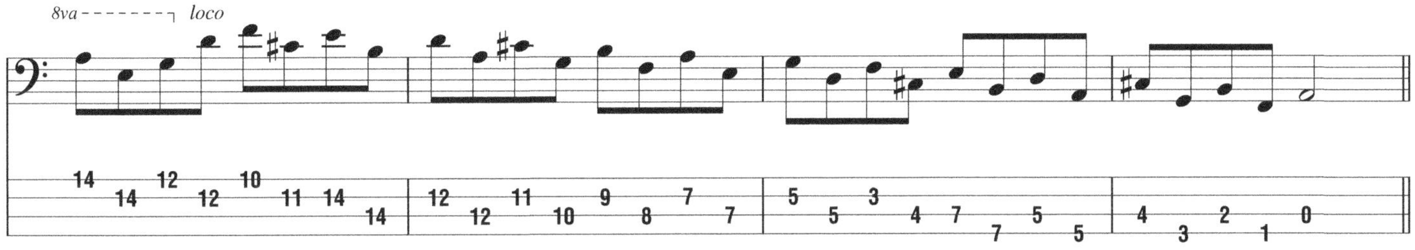

Now play the scale in four-note groupings starting on B♭.

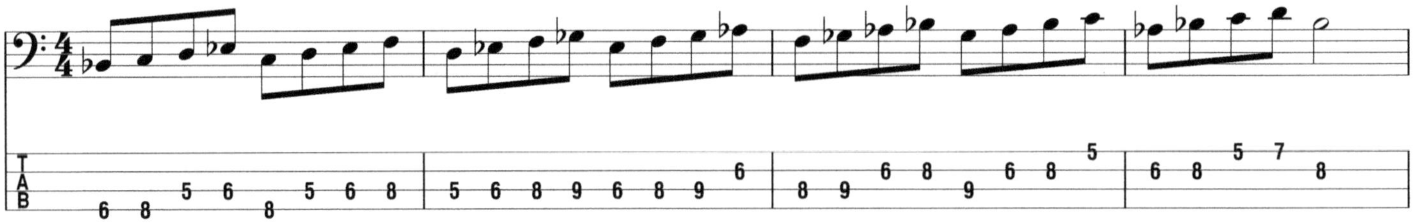

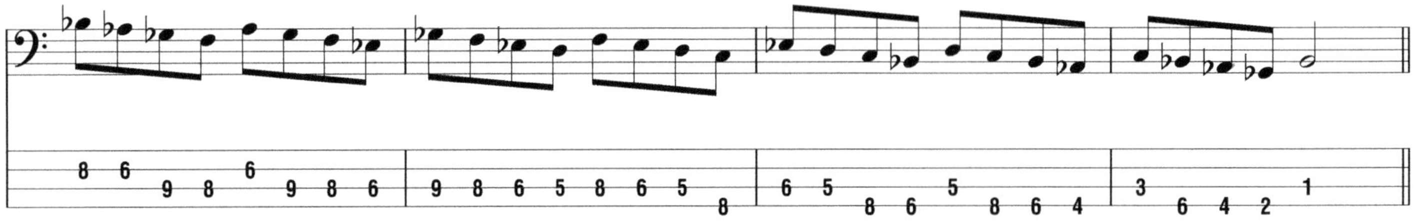

The E Mixolydian♭13 scale on the G string only, with the major third as the lowest starting note.

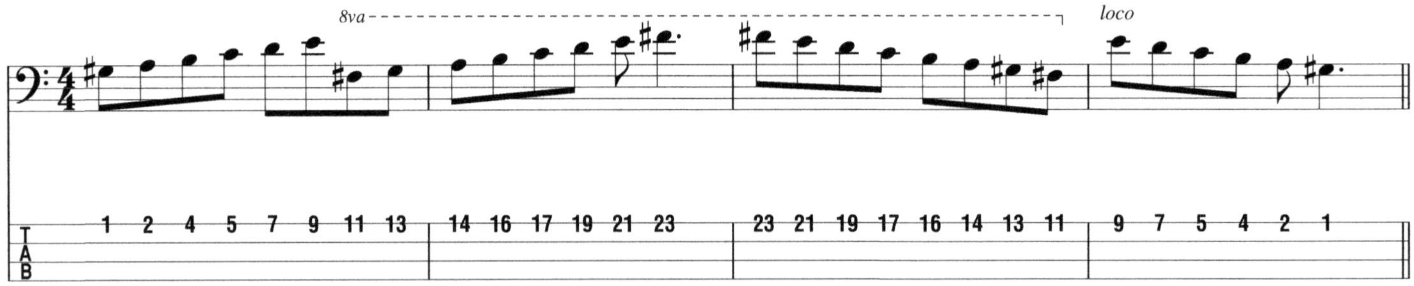

Solo Exercises

In this simple Imi7–IVmi7–V7 progression, we'll use Mixolydian♭13 on the V chord. The Imi7 chord can be Aeolian and the IVmi7 uses Dorian.

Track 43

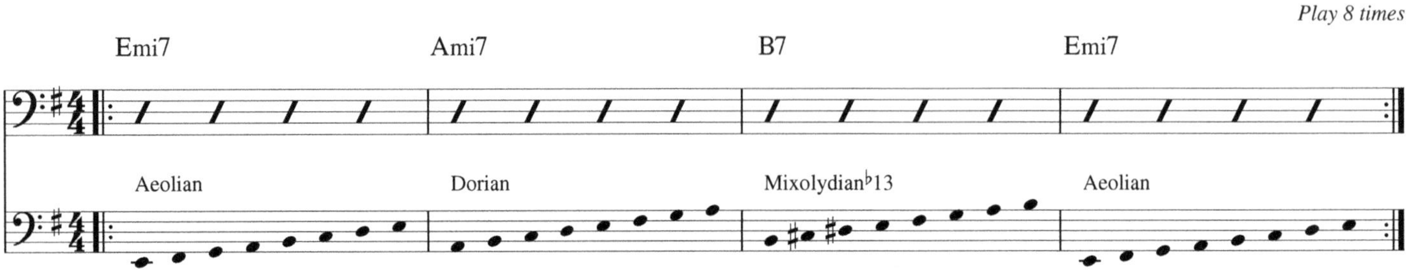

The following example consists of two descending IImi7–V7 progressions. The first IImi7(♭5)–V7 is in E minor and the second is in D major. We will use Locrian♮2 on F♯ and Mixolydian♭13 over B. On the second IImi7–V7 we'll use Dorian and Mixolydian.

Track 44

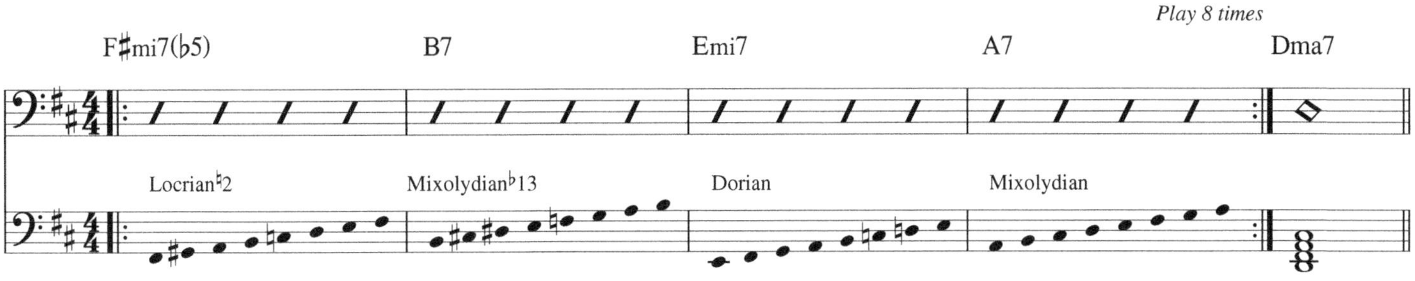

Additional Melodic Minor Modes

In addition to the five modes of melodic minor that we just discussed, there are two more; they are not commonly used for improvising.

The second degree outlines a mi7 chord that includes the passing notes ♭2 and 6. Since extensions are preferable to passing notes, Dorian is always a better choice than this scale, which is called *Dorian♭2*.

Degree: II
Chord: Cmi7(11)
Scale: Dorian♭2

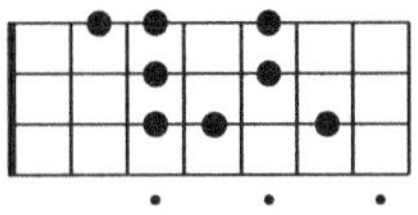

Degree three of melodic minor outlines a *major seventh (sharp five chord)* (ma7[♯5]). This chord is extremely rare. We call this scale *Lydian♯5*.

Degree: III
Chord: Cma7(♯5)(9/♯11)
Scale: Lydian♯5

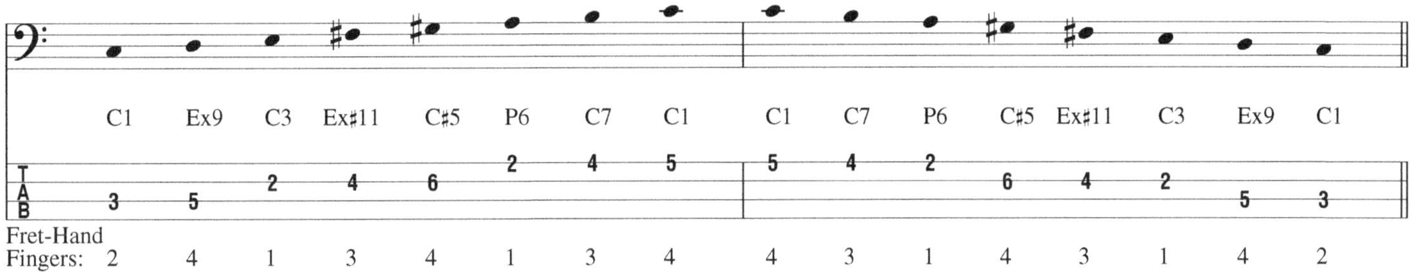

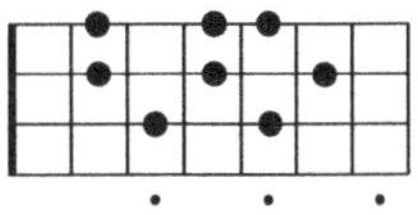

Combined Scale Exercise

Let's try to apply all the scales we have learned so far to a longer tune.

Track 45

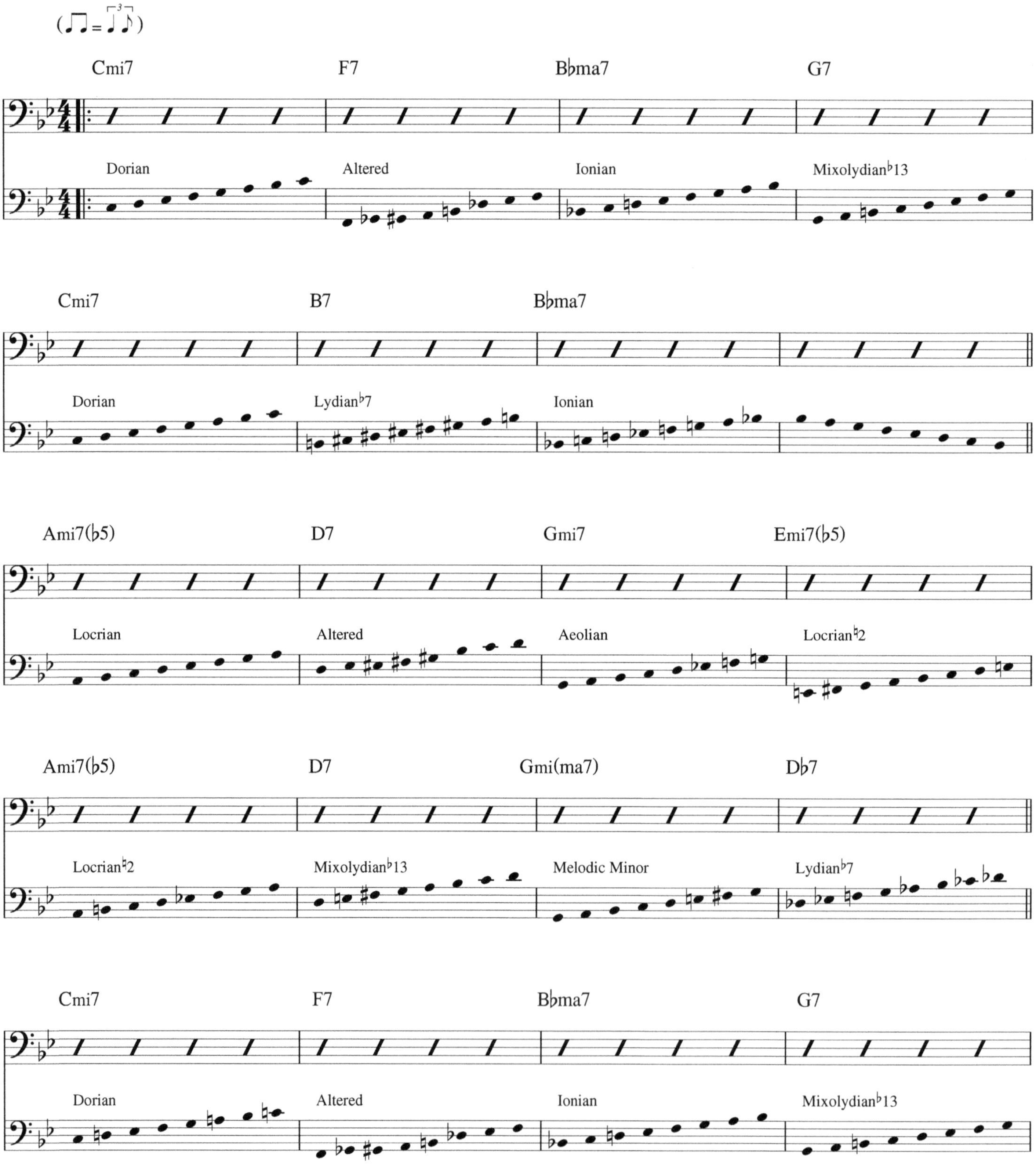

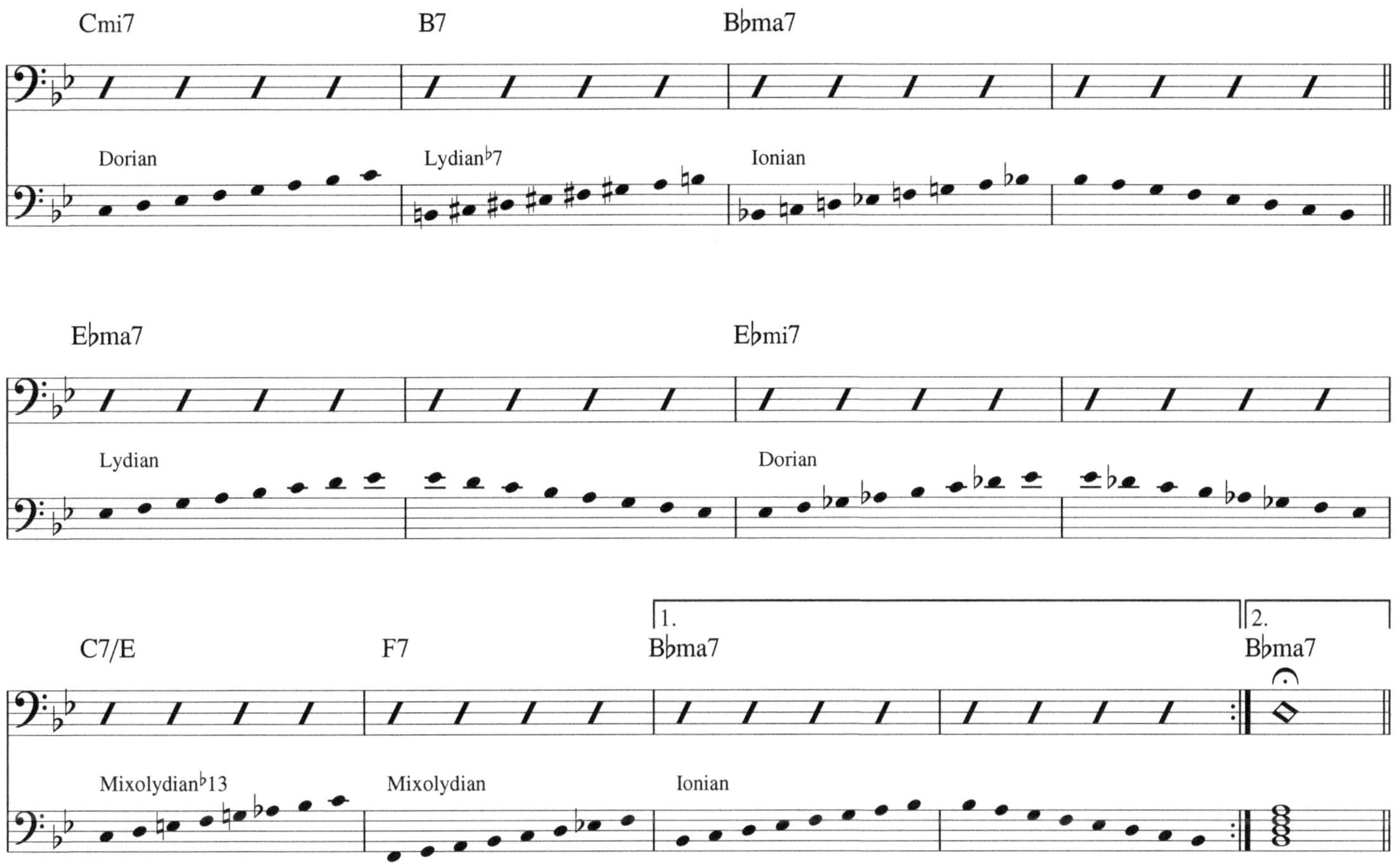
Cmi7
B7
B♭ma7
Dorian
Lydian♭7
Ionian
E♭ma7
E♭mi7
Lydian
Dorian
C7/E
F7
1.
B♭ma7
2.
B♭ma7
Mixolydian♭13
Mixolydian
Ionian

3 Harmonic Minor Modes

The harmonic minor scale consists of another set of seven modes of which the harmonic minor scale is the first degree.

Seven Modes of Harmonic Minor

Degree: I
Chord: Cmi(maj7)
Scale: Harmonic Minor

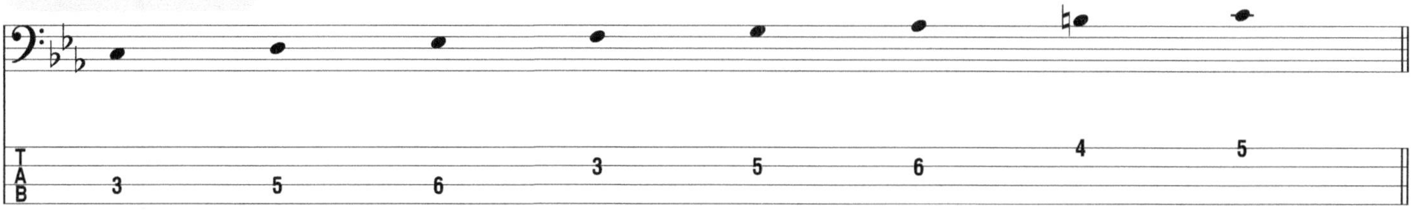

Degree: II
Chord: Dmi7
Scale: Locrian♮6

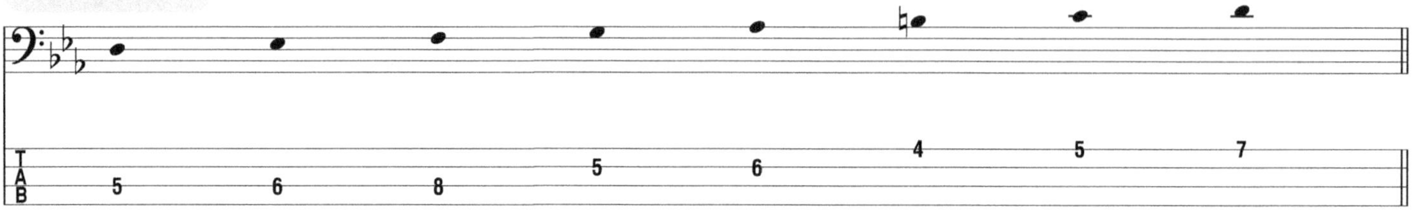

Degree: ♭III
Chord: E♭ma7(♯5)
Scale: Ionian♯5

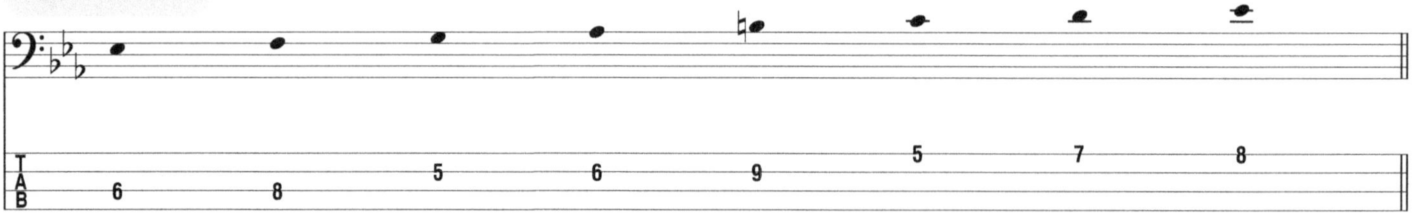

Degree: IV
Chord: Fmi7
Scale: Dorian♯4

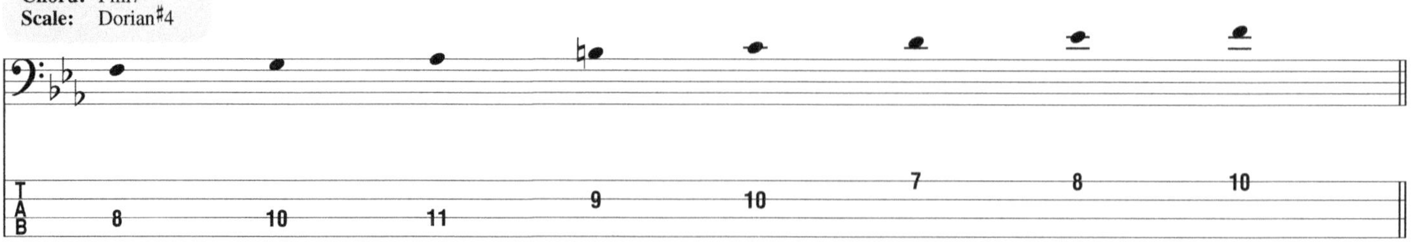

Degree: V
Chord: G7
Scale: Phrygian♯3

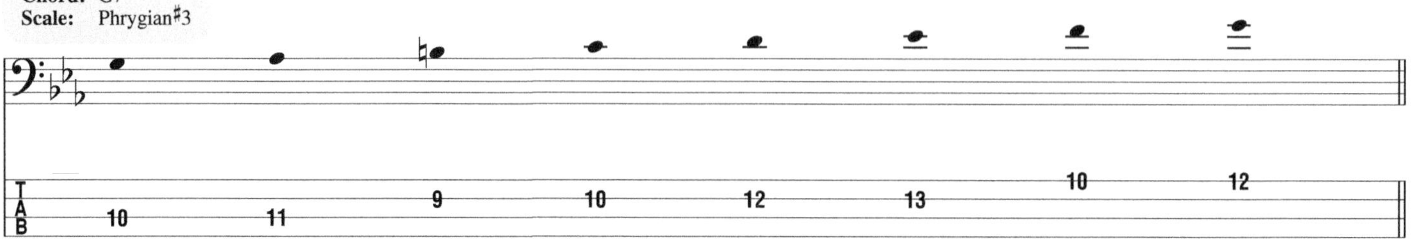

Degree: ♭VI
Chord: A♭ma7
Scale: Lydian♯2

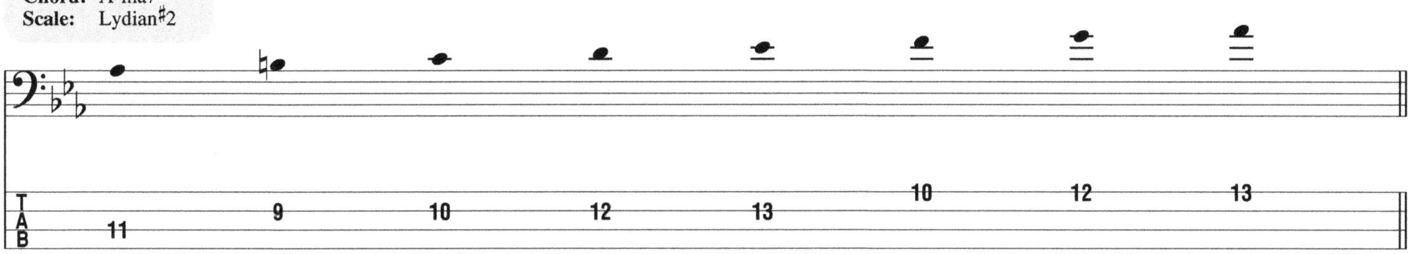

Degree: VII
Chord: B°7
Scale: No Name

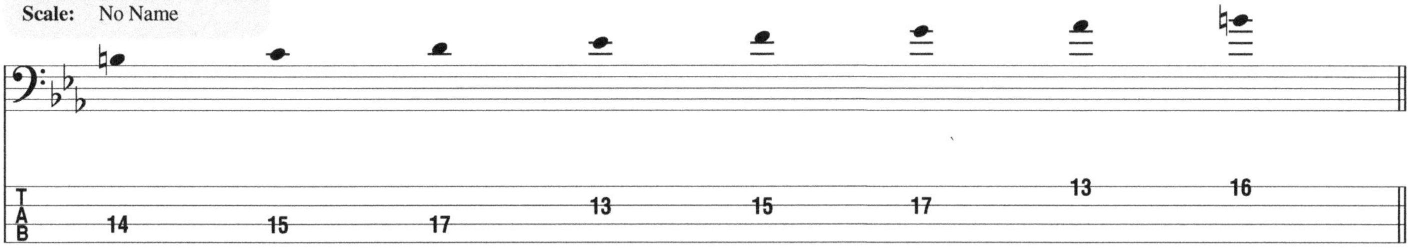

Harmonic Minor

Theory and Application

Harmonic minor is created by raising the seventh note of the Aeolian mode by a half step. This will result in a dominant chord on the fifth degree, which is usually preferred when playing in a minor key. This scale has the unusual interval of an *augmented second* between the sixth and seventh degrees. An augmented second sounds like a minor third; therefore, the scale sounds like it has a skip in it. This gives it a very unique and identifiable sound that is a bit "Middle Eastern."

Degree: I
Chord: Cmi(ma7)(9/11)
Scale: Harmonic Minor

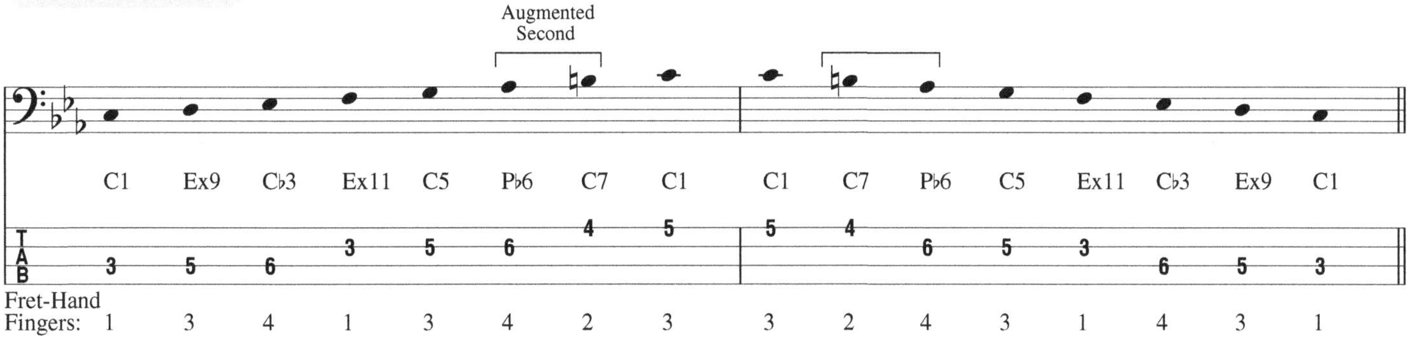

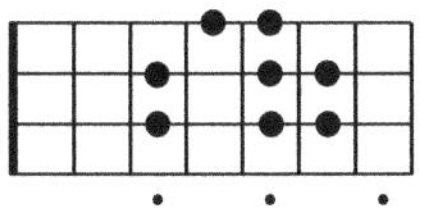

Harmonic minor is used to improvise over minor (major seventh) (mi[ma7]) chords. Like melodic minor, this scale is very tense and mainly seen in jazz. The scale itself is frequently used as a substitute over the tonic chord (Imi7) in a minor key.

Harmonic minor is the preferred scale choice for:
- Imi(ma7)chords
- a substitute scale for Aeolian and Dorian—especially if used over the Imi chord
- modal minor (major seventh) chords

Scale Exercises

D harmonic minor over two octaves.

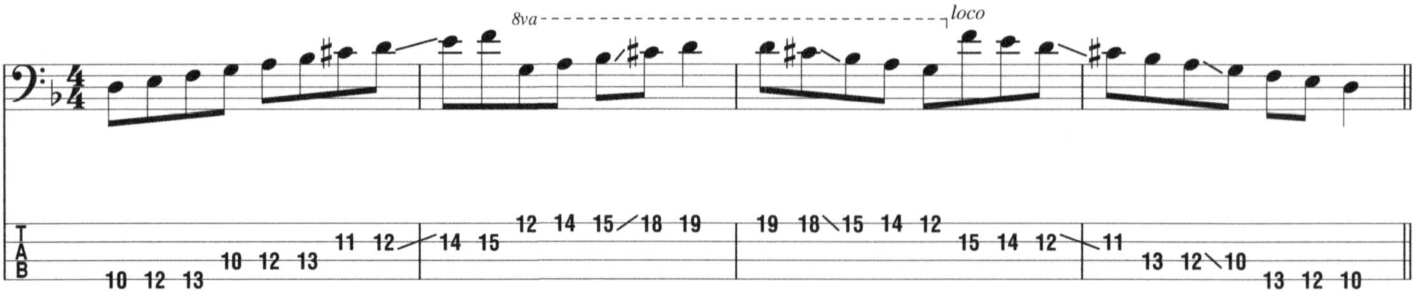

The scale from B♭ in thirds (two octaves).

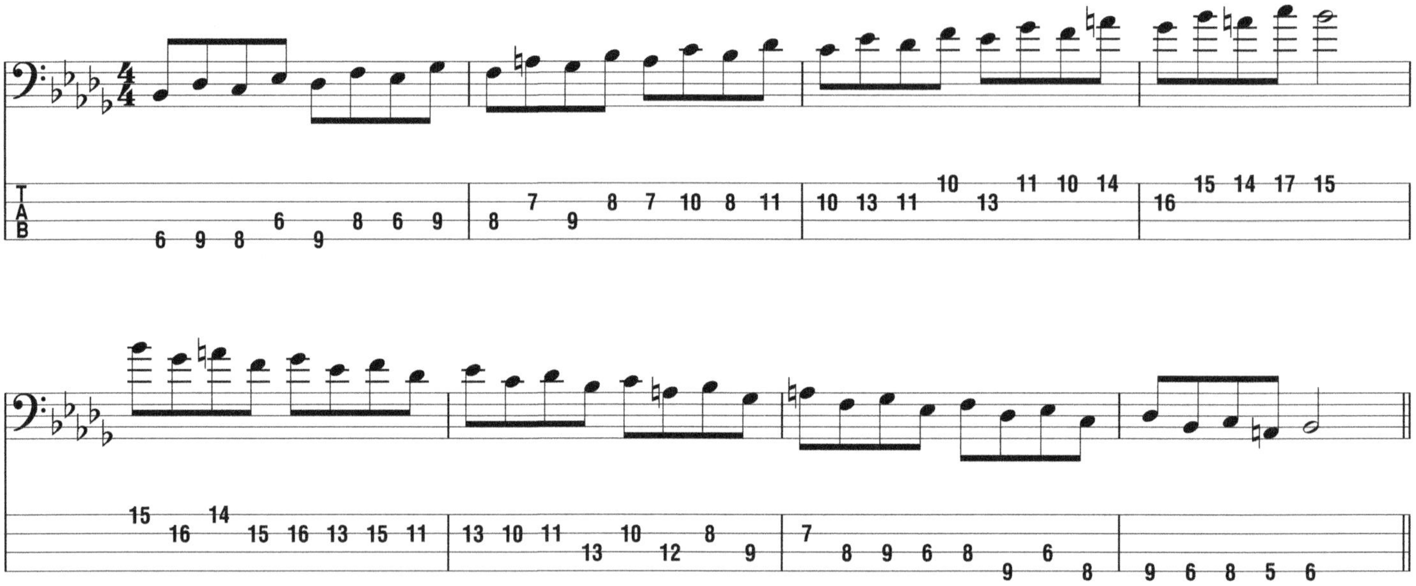

Here is the scale in a three-note grouping, starting on G.

From C♯, here is a three-note sequence consisting of two ascending fourths.

Solo Exercises

In this IImi7(♭5)–V7–Imi(ma7) progression, we'll use harmonic minor on the Imi(ma7) chord. The V7 chord could be Altered and the IImi7(♭5) calls for Locrian.

Track 46

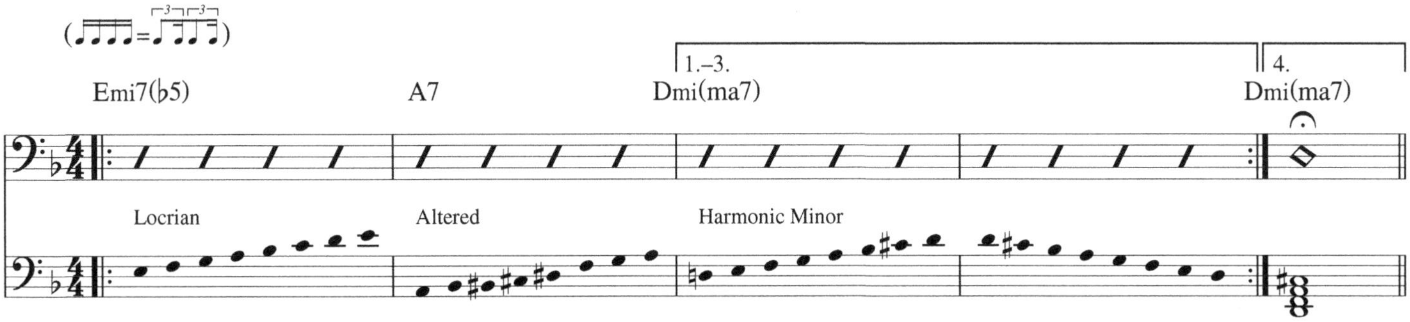

In this modal progression, we can play harmonic minor on each chord.

Track 47

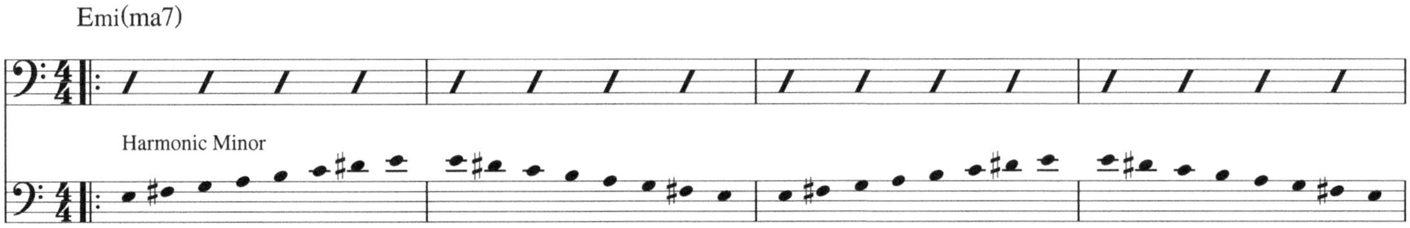

Phrygian♯3

Theory and Application

Phrygian♯3, also known as *Phrygian Dominant* (or *Mixolydian♭9♭13* in Europe), comes from degree five of harmonic minor. This scale has the interval of an augmented second between the second and third notes. When played over a V7 in a minor key, this mode is the closest you can come to staying in the natural minor system.

Degree: V
Chord: C7(♭9/♭13)
Scale: Phrygian♯3

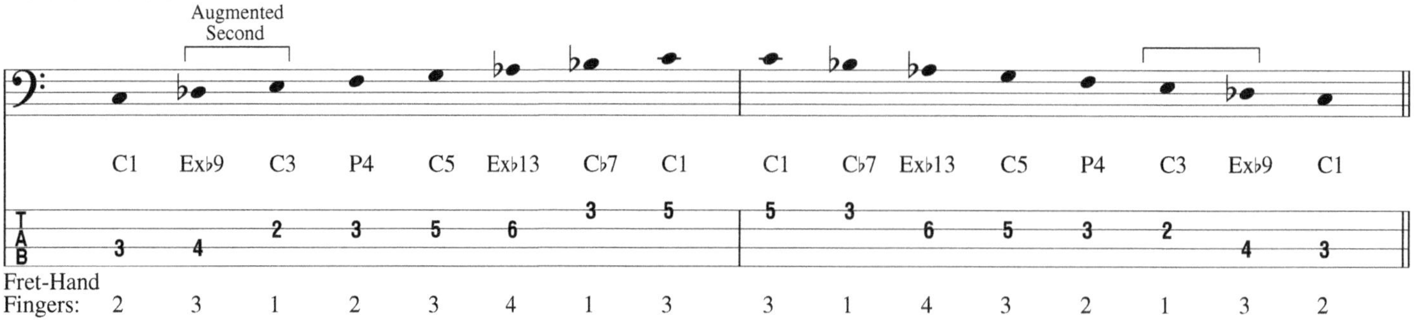

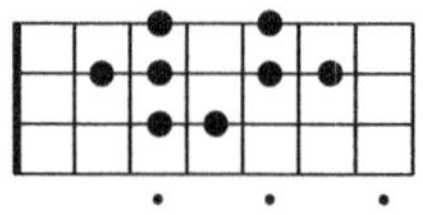

Phrygian♯3 is used to improvise over functioning dominant chords.

This scale is the preferred scale choice for:
- V7 chord in minor
- any functioning dominant chord resolving to major or minor

Scale Exercises

F Phrygian♯3 over two octaves.

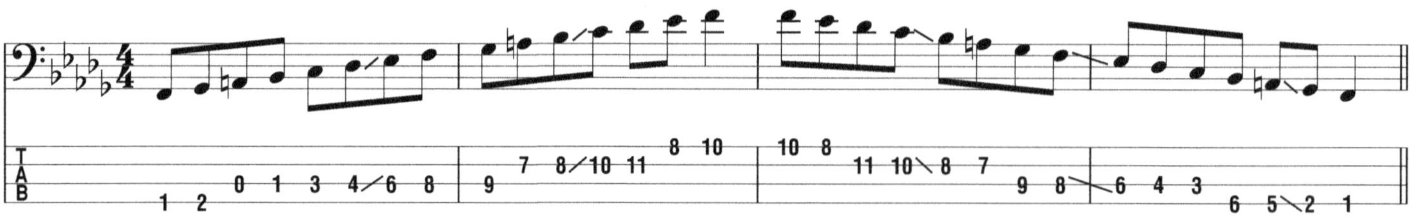

Here's the scale from G♯ in alternating ascending and descending thirds over two octaves.

Here, we play the scale in four-note groupings, starting on B.

Here is the scale in fourths.

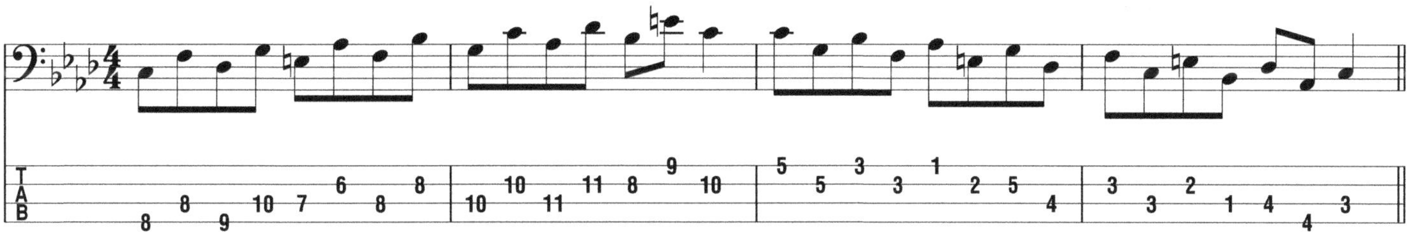

Solo Exercises

Let's play Phrygian♯3 on each dominant chord.

Track 48

In this Ima7–VI7–IImi7–V7 progression, we'll use Phrygian♯3 over the VI7 chord (which functions as the V7 of IImi7).

Track 49

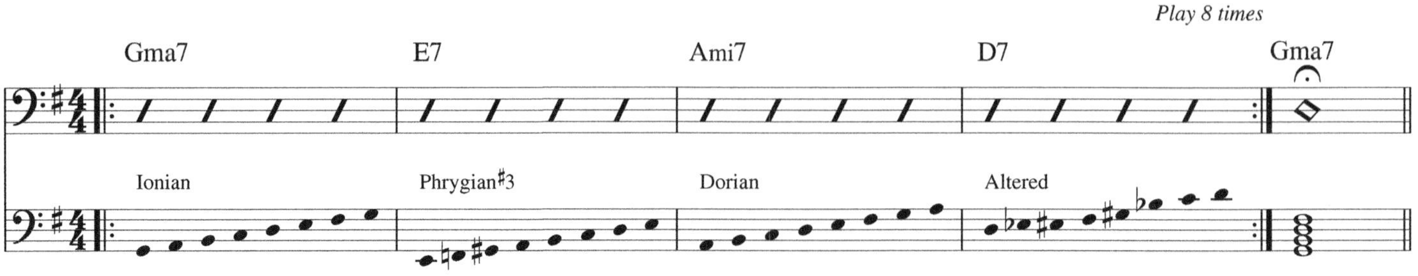

Additional Harmonic Minor Modes

In addition to the two scales of harmonic minor that we just talked about, there are five more. Although not commonly used for improvising, they are listed here for reference.

Degree: II of Harmonic Minor (HM)
Chord: Cmi7(♭5)(11)
Scale: Locrian♮6

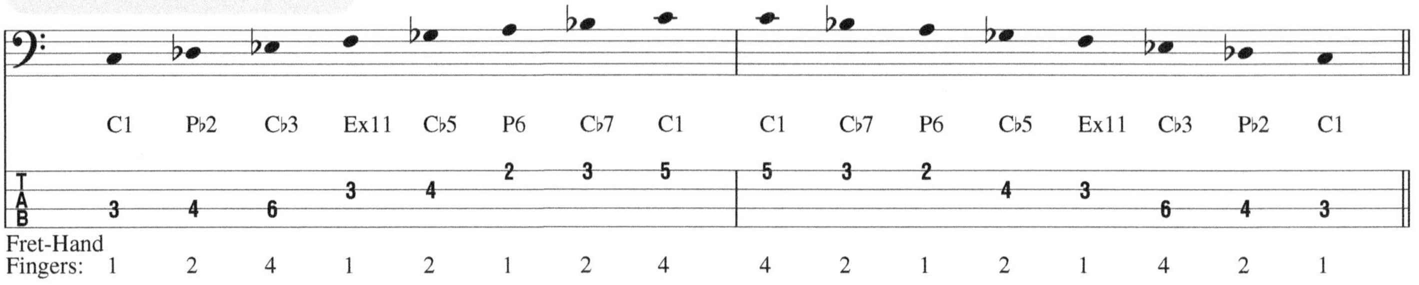

Degree: ♭III of HM
Chord: Cma7(♯5)(9)
Scale: Ionian♯5

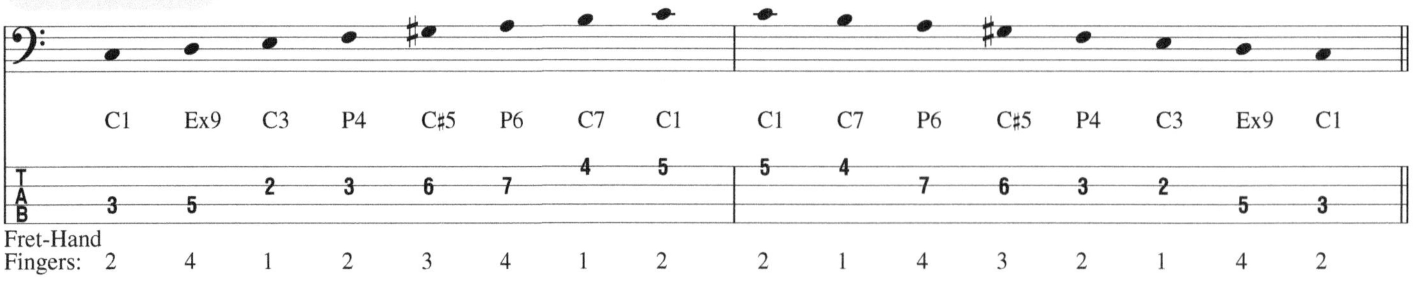

Degree: IV of HM
Chord: Cmi7(9)
Scale: Dorian♯4

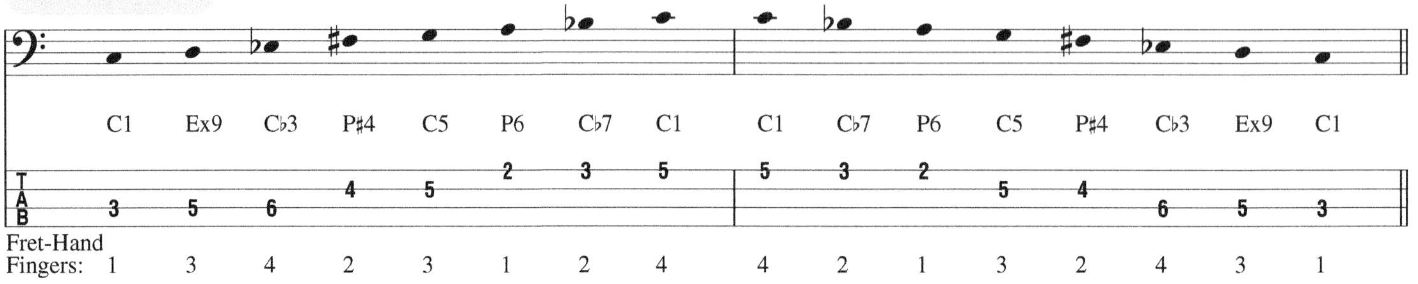

Degree: ♭VI of HM
Chord: Cma7(♯11/13)
Scale: Lydian♯2

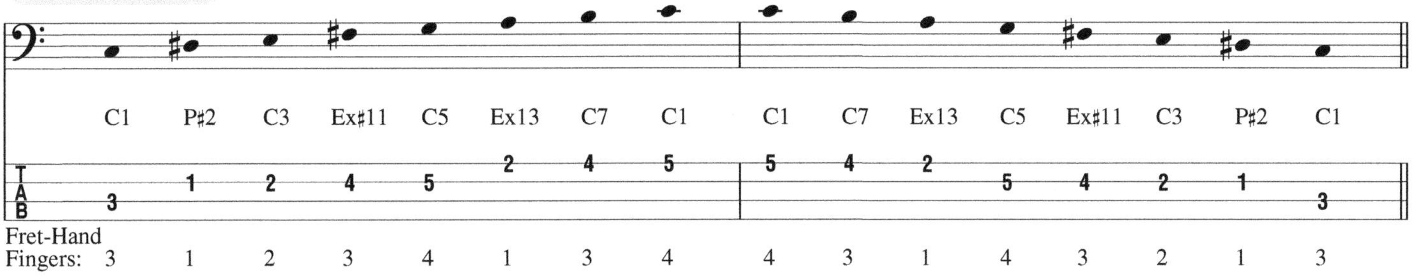

Degree: VII of HM
Chord: C°7(♭13)
Scale: No Name

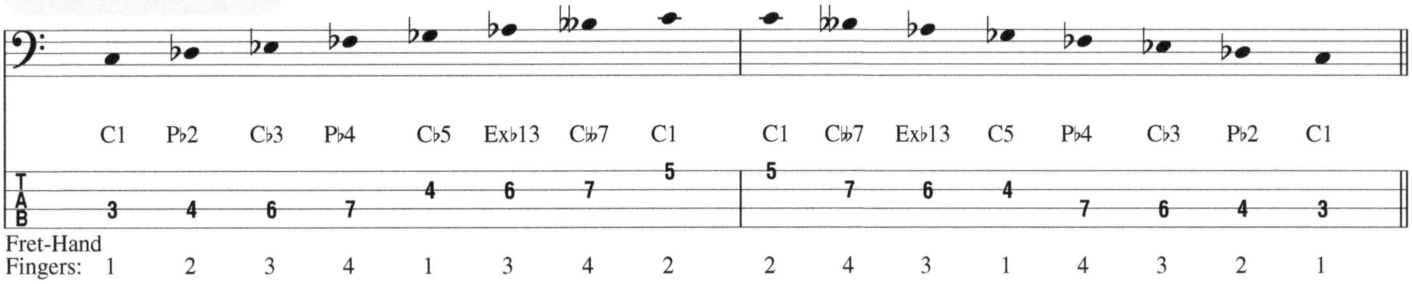

Combined Scale Exercise

Let's try soloing over a progression that uses a mixture of all the scales we know so far.

Track 50

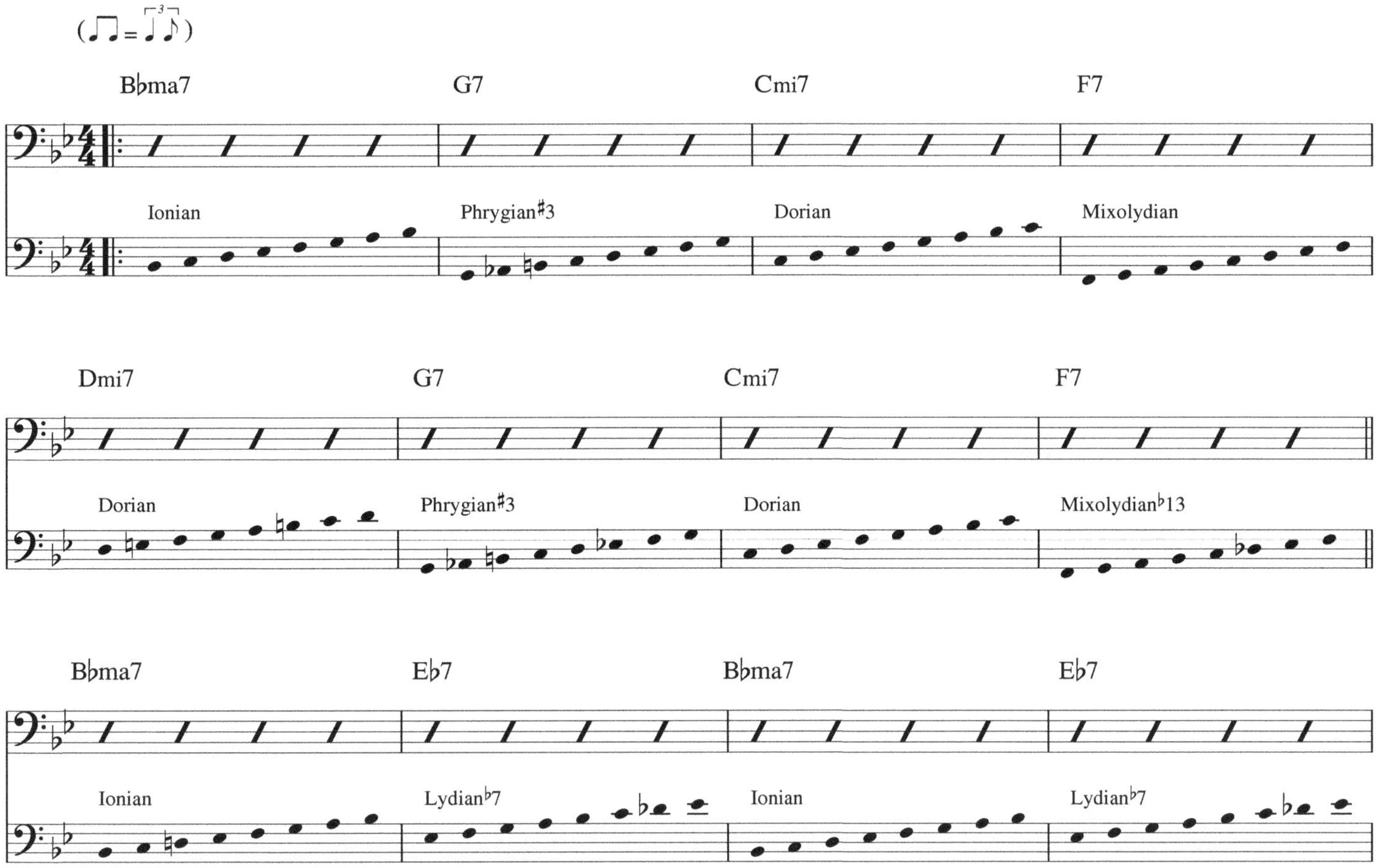

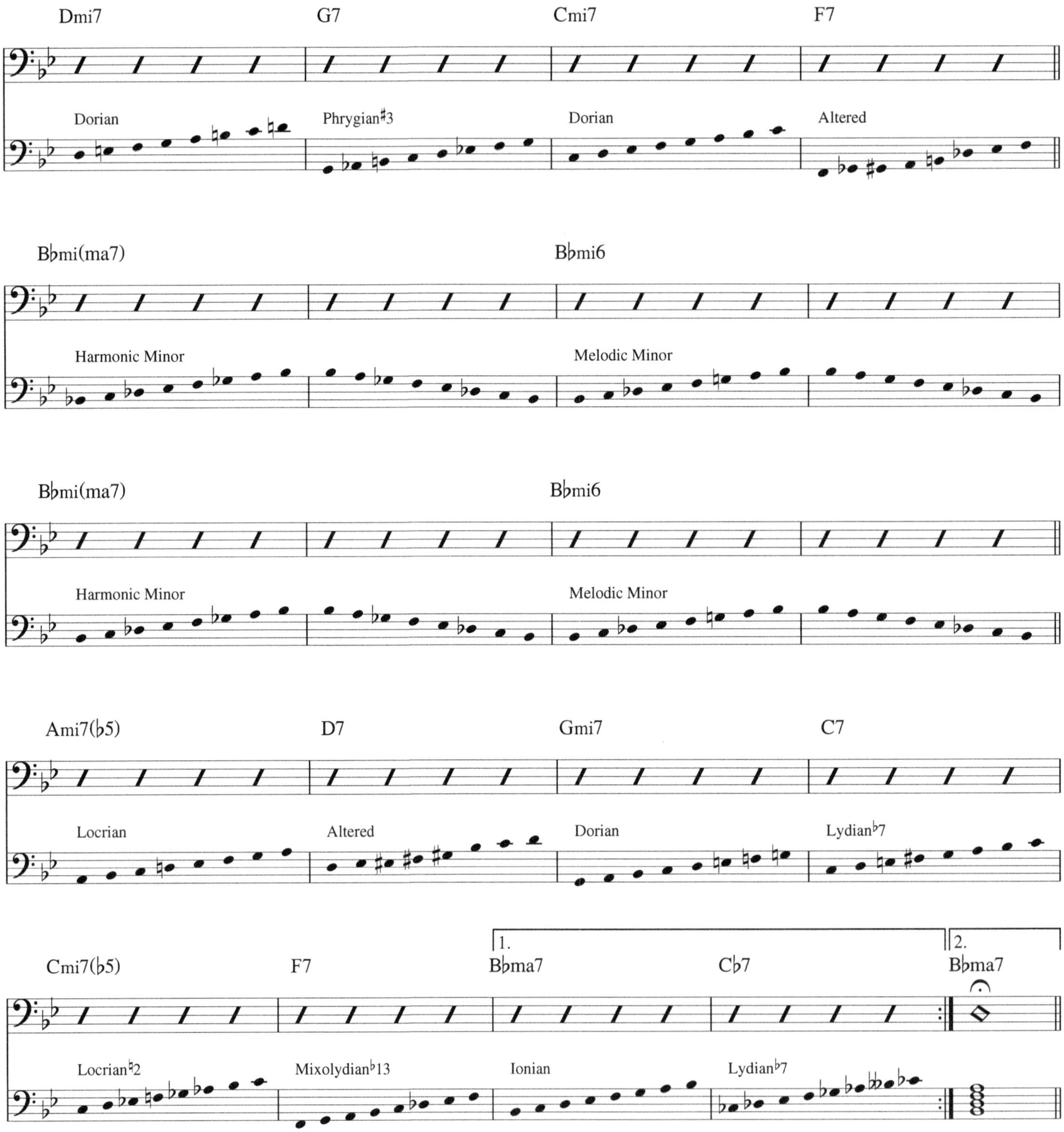
Dmi7
G7
Cmi7
F7
Dorian
Phrygian♯3
Dorian
Altered
B♭mi(ma7)
B♭mi6
Harmonic Minor
Melodic Minor
B♭mi(ma7)
B♭mi6
Harmonic Minor
Melodic Minor
Ami7(♭5)
D7
Gmi7
C7
Locrian
Altered
Dorian
Lydian♭7
1.
2.
Cmi7(♭5)
F7
B♭ma7
C♭7
B♭ma7
Locrian♮2
Mixolydian♭13
Ionian
Lydian♭7

4 Symmetrical Scales

Any scale that equally divides the octave is *symmetrical*. This means that the scale can be started from any one of its notes and have all the same half- and whole-step relationships. If the octave is divided into twelve equal parts, you get the chromatic scale, which includes all half steps in traditional Western music. Not all symmetrical scales are exceptionally useful in functional music, but the following three are the ones used most often.

Whole-Half Tone Scale

Theory and Application

The *whole-half tone* scale (also known as the *diminished* or *octatonic* scale) repeats its interval scheme every minor third. It consists of alternating major and minor seconds. This scale outlines a *diminished seventh* chord.

Since this scale is symmetrical and divides the octave into four equal parts, the sound of C°7, E♭°7, G♭°7, and A°7 chords and scales are all the same. Whole-half tone is the only scale that is commonly used to improvise over any diminished seventh chord.

Another unique feature of this scale is the fact that it consists of eight notes, featuring both a diminished and major seventh. Therefore, this scale also outlines the exotic *major seventh (flat five)* chord, which can be notated as Cma7(♭5) or B/C. Most often, the function of this chord is VII°7 to I, meaning that the diminished chord resolves up by a half step to either a minor or major chord.

The whole-half tone scale is used to improvise over any diminished seventh or diminished major seventh chord.

Chord: C°7(9/11/♭13) [C°ma7 = B/C]
Scale: Whole-Half Tone

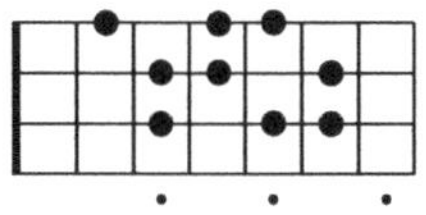

Scale Exercises

Here is the two-octave G diminished whole-half tone scale.

If we play the scale in thirds, we will get all minor thirds.

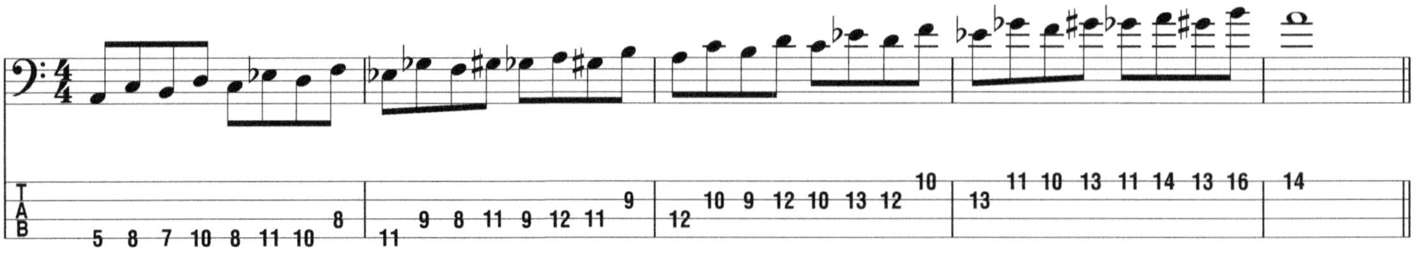

When played in fourths, the scale gives alternating perfect and diminished intervals.

Here is D whole-half tone on the A string only.

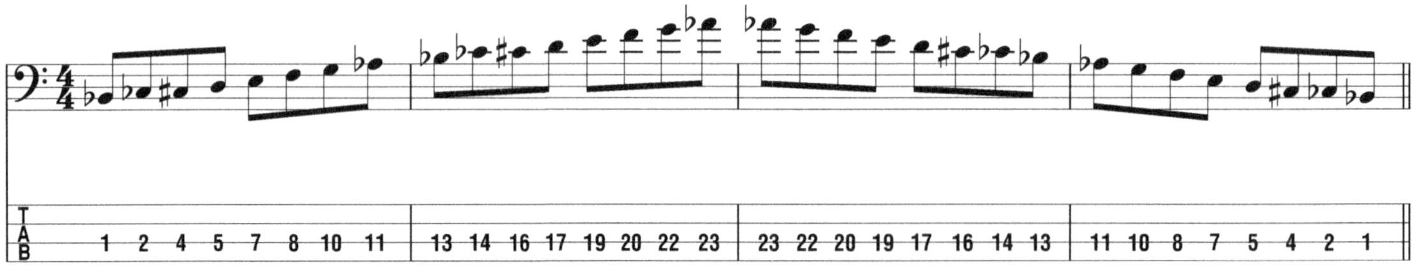

Solo Exercises

In this first exercise, the diminished chord resolves up by a half step.

Track 51

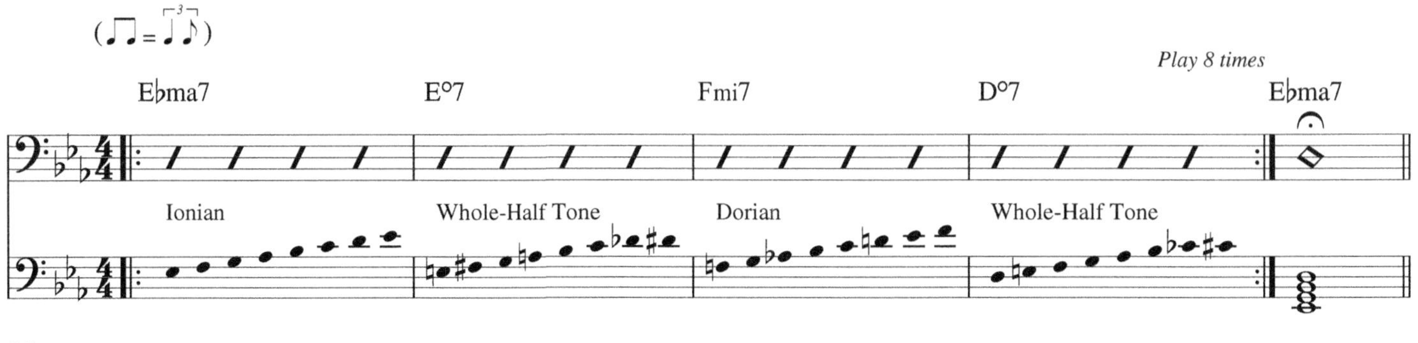

In this jazz progression, the diminished chord resolves down a half step, and then to a major seventh chord.

Track 52

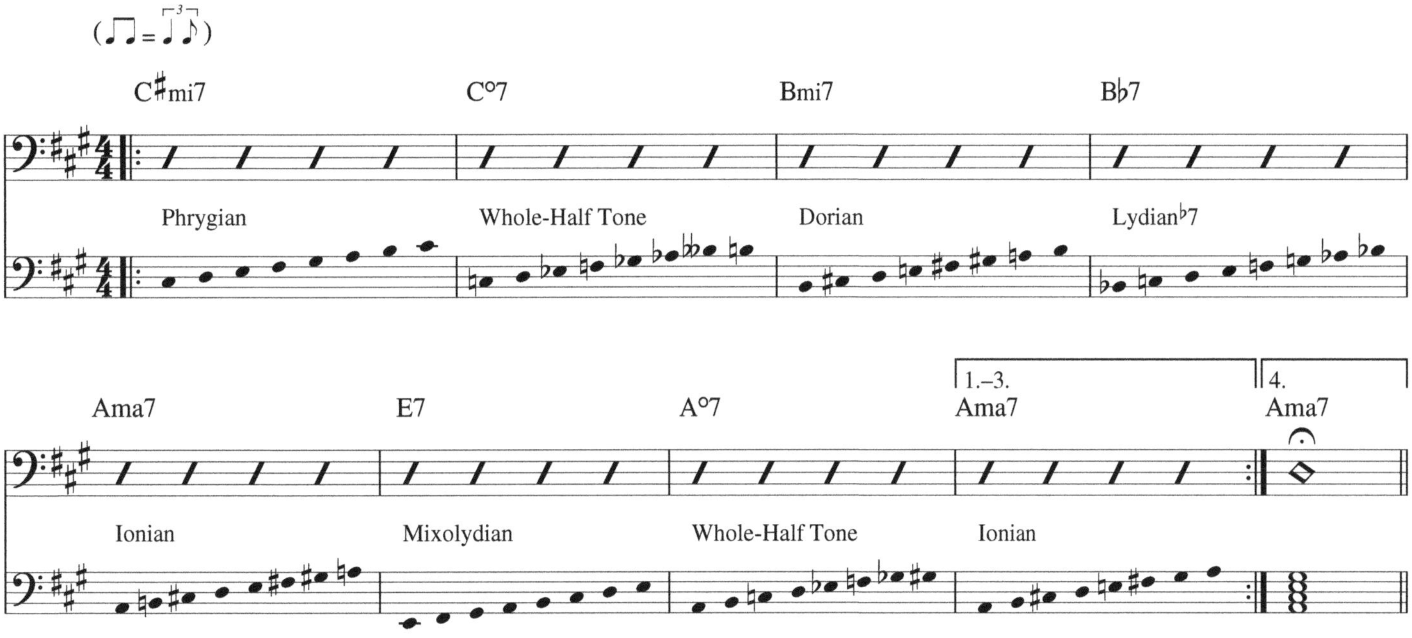

Half-Whole Tone Scale

Theory and Application

The *half-whole tone* scale (also known as the *dominant diminished scale*) also repeats every minor third, and consists of alternating minor and major seconds. This scale enharmonically outlines a dominant chord. Like the previous scale, this one also consists of eight notes, but features both flat and sharp ninths.

The half-whole tone scale is used to improvise over functioning dominant chords and dominant chords resolving down a half step. It can resolve to either major or minor.

Chord: C7(♭9/♯9/♯11/13)
Scale: Half-Whole Tone

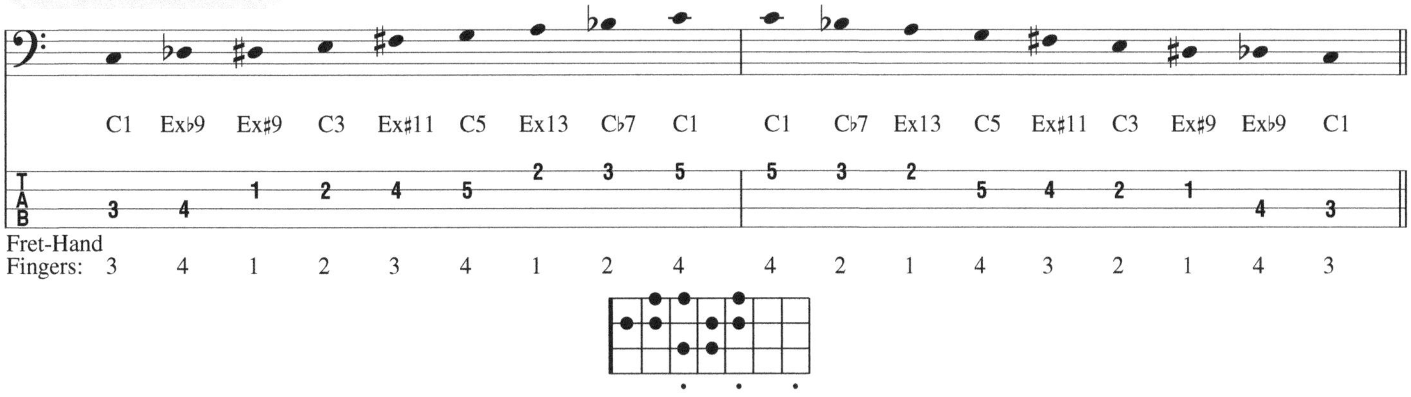

Scale Exercises

Here is the half-whole tone scale from F over two octaves.

The scale in fifths.

The scale in four-note groupings.

G dominant diminished on the G string only.

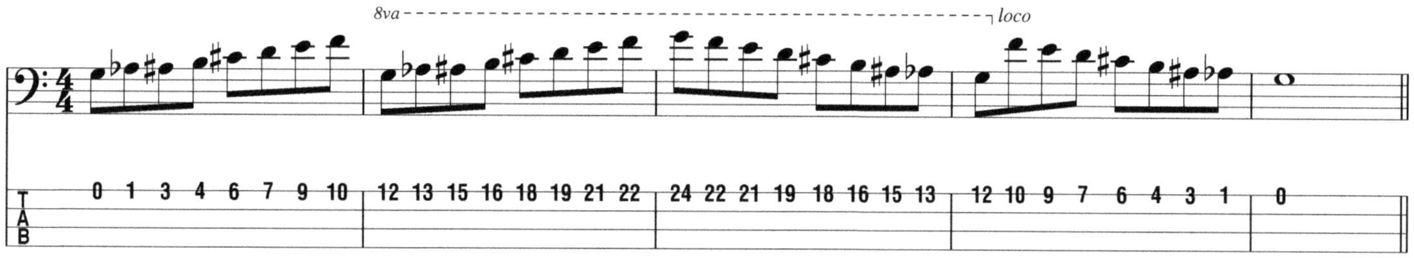

Solo Exercises

A modal jam using only dominant chords.

Track 53

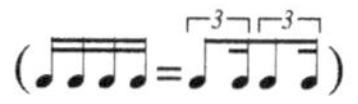

This is a Ima7–I7–IVma7–V7 progression, and the I7 serves as a *secondary dominant* chord that sets up the IVma7 chord.

Track 54

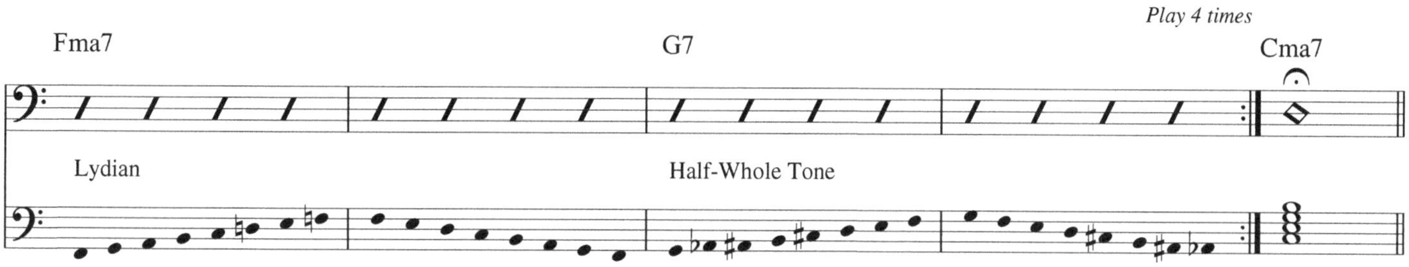

Whole-Tone Scale

Theory and Application

The *whole-tone* scale consists only of major seconds. It outlines *dominant seventh (sharp five)* and *dominant seventh (flat five)* chords, and is used to improvise over functioning dominant chords and those resolving down a half step. This scale contains three tritones (six half steps) and no minor seconds, which gives it a dissonant, dreamy sound. Its uniqueness also stems from the fact that this scale has only six notes. This is the reason why you see this scale notated with either ♭5 and ♭13, or ♯11 and ♯5.

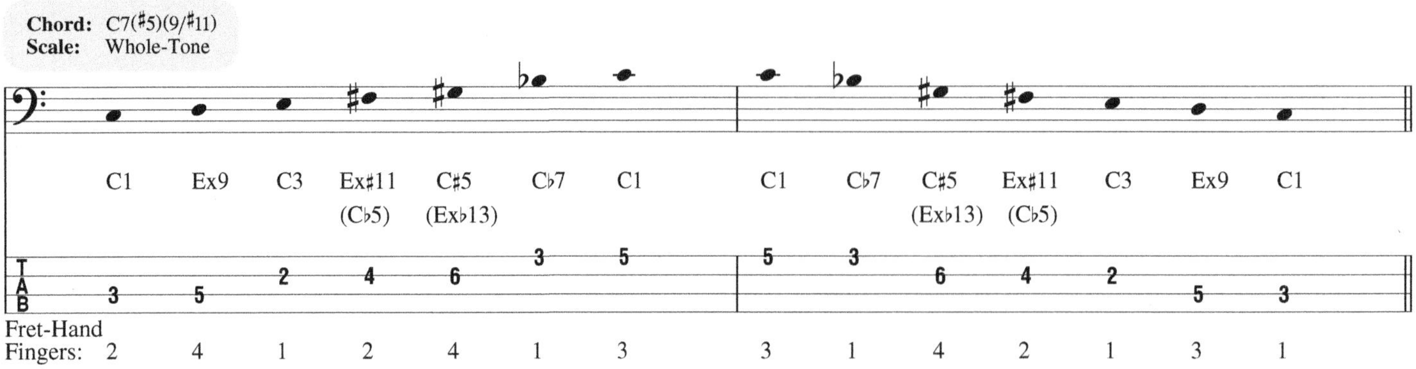

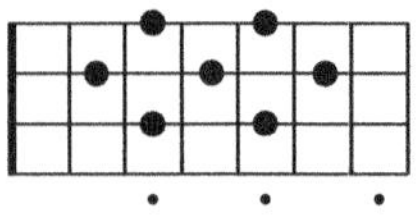

Scale Exercises

Here is the whole-tone scale over two octaves.

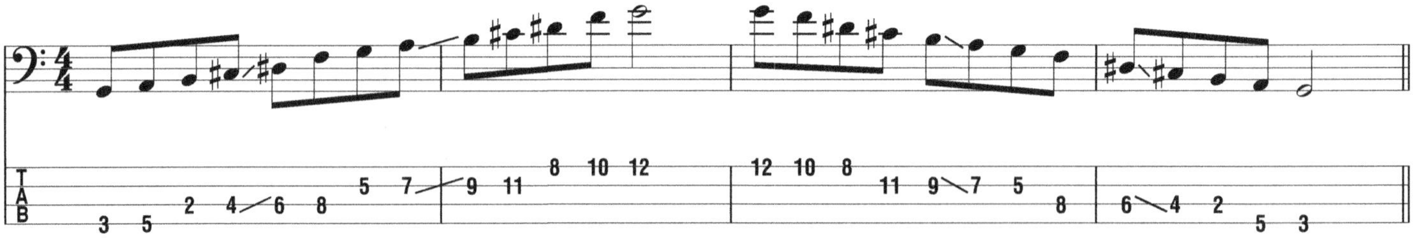

Here's the scale in thirds.

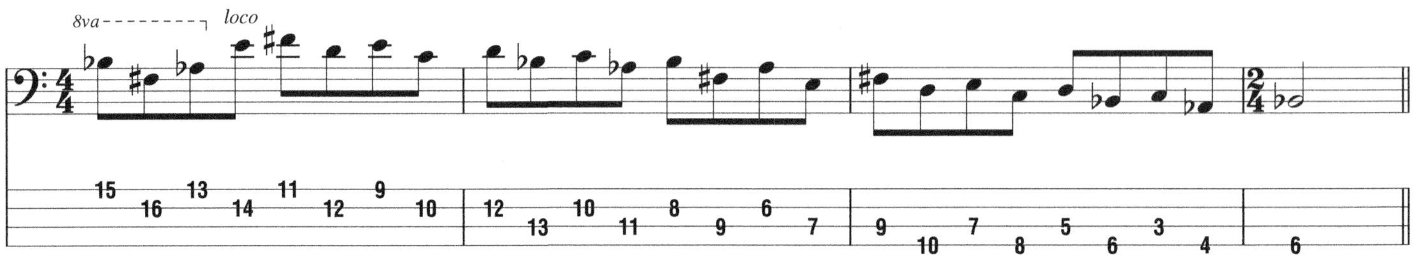

This is the A scale in three-note groupings.

Here's the C whole-tone scale in seventh position.

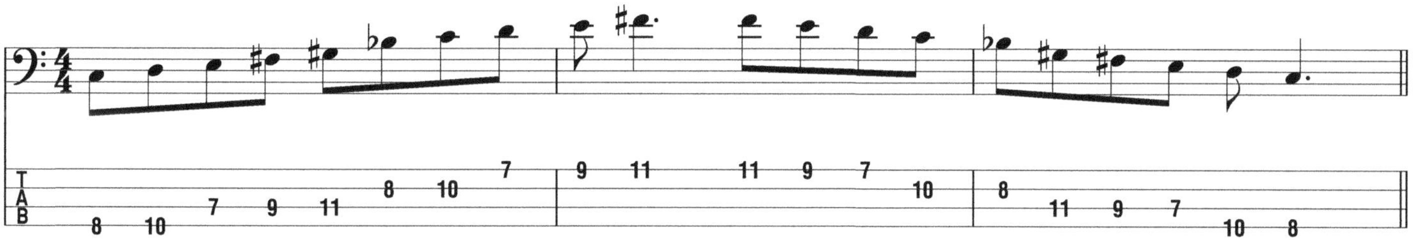

Solo Exercises

Using only dominant chords, here's another modal jam.

Track 55

A IImi7(♭5)–V7–Imi7 progression in minor.

Track 56

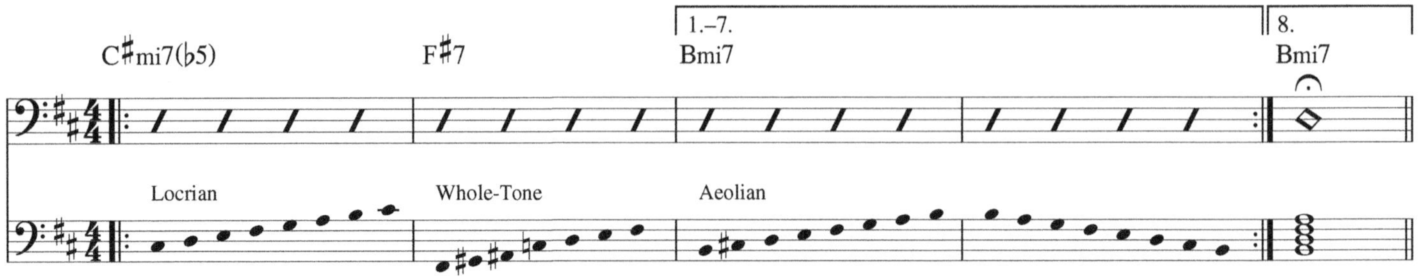

Combined Scale Exercises

Let's try a progression that uses scales from the previous chapters. For some of these chords, you can play more than one scale, especially over dominant chords. Try to experiment with different scales; just make sure they outline the correct seventh chord type (mi7, ma7, etc.).

Track 57

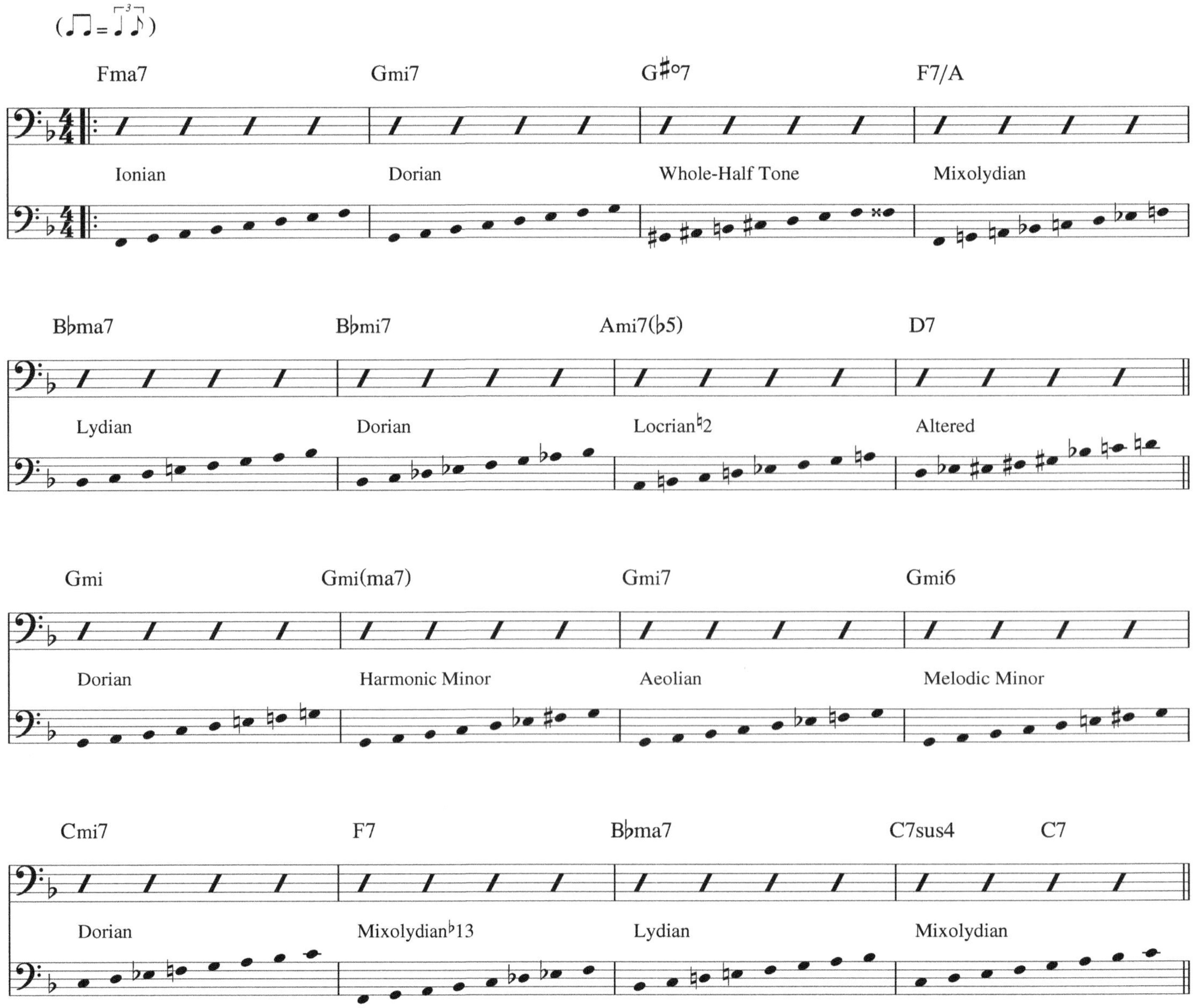

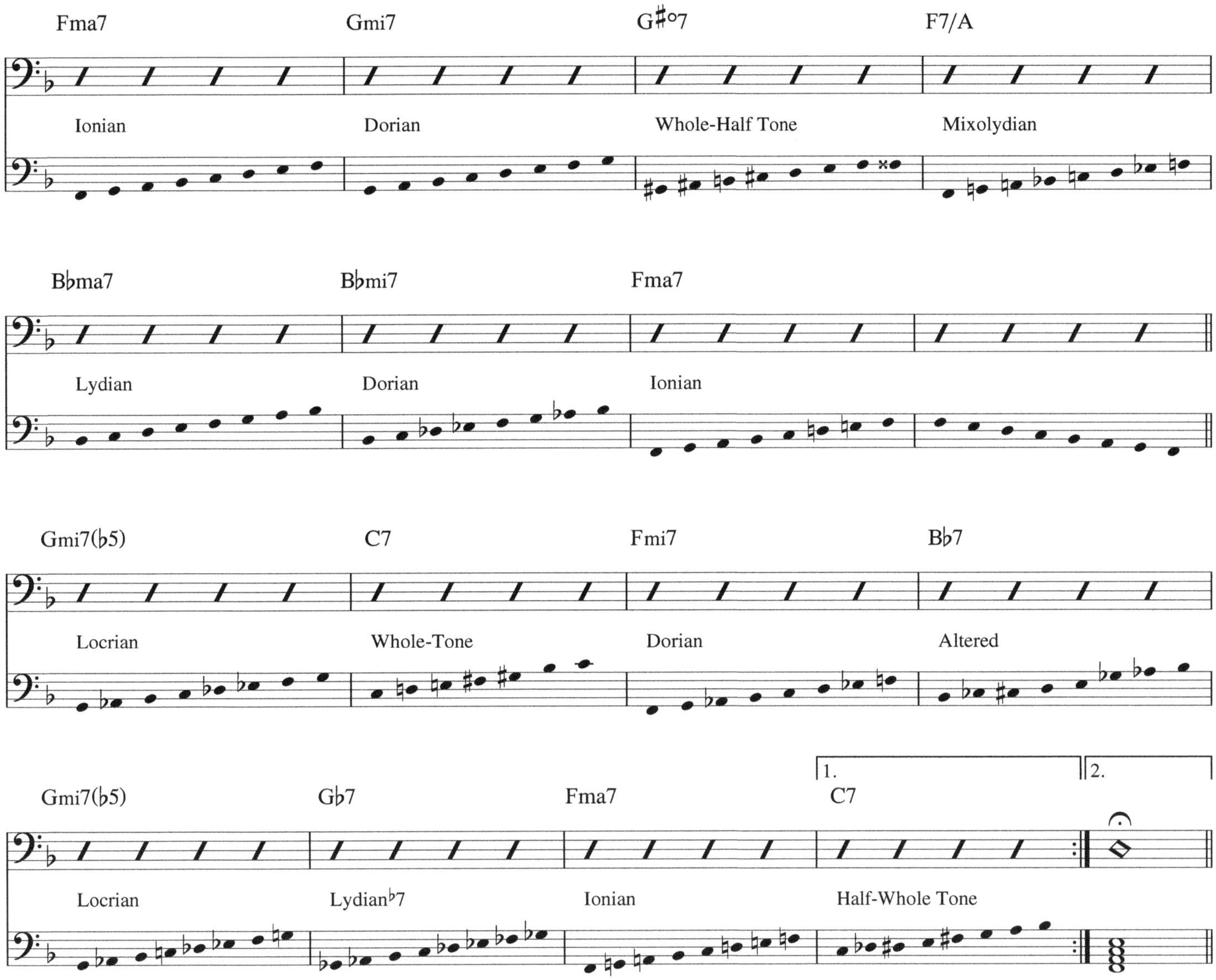
Fma7
Gmi7
G♯°7
F7/A
Ionian
Dorian
Whole-Half Tone
Mixolydian
B♭ma7
B♭mi7
Fma7
Lydian
Dorian
Ionian
Gmi7(♭5)
C7
Fmi7
B♭7
Locrian
Whole-Tone
Dorian
Altered
1.
2.
Gmi7(♭5)
G♭7
Fma7
C7
Locrian
Lydian♭7
Ionian
Half-Whole Tone

5 Modal Interchange

Modal interchange is not a scale or soloing approach. It describes a chord progression that substitutes chords from its parallel major or minor key.

If you have a tune that is in C major, you have seven diatonic chords available in that key. In this example:

Cma7–Dmi7–Emi7–Fma7–G7–Ami7–Bmi7(♭5)

If you have a tune that is in C minor the available chords are:

Cmi7–Dmi7♭5–E♭ma7–Fmi7–Gmi7–A♭ma7–B♭7

The relationship between the keys of C major and C minor is called *parallel*. Substituting a chord from the minor system while you're in a major key (and vice versa) is called *modal interchange*. It's important to recognize this when analyzing a progression to figure out the correct scales to use.

The following example uses a modal interchange chord on the fourth and sixth degree.

Track 58

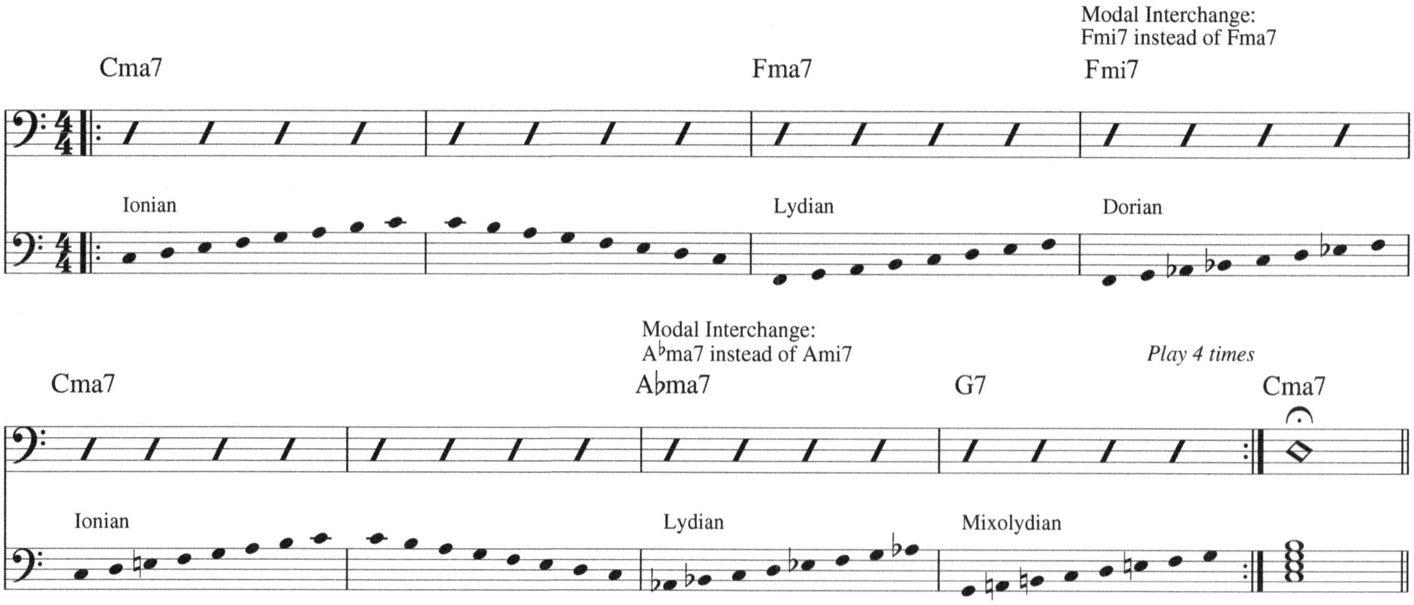

6 Key-Center Playing

Theory and Application

Until now, we have assigned different scales to different chords. This approach is very useful when you have chord progressions with lots of *modulations* (key changes), modal interchanges, or *chromaticism* (half-step movement).

If the music you're soloing over is more diatonic, it can be much easier to think of one scale that fits all chords.

Here is an example: if you are in the key of C major and have a I–IVma7–V7 progression, the appropriate chords are Cma7, Fma7, and G7. The corresponding scales would be Ionian, Lydian, and Mixolydian.

Looking at these scales a bit closer, you notice that they all contain the same seven notes: C–D–E–F–G–A–B. The only difference lies in the notes that you start with or resolve to for each chord.

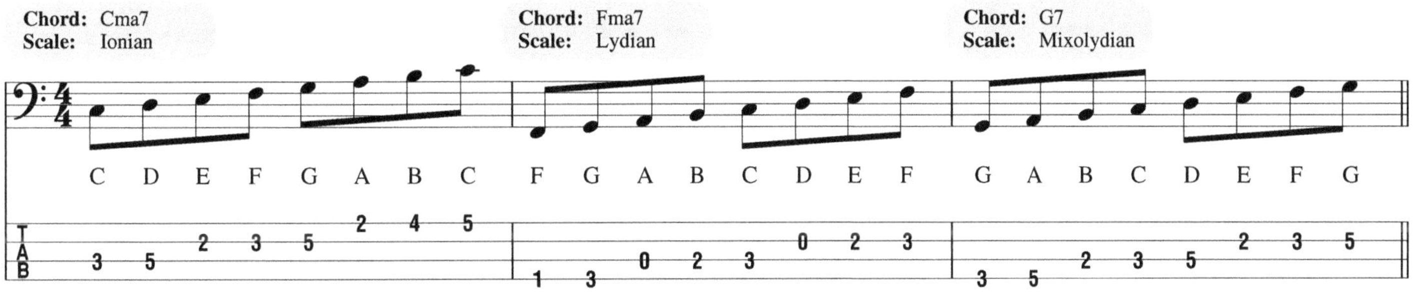

Now, you think to yourself, "Why bother with all the changing scales if they are all the same?" You are right—it's much easier to only play the C major scale over all three chords.

This approach has pros and cons if weighed against the scale approach:

- The positive side is that you can focus on just one scale for a while and not constantly have to worry about making every chord change. This gives you a much freer way of soloing, which will also sound simpler since the melodies you'll be playing stay in one key. This approach is heard a lot in blues, pop, and rock.
- The negative side of this approach is that you can't control what you're playing that well. Since you are focusing on one scale, you don't really know the exact relationship of the notes you're playing against the chords as they go by.

Of course, both ways of improvising are great and just yield different results.

Major and Minor Pentatonic Scales

In key-center playing, pentatonic scales are quite common. A *pentatonic scale* is a five-note scale that contains no half steps.

The *major pentatonic* scale is derived from the Ionian mode with the fourth and seventh degrees removed. This makes the scale less dissonant than any of the seven-note scales, which is why you hear this sound a lot in rock and pop music. In the key-center approach, major pentatonic is used to improvise over major chord progressions.

Chord: Cmi
Scale: Major Pentatonic

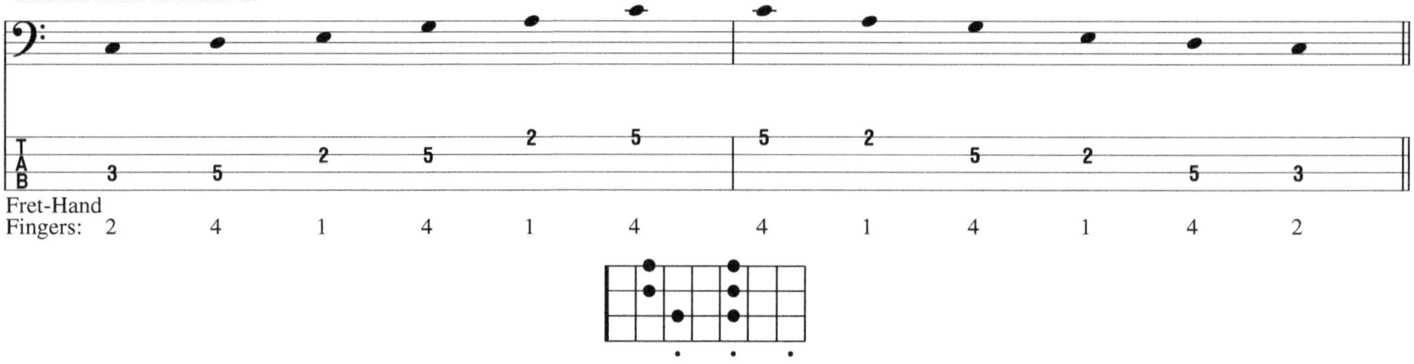

The *minor pentatonic* scale starts on the fifth note of the major pentatonic (C major pentatonic = A minor pentatonic), and you can think of it as the Aeolian or natural minor scale with the second and sixth note removed. In the key-center approach, this scale is used to improvise over minor chord progressions.

Chord: Cmi
Scale: Minor Pentatonic

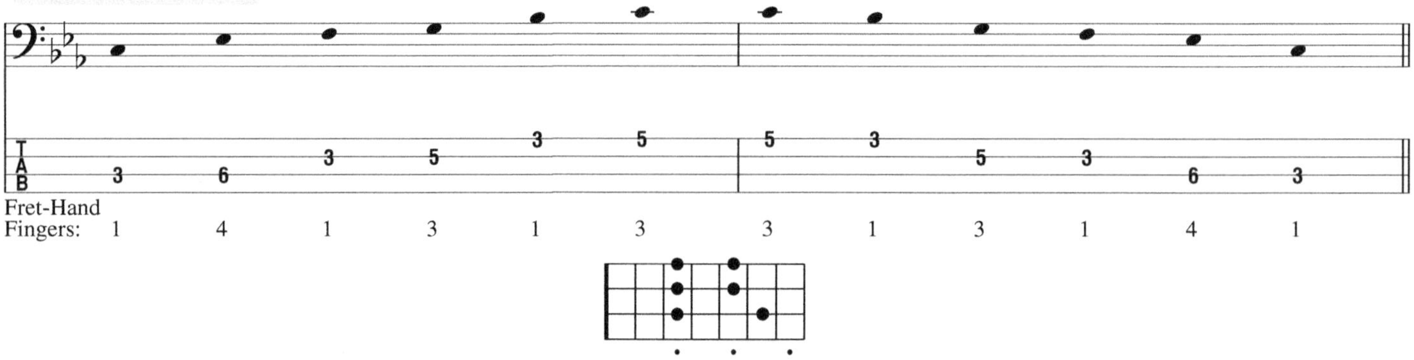

Major and Minor Blues Scales

The *blues scales* are derived from the pentatonic scales. They add a chromatic passing note that results in a six-note scale with two consecutive minor seconds.

The *major blues* scale adds a passing note between the second and third note. The added passing note is the minor third of the scale. This will make the scale sound bluesy, but it's also an important sound for country and rock. With the key-center approach, this scale is used to improvise over major chord progressions with the intent to give a down-home feel.

Chord: C
Scale: Major Blues

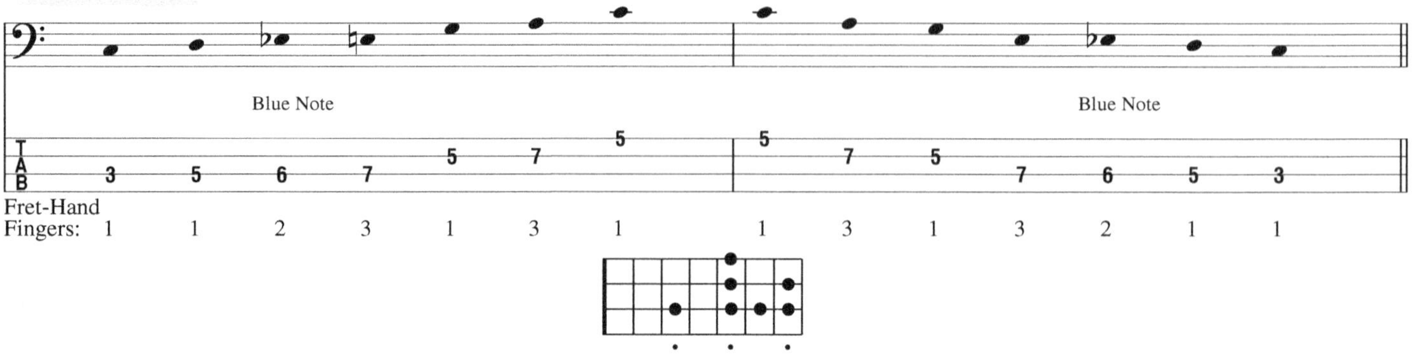

The *minor blues* scale adds a passing note between the fourth and fifth note; the added passing note is the ♭5 (♯4) of the scale. Again, this will make the scale sound quite bluesy. With the key-center approach, this scale is used to improvise over minor and blues progressions.

Chord: Cmi
Scale: Minor Blues

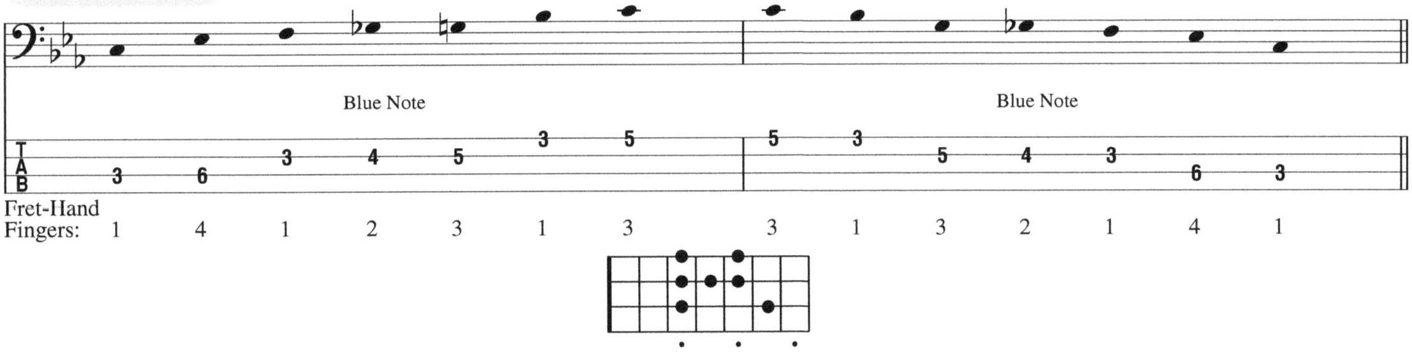

The two pentatonic and blues scales share the same relationship that exists between major and natural minor scales. Just as C major has the same notes as A minor, C major pentatonic shares its notes with A minor pentatonic. Similarly, C blues shares its notes with A minor blues. This means you can move a major blues scale down three frets on your bass and get the minor blues scale. The opposite also applies: move the minor blues scale up a minor third and you get the major blues shape. Be sure to practice making this connection for other keys.

Solo Exercises

This example is in the key of A major. Solo over it using only the A Ionian mode.

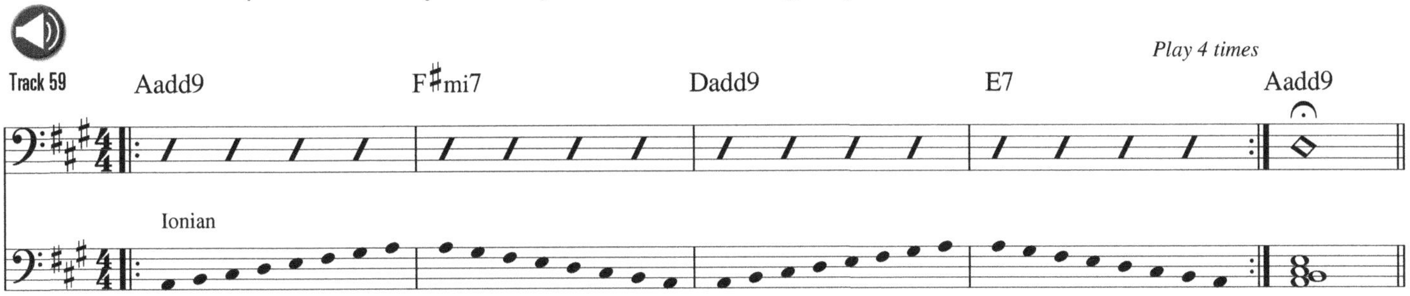

This progression uses A♭ major pentatonic for the first four measures and then shifts to F minor pentatonic for the last four measures.

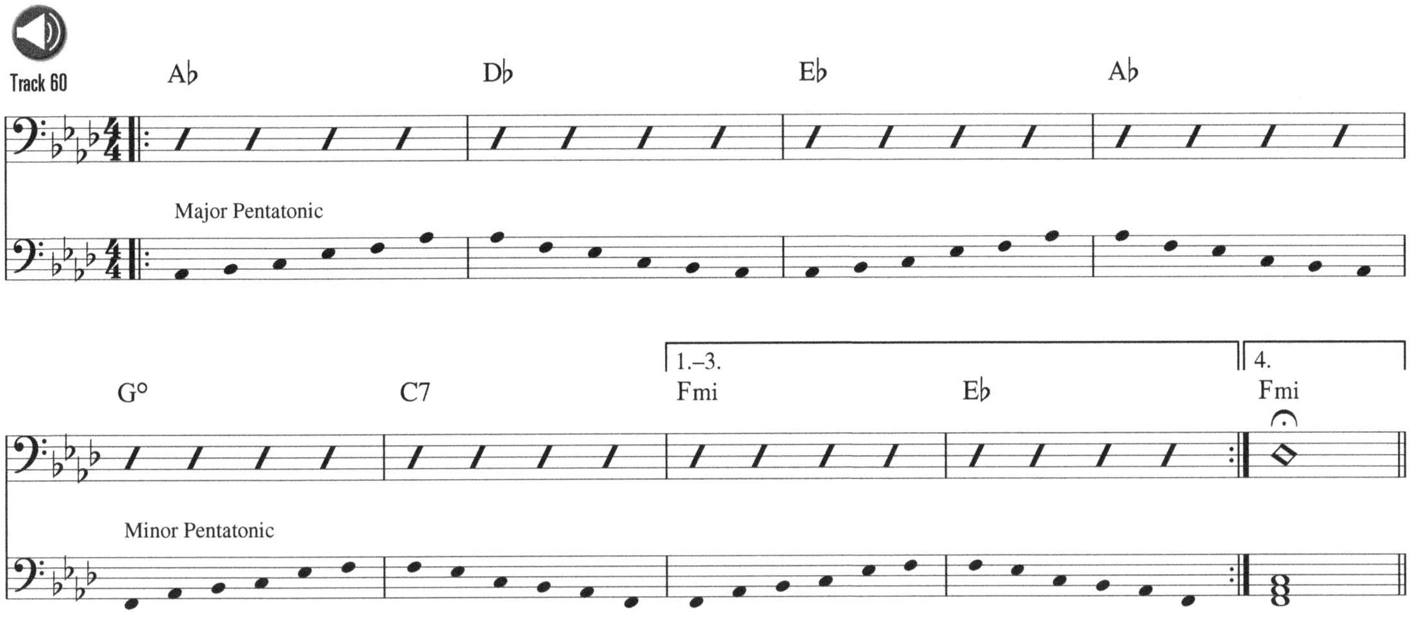

Track 61

This example is a 12-bar jazz-blues. Try sticking with just one minor blues scale for all the chords.

Track 62

In this minor progression, we'll use only the minor blues scale.

This last example uses the major blues scale. Notice how the blue note sounds really good over the D♭7 chord.

Track 63

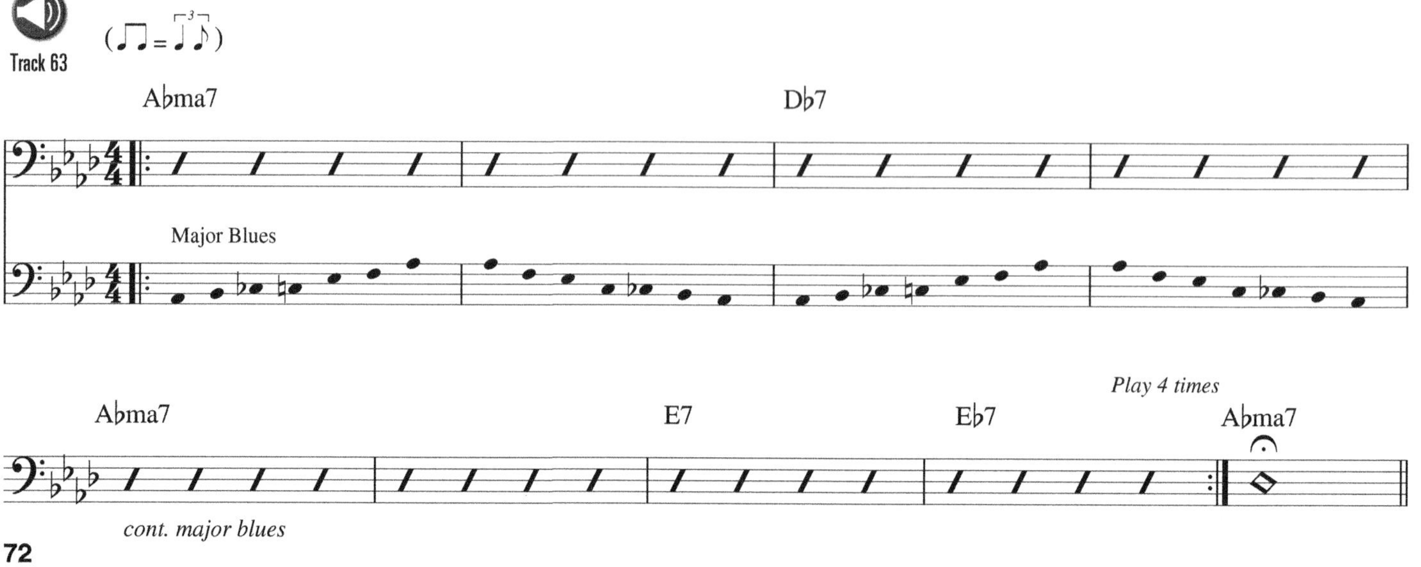

7 Scale Substitutions

Now that we know all the common scales, it's a good idea to categorize them by chord type. When you don't always have to stick with the same scale, you can create variations in your solos.

Choices for Major

- For a Ima7, ♭IIma7, and ♭IIIma7 chords:
  Ionian, Lydian, major pentatonic, and major blues
- For a IVma7 and ♭VIma7 chords:
  Lydian, major pentatonic, and major blues

Choices for Dominant

- For functioning dominants resolving to major seventh chords:
  Mixolydian, Mixolydian♭13, Phrygian♯3, whole-tone, half-whole tone, Altered, major pentatonic, and major blues
- For functioning dominants resolving to minor seventh chords:
  Phrygian♯3, Mixolydian♭13, whole-tone, half-whole tone, and Altered
- For non-functioning dominants:
  Lydian♭7, Mixolydian, major pentatonic, and major blues
- For dominants resolving down a half step:
  Lydian♭7, whole-tone, and half-whole tone

Choices for Minor

- For a Imi7 chord:
  Melodic minor, harmonic minor, Aeolian, Dorian, minor blues, and minor pentatonic
- For a IImi7 chord:
  Dorian, minor blues, and minor pentatonic
- For a IIImi7 chord:
  Phrygian, minor blues, and minor pentatonic
- For a IVmi7 chord:
  Dorian, melodic minor, minor blues, and minor pentatonic
- For a Vmi7 chord:
  Phrygian, Aeolian, minor blues, and minor pentatonic
- For a VImi7 chord:
  Aeolian, minor blues, and minor pentatonic

Choices for Minor Seventh (Flat Five)

- For a IImi7(♭5) chord:
  Locrian, Locrian♮2, and Locrian♮6
- For a ♯IVmi7(♭5), VImi7(♭5), and VIImi7(♭5) chords:
  Locrian, Locrian♮2

8 Superimposition

Theory and Application

To *superimpose* means to play a different scale or arpeggio over a given chord than the one that starts on its root.

For example, let's assume that you have a Cma7 chord in front of you. The correct scale would be Ionian (C–D–E–F–G–A–B). By playing the F Lydian scale, you will still play the same notes, but they will now center around the note F. It also will look different on your neck and the position you're playing it in will most likely change.

If you apply this concept to the pentatonic scale, you can choose to play a G major pentatonic scale over the Cma7 chord, outlining the 5–6–7–9–3 of C.

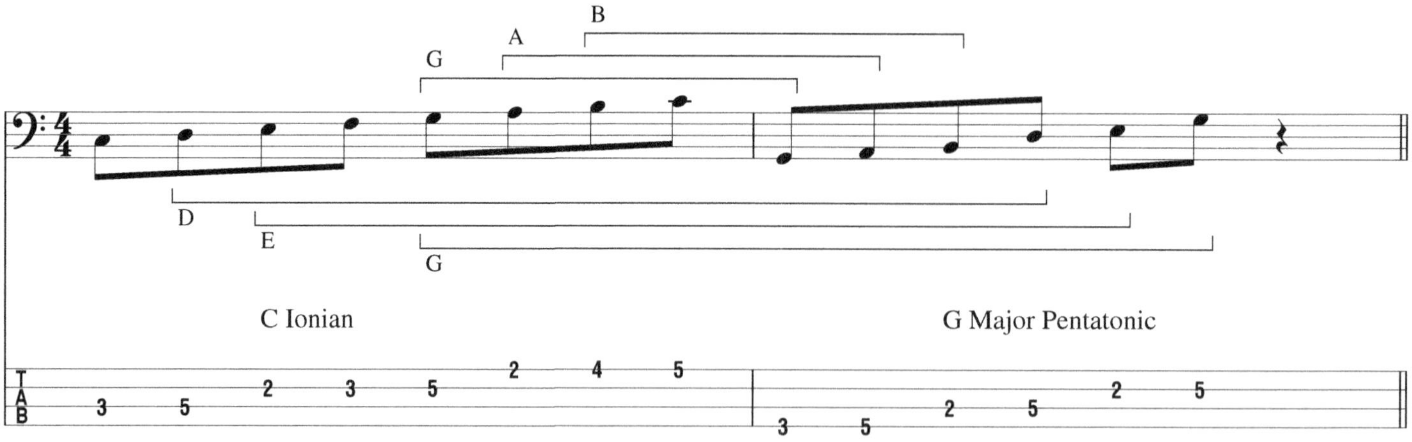

This concept can also be applied to arpeggios. Let's say that you have a Cma7 chord in front of you, and the correct scale is Lydian (C–D–E–F♯–G–A–B). You could choose to outline a D7 chord in your solo which would correspond to the 9–♯11–13–1 of C.

Let me show you an example where we take a IImi7–V7–Ima7 progression and superimpose different minor pentatonic scales over it.

Our chord progression is Dmi7–G7–Cma7. The basic scale choices would be D Dorian, G Mixolydian, and C Ionian. Using chord substitutions could result in D Dorian, G Altered, and C Lydian. Outlining only the minor pentatonic scales could give you A, B♭, and B. Now you have chromatic ascending scales that you can play against a descending chord progression.

Base Scales:

Chord: Dmi7
Scale: D Dorian

Chord: G7
Scale: G Mixolydian

Chord: Cma7
Scale: C Ionian

Substitutions:

Chord: Dmi7
Scale: D Dorian

Chord: G7
Scale: G Altered

Chord: Cma7
Scale: C Lydian

Implied Pentatonic Scales:

Chord: Dmi7
Scale: A Minor Pentatonic

Chord: G7
Scale: B♭ Minor Pentatonic

Chord: Cma7
Scale: B Minor Pentatonic

Pentatonic Scales:

Chord: Dmi7
Scale: A Minor Pentatonic

Chord: G7
Scale: B♭ Minor Pentatonic

Chord: Cma7
Scale: B Minor Pentatonic

Solo Exercise

Try soloing over the previous progression now using only minor pentatonic scales. Substituting the blues scale for the pentatonic scale seems to work most of the time too.

Track 64

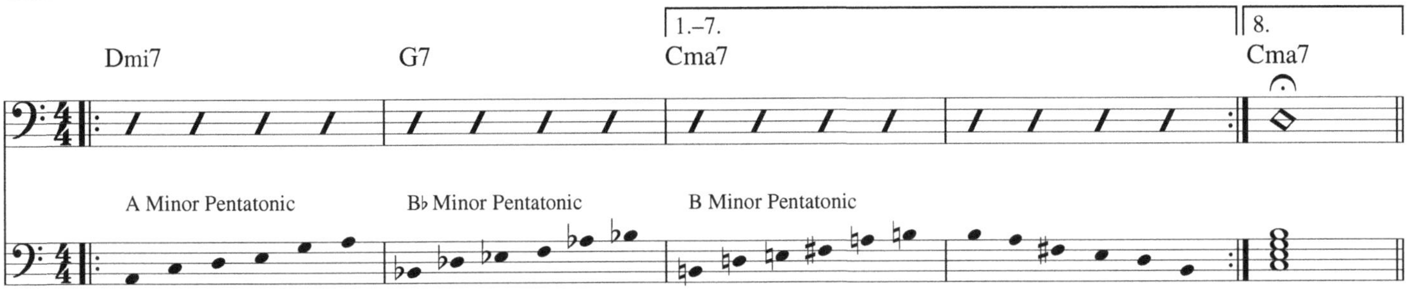

9 II–V–I Progression

The II–V–I progression is the most common progression in jazz. If you're trying to get better at improvising in that style, studying these chords will help you a lot. This involves knowing the different scale choices by heart (as well as the key centers). Let's look at all the different variations and scale choices.

Key-Center Choices

It is possible to play only one scale for all three chords, which is the key-center approach from Chapter 6. There are four different II–V–I progressions:

1. Dmi7–G7–Cma7: C Ionian
2. Dmi7(♭5)–G7–Cma7: C harmonic major, which is a new scale in this book and rarely used
3. Dmi7(♭5)–G7–Cmi: C harmonic minor
4. Dmi7–G7–Cmi: C melodic minor

1

Degree: IImi7 **Chord:** Dmi7 **Scale:** C Ionian	**Degree:** V7 **Chord:** G7 **Scale:** C Ionian	**Degree:** Ima7 **Chord:** Cma7 **Scale:** C Ionian

2

Degree: IImi7(♭5) **Chord:** Dmi7(♭5) **Scale:** C Harmonic Major	**Degree:** V7 **Chord:** G7 **Scale:** C Harmonic Major	**Degree:** Ima7 **Chord:** Cma7 **Scale:** C Harmonic Major

3

Degree: IImi7(♭5) **Chord:** Dmi7(♭5) **Scale:** C Harmonic Minor	**Degree:** V7 **Chord:** G7 **Scale:** C Harmonic Minor	**Degree:** Imi(ma7) **Chord:** Cmi(ma7) **Scale:** C Harmonic Minor

4

Degree: IImi7 **Chord:** Dmi7 **Scale:** C Melodic Minor	**Degree:** V7 **Chord:** G7 **Scale:** C Melodic Minor	**Degree:** Imi6 **Chord:** Cmi6 **Scale:** C Melodic Minor

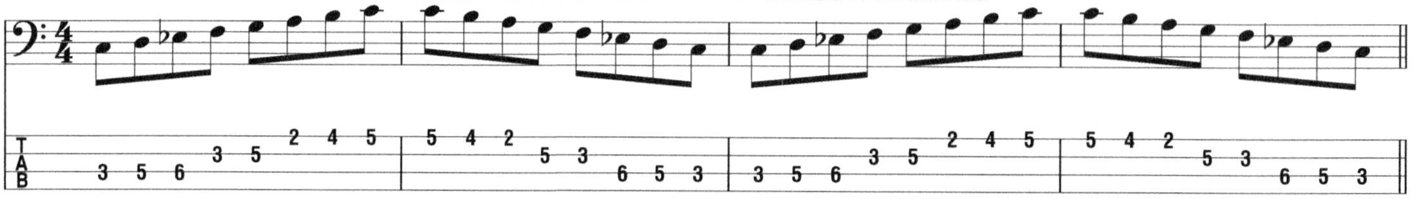

Scale Choices

If you choose to play a different scale for each chord, it'll help to know what all your options are. The following list shows the most common possibilities:

Scale Choices in Major Keys:

IImi7	**V7**	**Ima7**
Dorian	Mixolydian*	Ionian
	Mixolydian♭9 (H Major5)	Lydian
	Mixolydian♭9(MM5)	Major pentatonic
	Phrygian♯3 (HM5)	Major blues
	Whole-tone	
	Half-whole tone	
	Altered**	

*For the V chord, Mixolydian sounds the most inside, since it has the same notes as Ionian.
**Altered sounds the most outside, since it shares the fewest notes with Ionian (three).

Scale Choices in a Minor Key:

Imi7(♭5)	**V7**	**Imi7**
Locrian	Phrygian♯3 (HM5)*	Aeolian
Locrian♮2	Mixolydian♭9 (H Major5)	Dorian
Locrian♮6 (HM2)	Mixolydian♭13 (MM5)	Melodic minor
	Altered	Harmonic minor
	Whole-tone	Minor pentatonic
	Half-whole tone	Minor blues

*For the V chord, Phrygian♯3 sounds the most inside, since it shares six out of seven notes with Aeolian. Mixolydian is not used in minor keys.

Solo Exercise

This track consists of two II–V–I progressions. The first four measures are in C major and the last four are in A minor. Apply the information from this chapter to your soloing and experiment with different scales and key centers.

Track 65

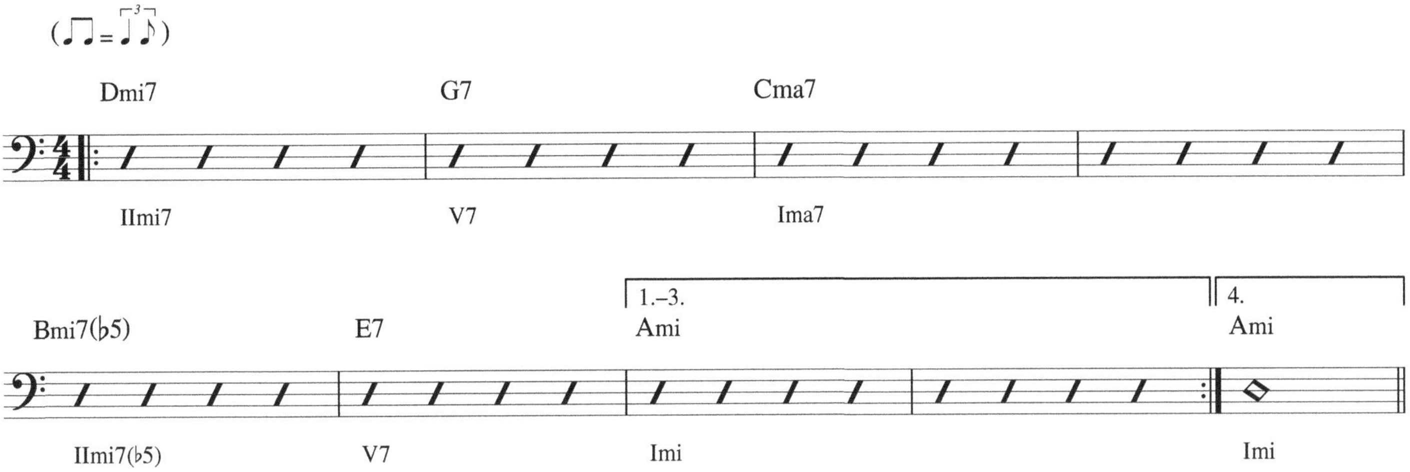

10 Chromatic Notes

A *chromatic note* (Cr) is any tone that is not part of the key or scale. In C major, the chromatic pitches are C♯/D♭, D♯/E♭, F♯/G♭, G♯/A♭, and A♯/B♭.

- Ascending chromatic notes are always notated with either sharps or naturals
- Descending chromatic notes are always notated with either flats or naturals

Sustaining these notes by themselves against a C major chord would essentially sound wrong. The only way to incorporate these pitches would be in passing. This means that they can be used to connect notes from the scale, but they always need to resolve by half step.

Track 66

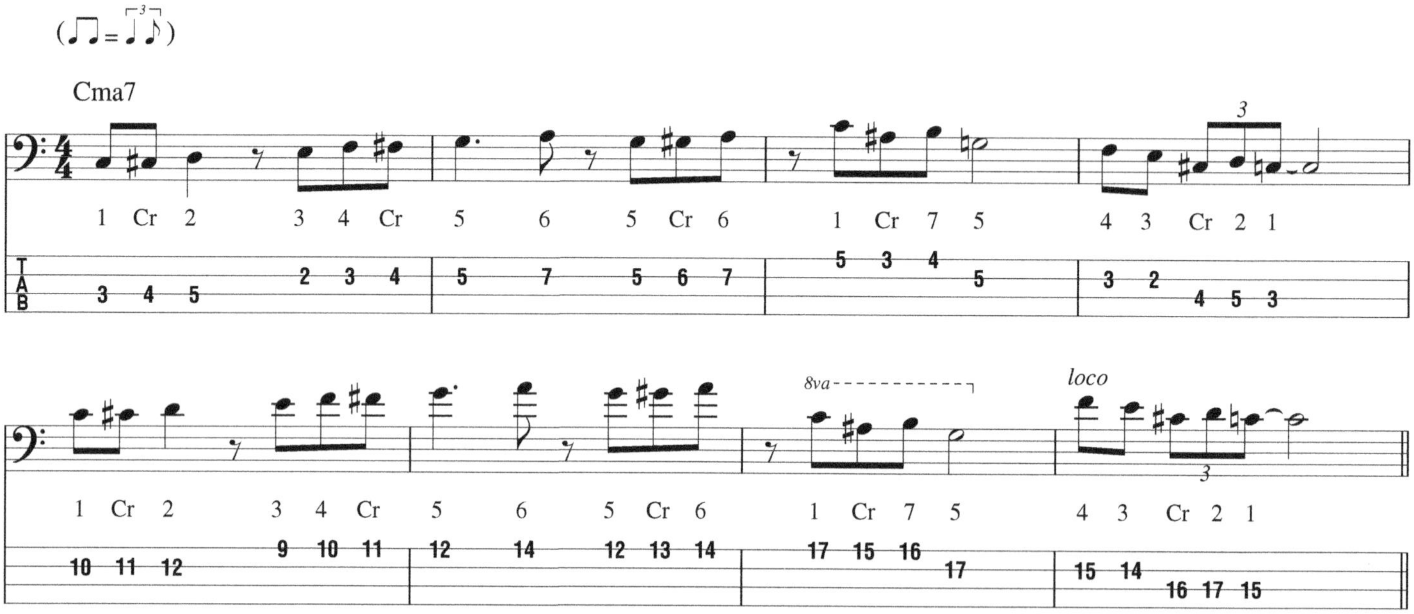

Bebop Dominant Scale

It is so common to add a chromatic note between the ♭7th and octave of the Mixolydian mode, that the result gets its own name: the *bebop seventh* or *bebop dominant scale.*

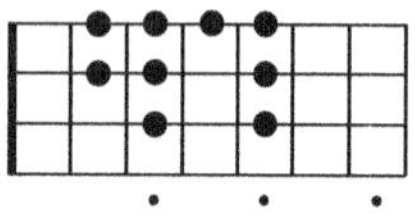

In this instance, there has been only one chromatic note added to the scale, but you could add a chromatic note between any two notes that are a whole step apart.

You can create scales with one to five chromatic notes. Try experimenting with this idea, and you'll notice how much this can enrich your soloing. Going back to some of the earlier exercises with the chromatic notes in mind will completely change your sound.

This next playing example uses the Dorian, Mixolydian, and Ionian modes, but I added one or two chromatic notes to each.

- Dorian uses a passing tone between the fourth and fifth notes
- Mixolydian uses a passing tone between the seventh and octave (giving us the bebop dominant scale)
- Ionian uses a passing tone between the second and third, and the fifth and sixth notes

Track 67 shows you how this approach could sound and Track 68 is for you to try.

Track 67–68

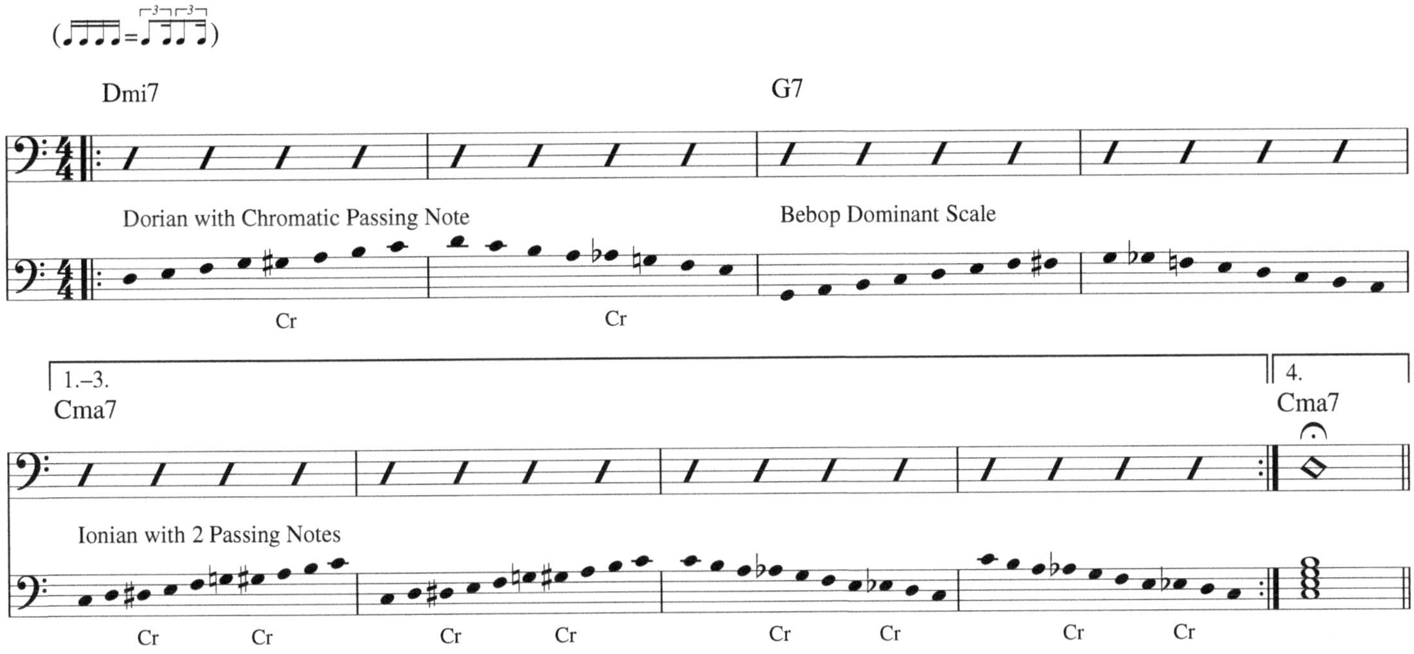

11 Exercise Glossary

In this section, there are many different ways to practice a scale. The better you can visualize the scale on the neck, the easier it will be to solo and make music out of it. These exercises really help you learn the fretboard shapes and break you out of continuous stepwise motion.

All the examples are shown in C Ionian, but they should be applied to all scales that you learned in this book.

#1 One-Octave Range

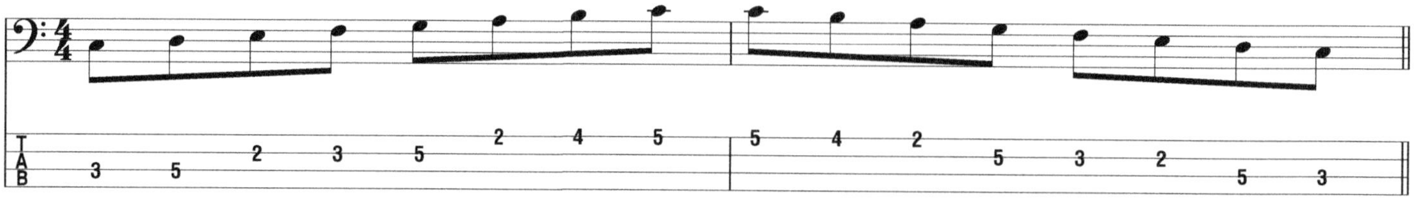

#2 Two-Octave Range

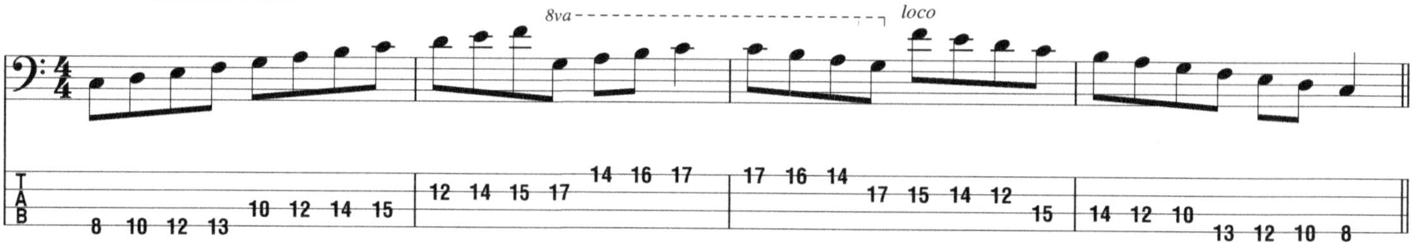

#3 Across the Whole Neck

#4 On the G String Only

#5 On the D String Only

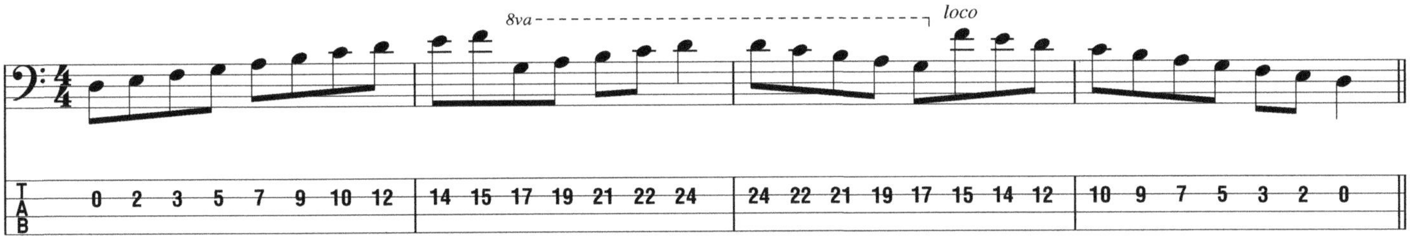

#6 On the A String Only

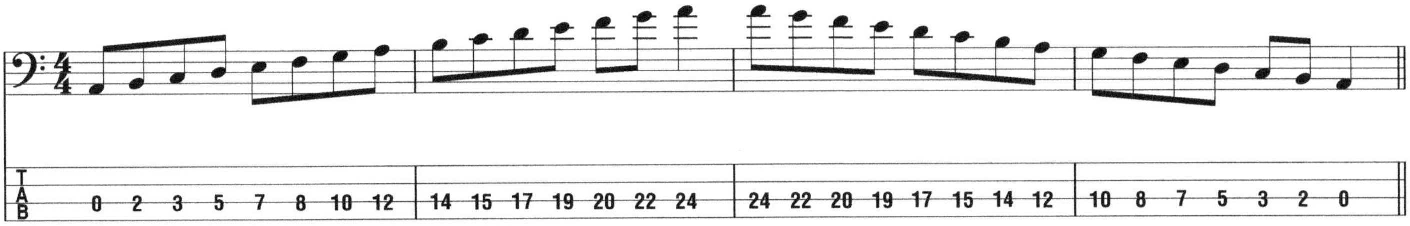

#7 On the E String Only

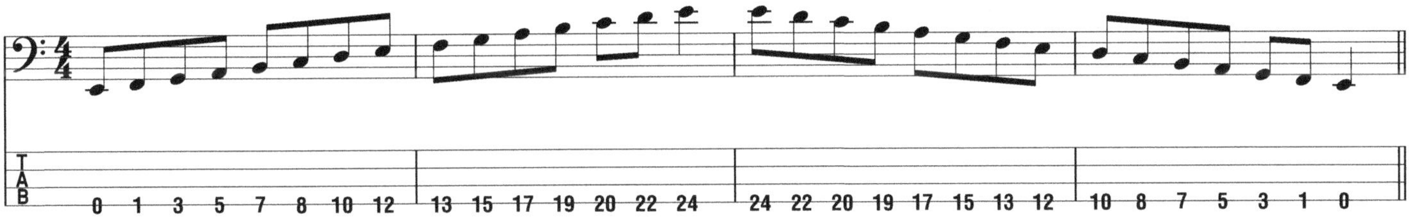

#8 Two-Note Groupings

#9 Three-Note Groupings

#10 Four-Note Groupings

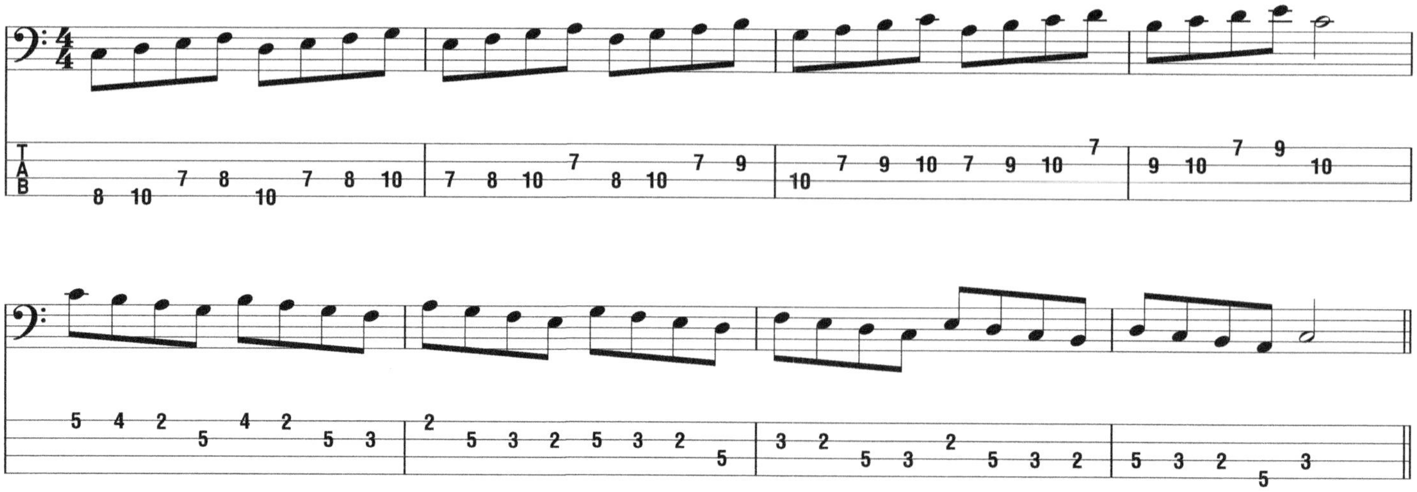

#11 Five-Note Groupings

This concept can be extended up the seven-note-grouping pattern.

#12 Thirds

#13 Fourths

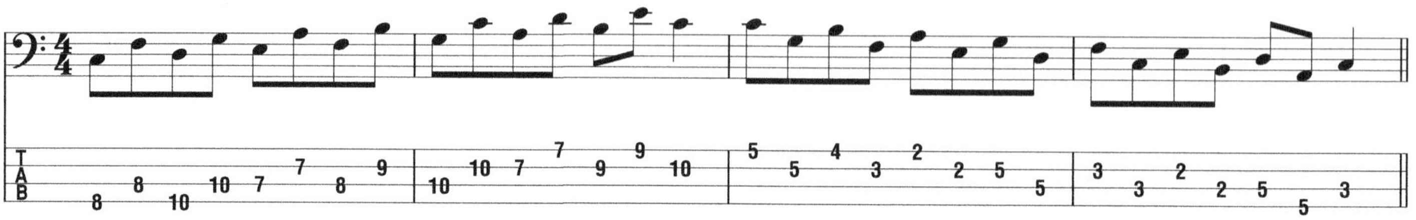

#14 Fifths

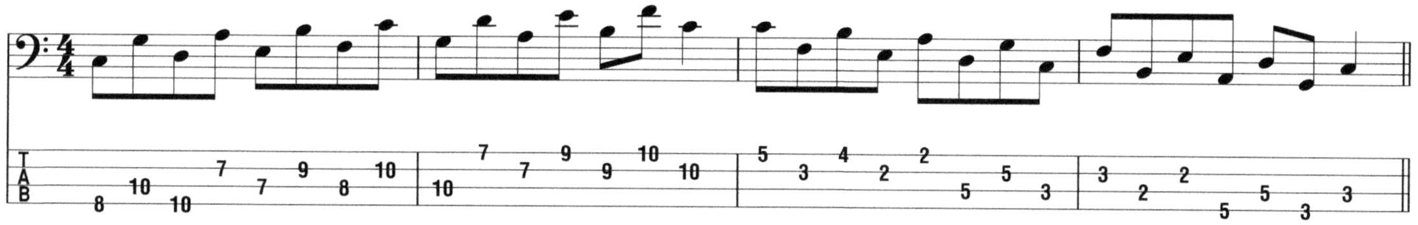

#15 Sixths

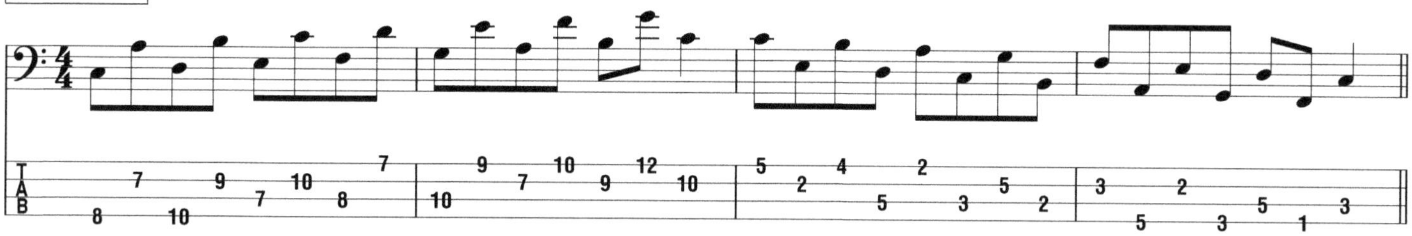

#16 Sevenths

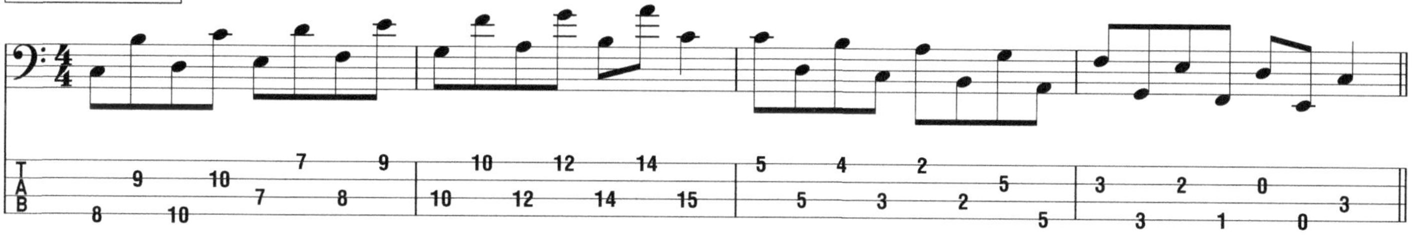

#17 Alternating Ascending and Descending Thirds

This concept can also be applied to fourths, fifths, sixths, and sevenths.

#18 Triads

#19 Alternating Ascending and Descending Triads

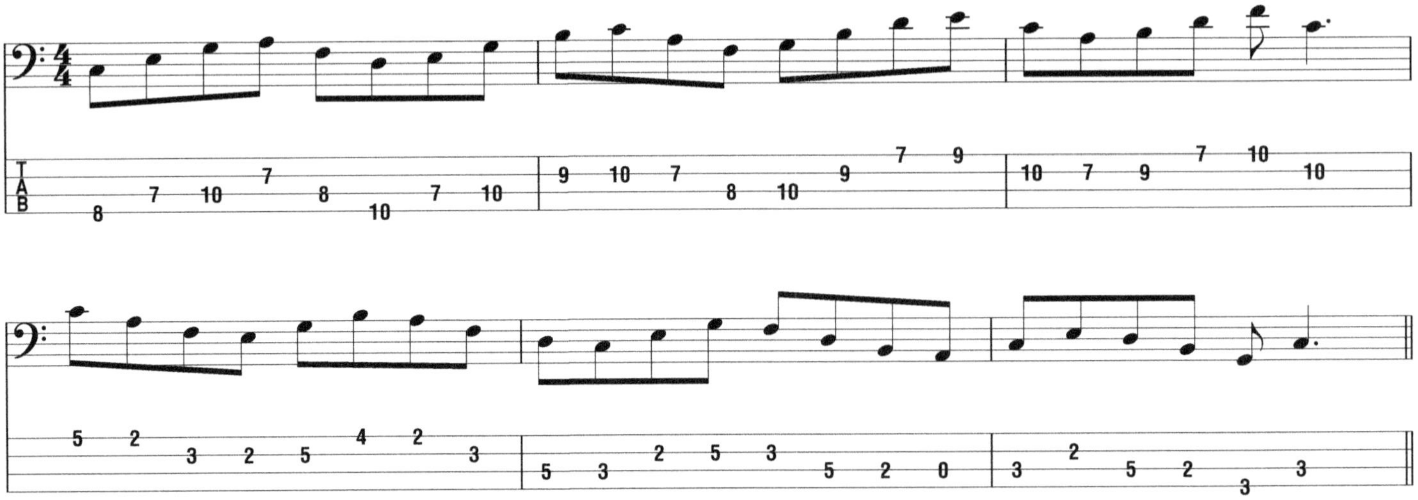

#20 Seventh Chords

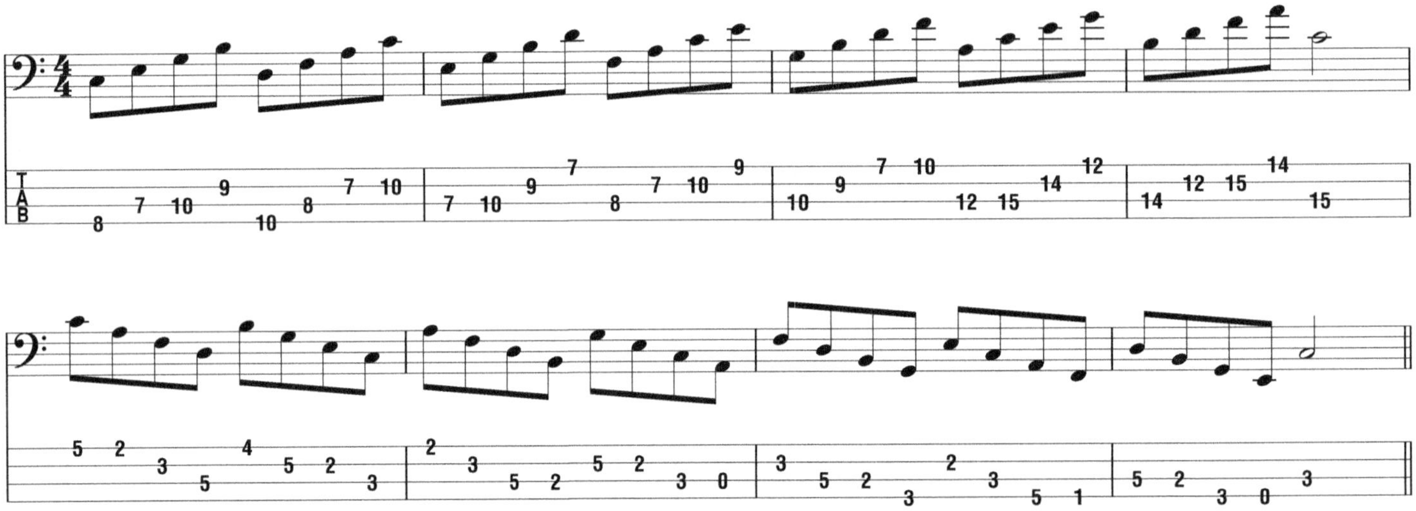

#21 Alternating Ascending and Descending Seventh Chords

#22 Surrounding Scale Notes Diatonically:
from Above and Below, Four-Note Groupings

#23 Surrounding Scale Notes Diatonically:
from Below and Above, Four-Note Groupings

#24 Surrounding Scale Notes Diatonically:
from Above and Below, Three-Note Groupings

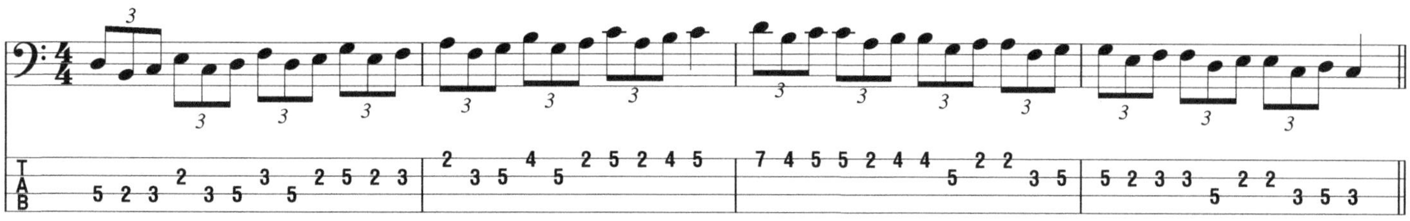

#25 Surrounding Scale Notes Diatonically:
from Above and Chromatically Below, Three-Note Groupings

#26 Thirds:
Skipping Every Other Note

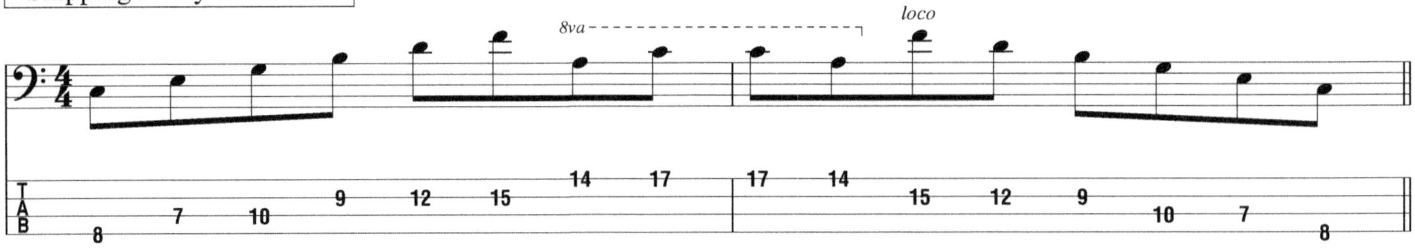

#27 In One Position:
V Position

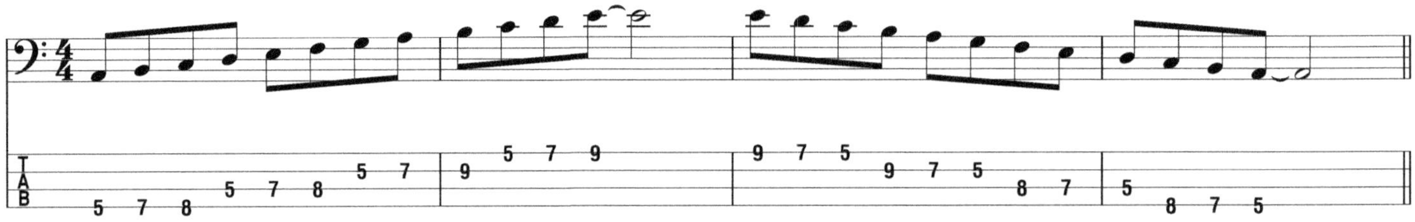

12 Scale Glossary

Here are all the scales we talked about, with a few additional scales for reference (rarely used in soloing). All scales start from C.

Major Scales

Ionian

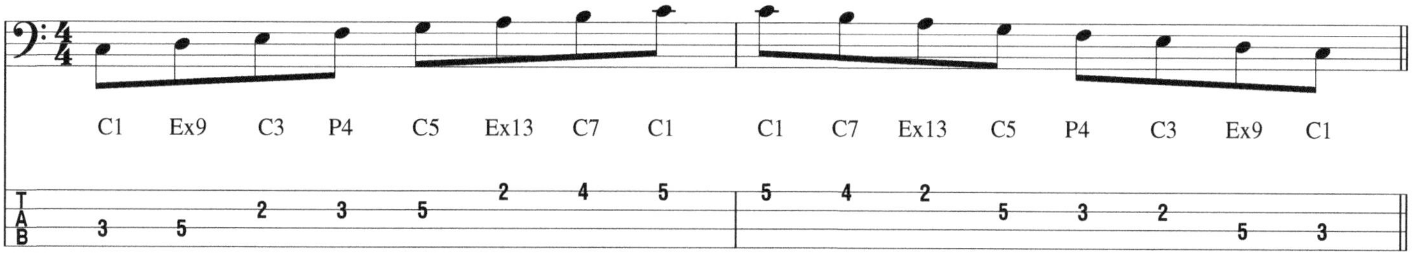

Dorian

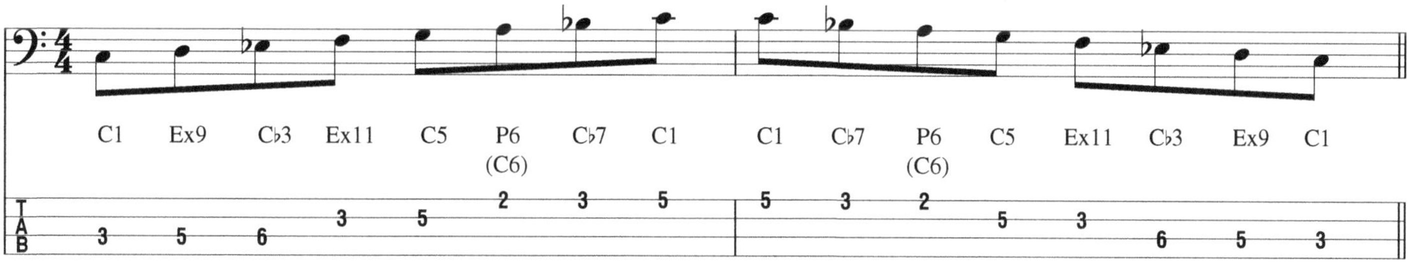

Phrygian

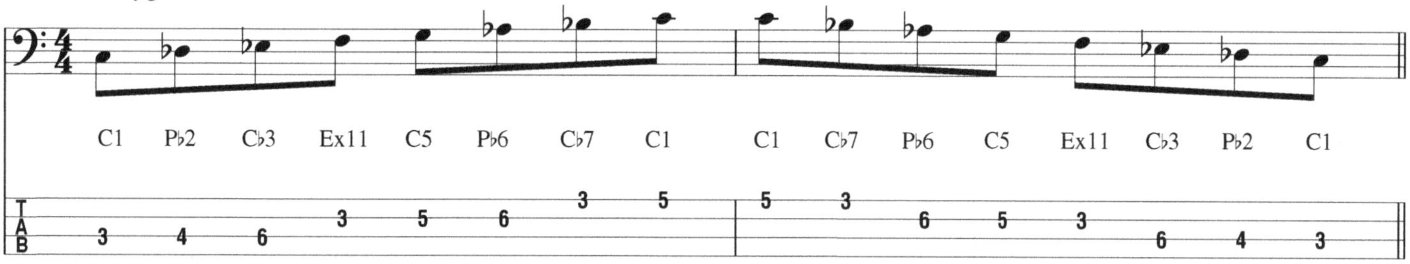

Lydian

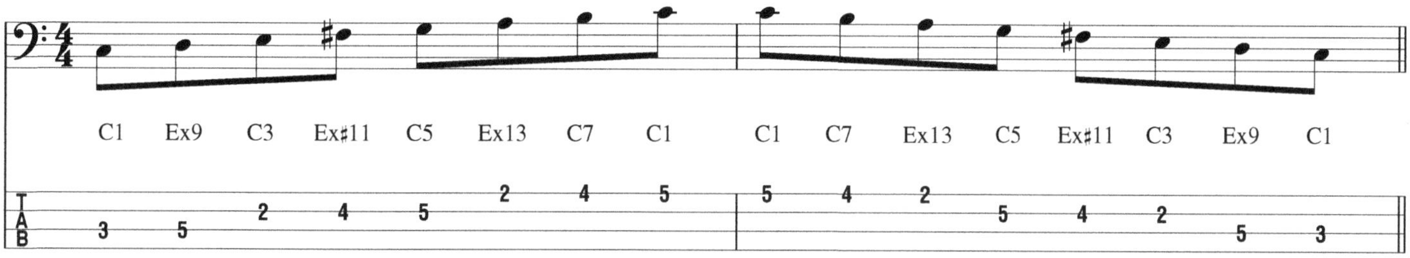

Mixolydian

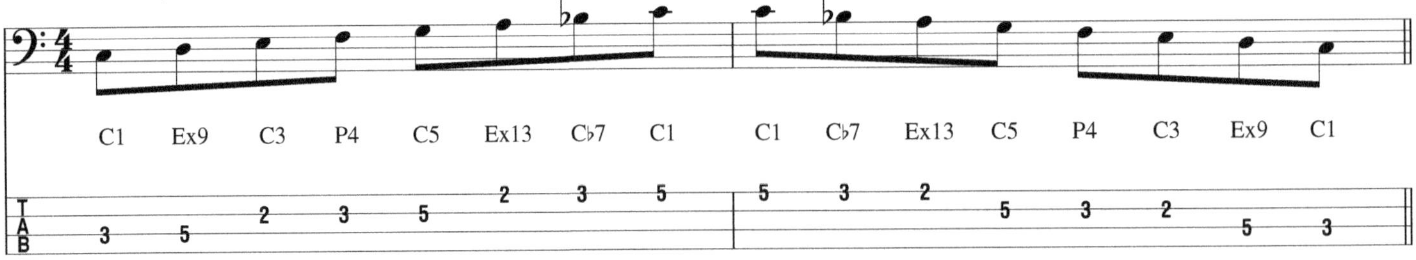

Aeolian

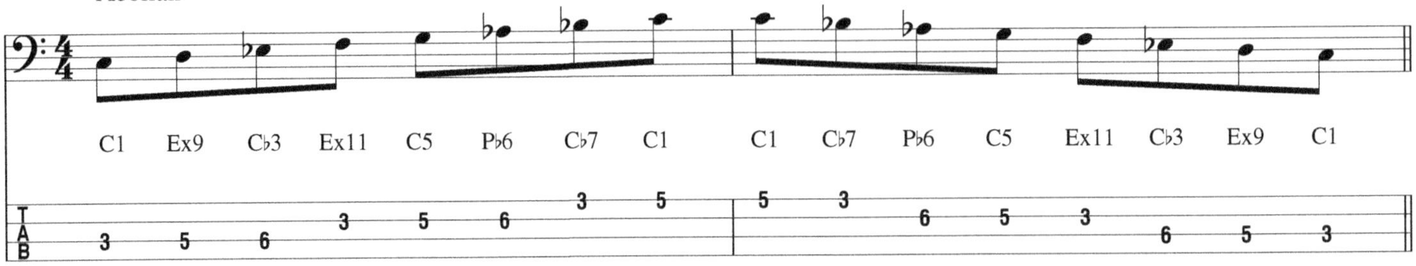

Locrian

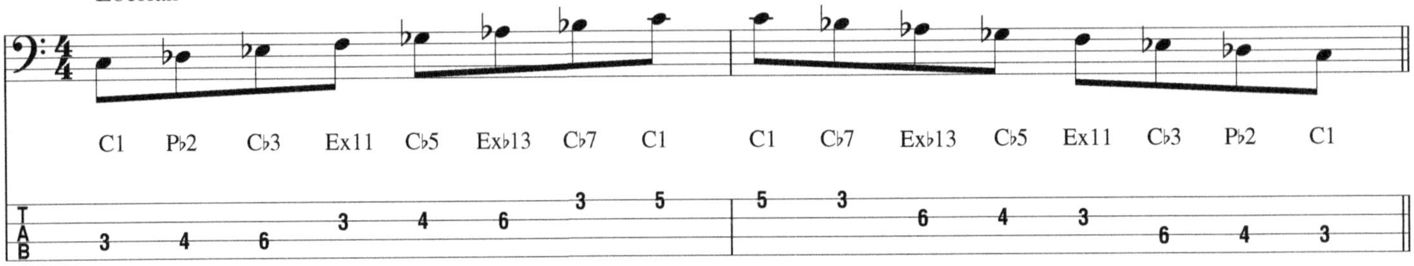

Melodic Minor Scales

Melodic Minor

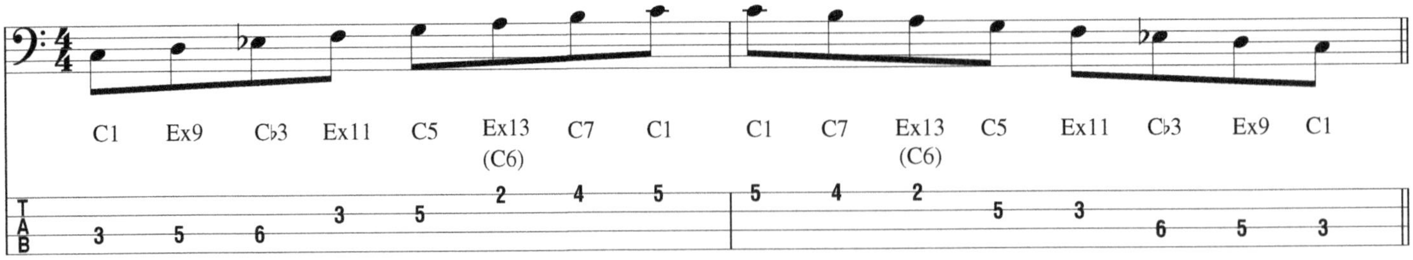

Dorian♭2

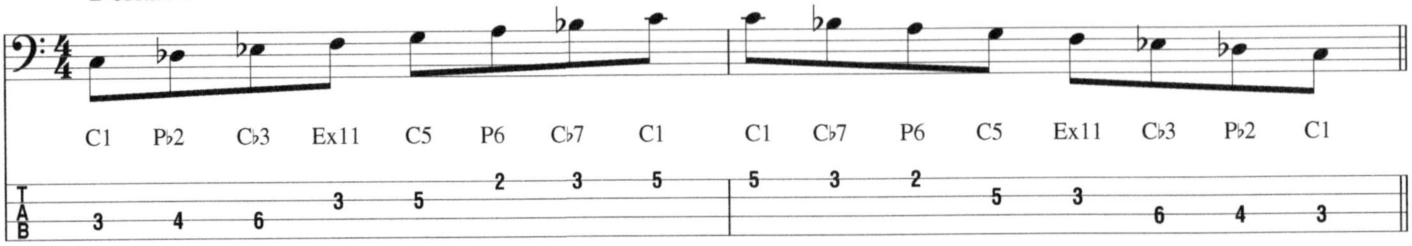

Lydian♯5

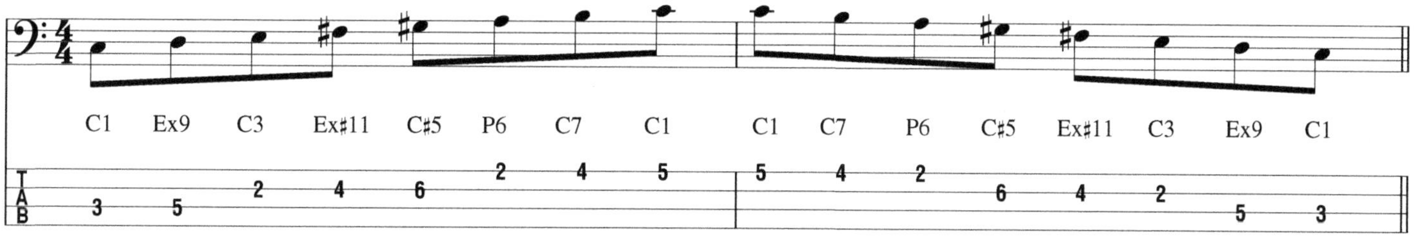

Lydian♭7

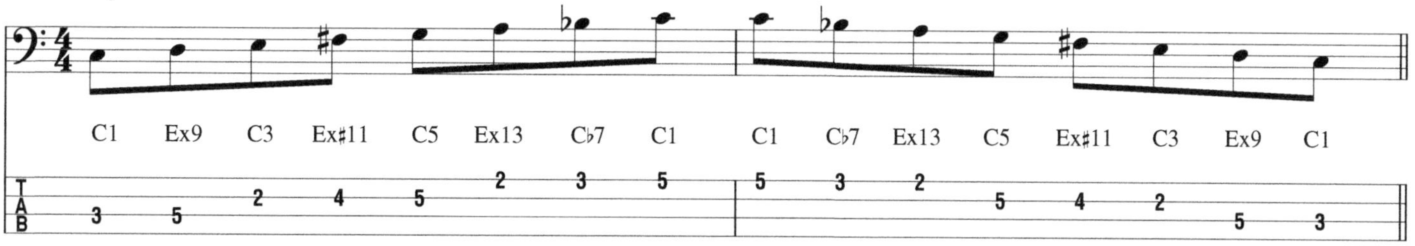

Mixolydian♭13

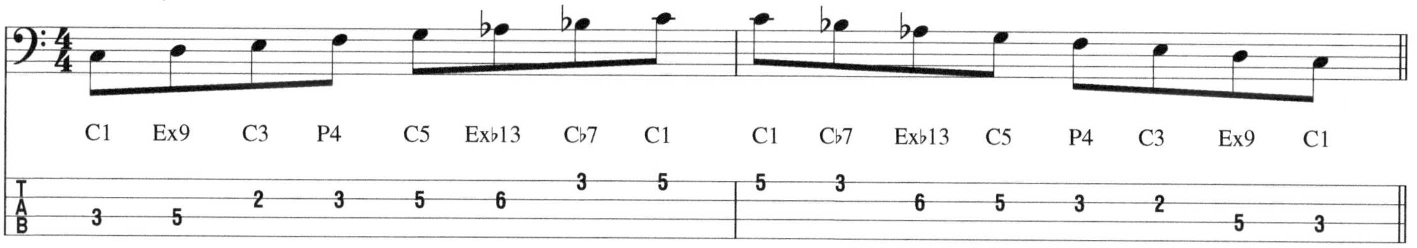

Locrian♮2

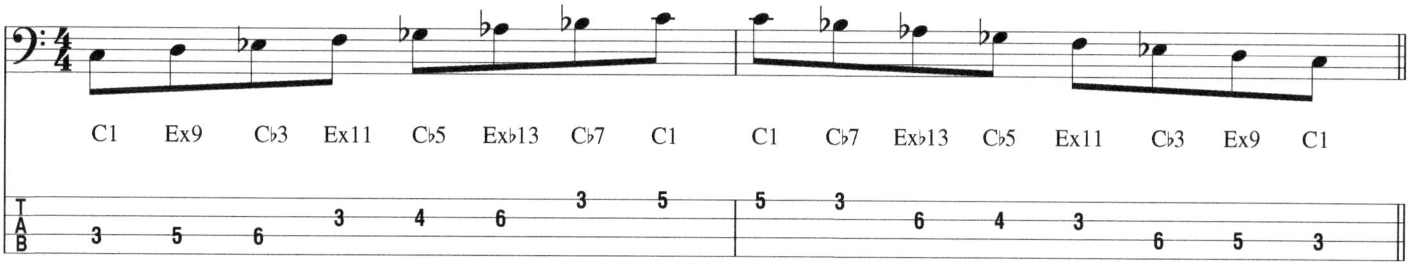

Altered

Harmonic Minor Scales

Harmonic Minor

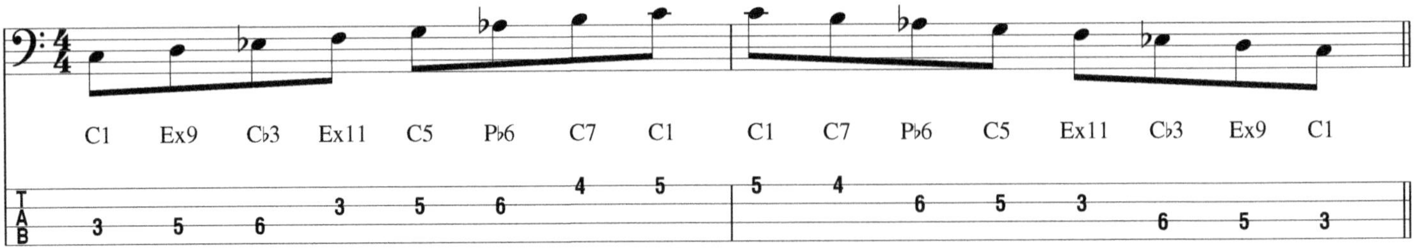

Locrian♮6

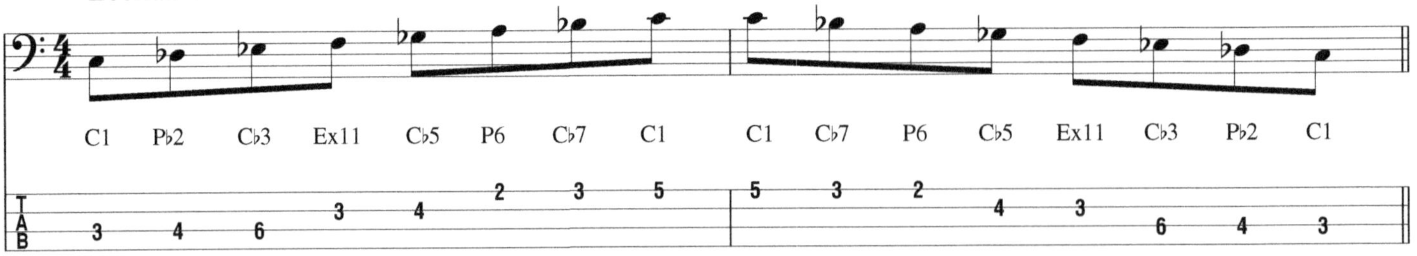

Ionian♯5

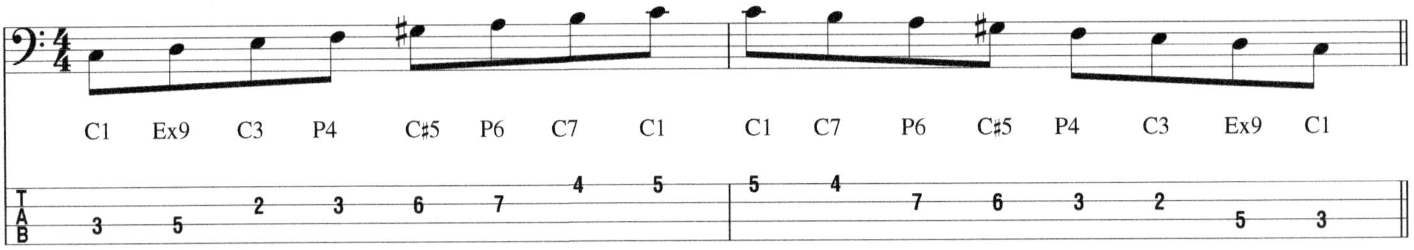

Dorian♯4

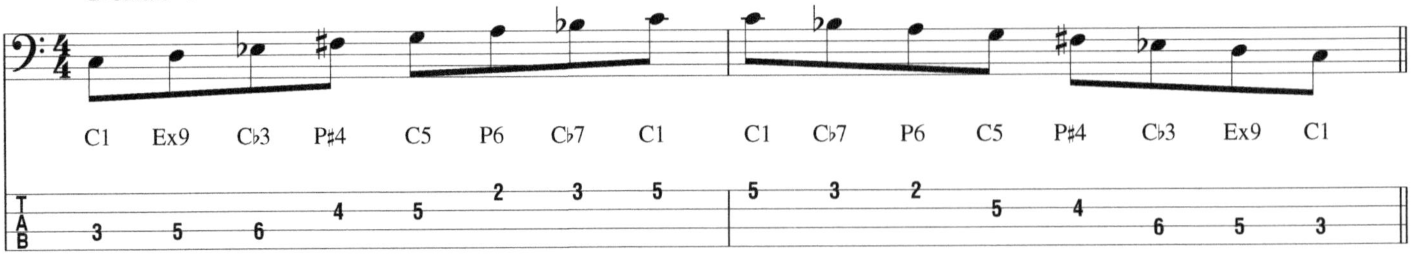

Phrygian♯3

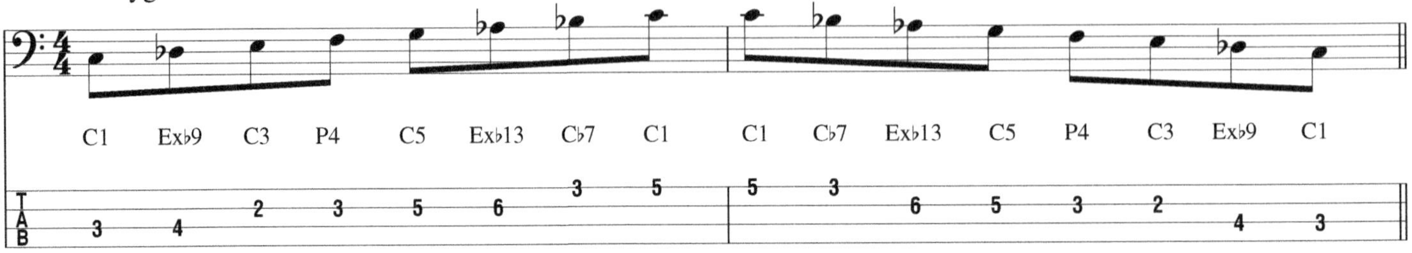

Lydian♯2

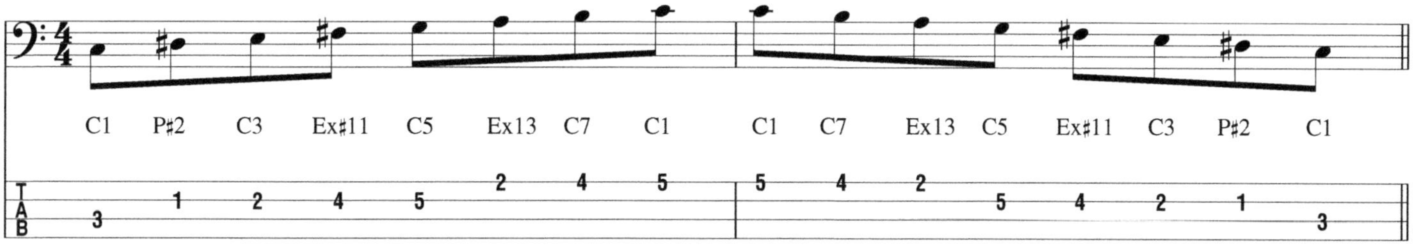

VII Degree of HM

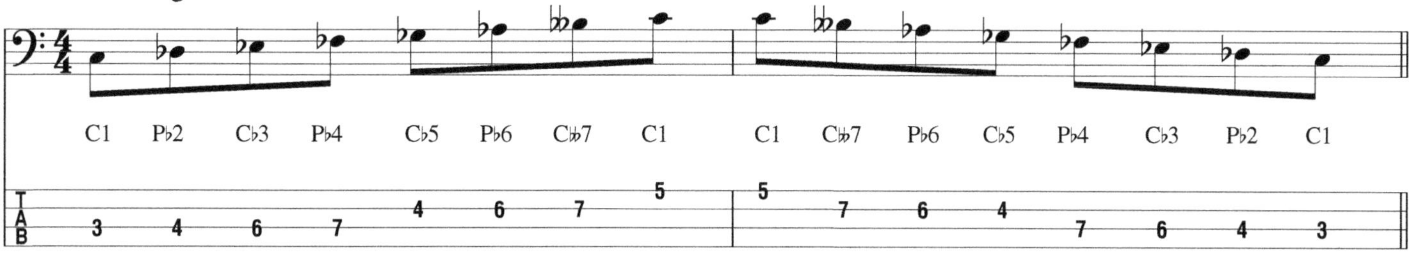

Harmonic Major Scales

This scale is very unusual; the given mode names are only for convenience and are not really used.

Harmonic Major

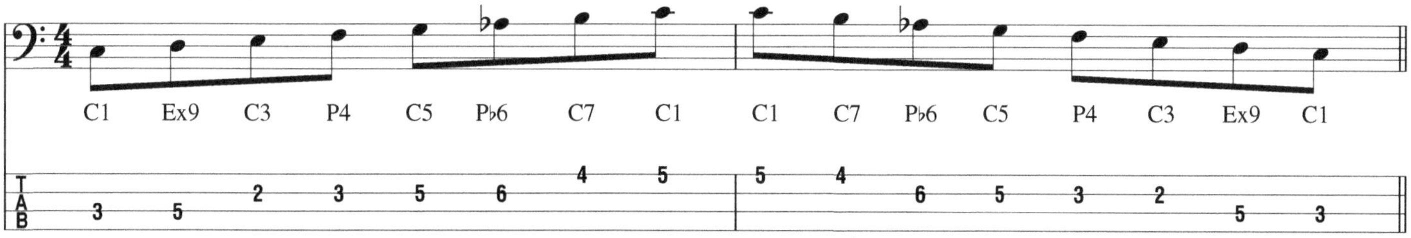

Dorian♭5

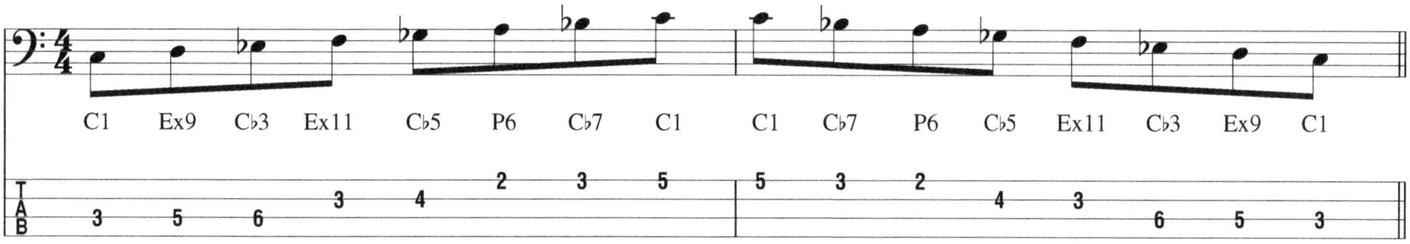

Phrygian♭4

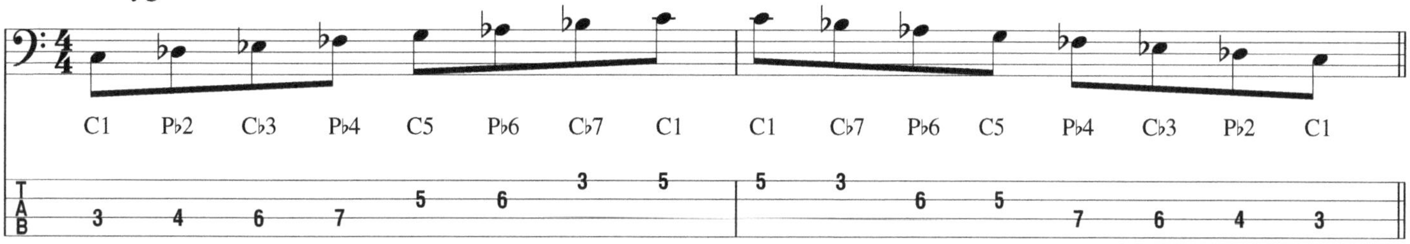

Altered♮5
(Enharmonic Spelling of Phrygian♭4)

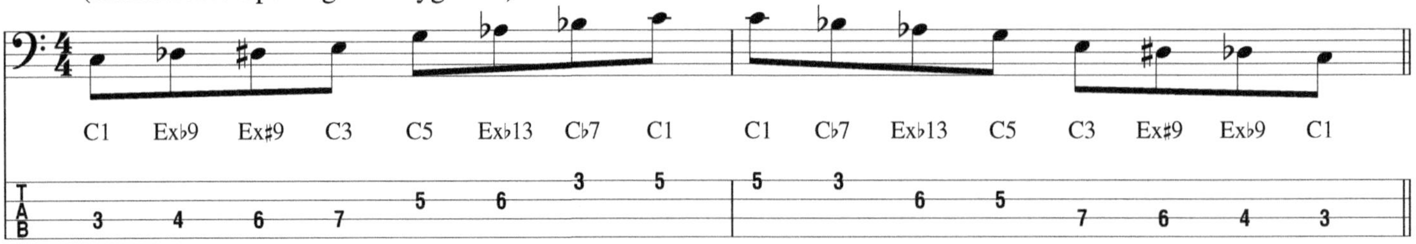

Melodic Minor♯4

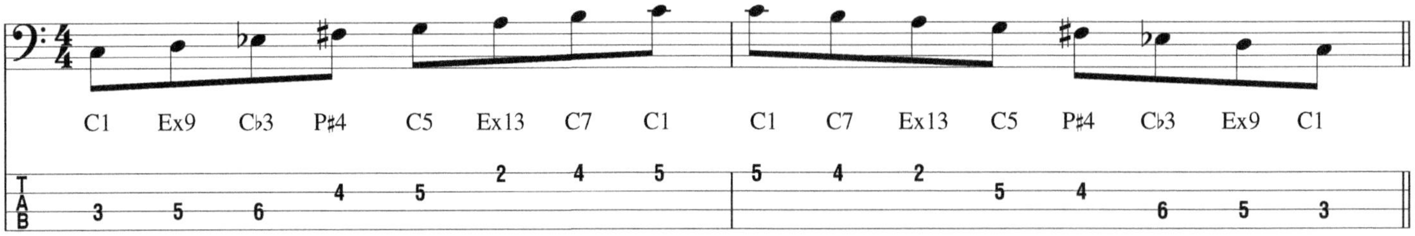

Mixolydian♭9

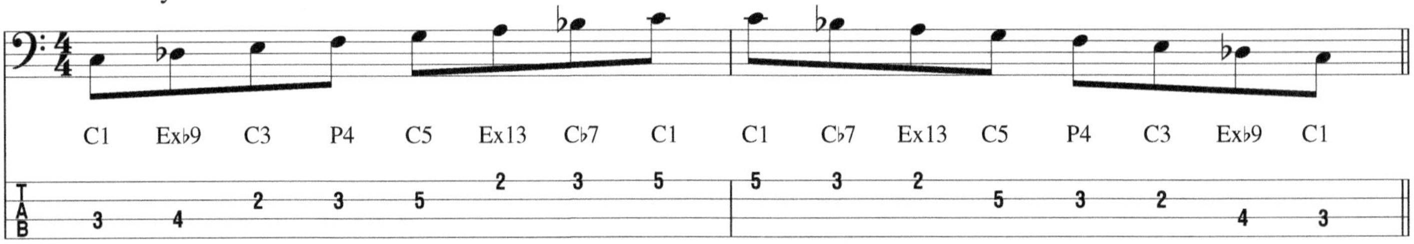

Lydian♯2♯5

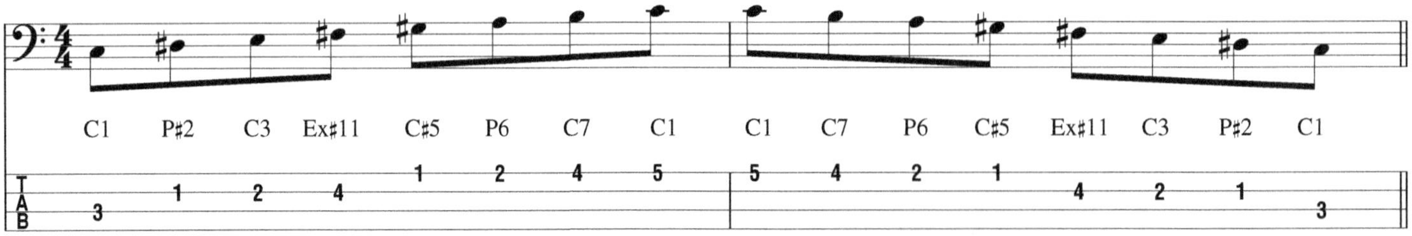

Locrian♭♭7

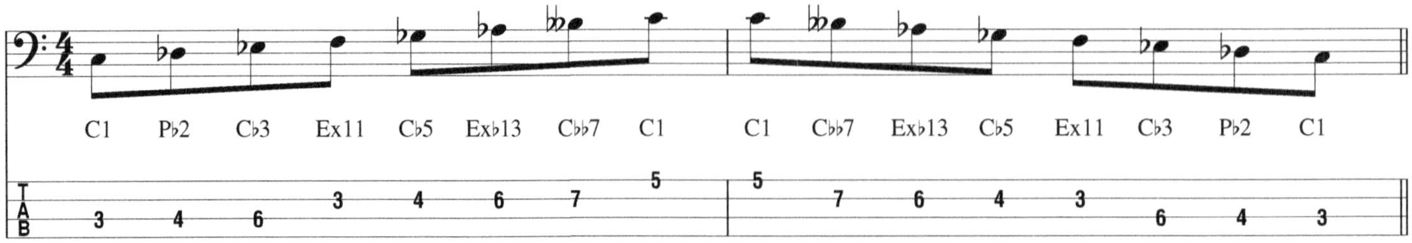

Chapter 12

Symmetrical Scales

Whole-Half Tone

Half-Whole Tone

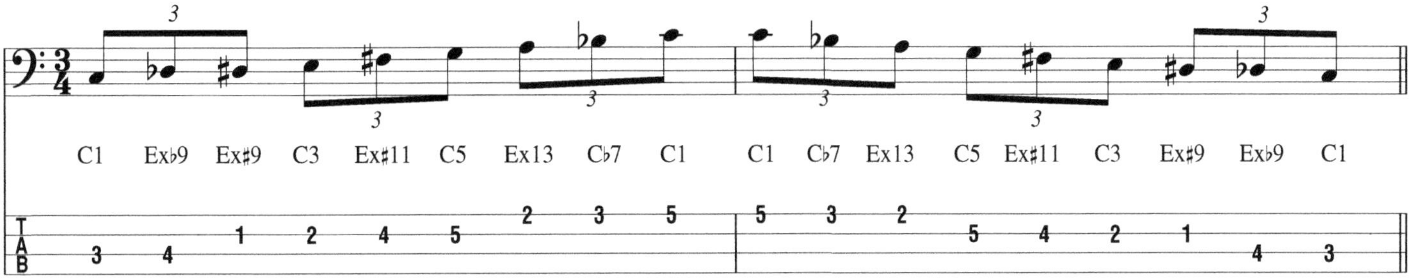

Whole-Tone

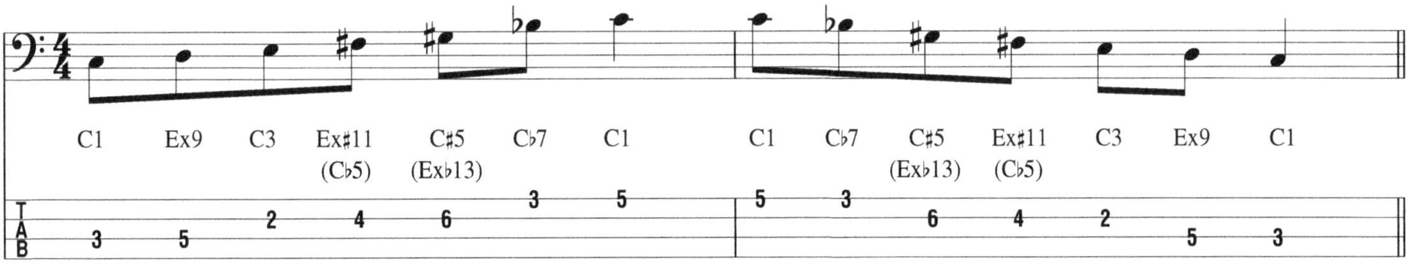

Augmented

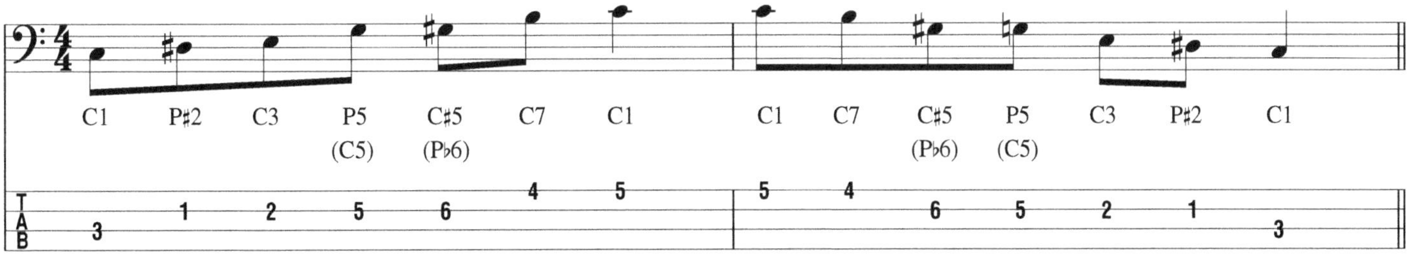

Pentatonic and Blues Scales

Major Pentatonic

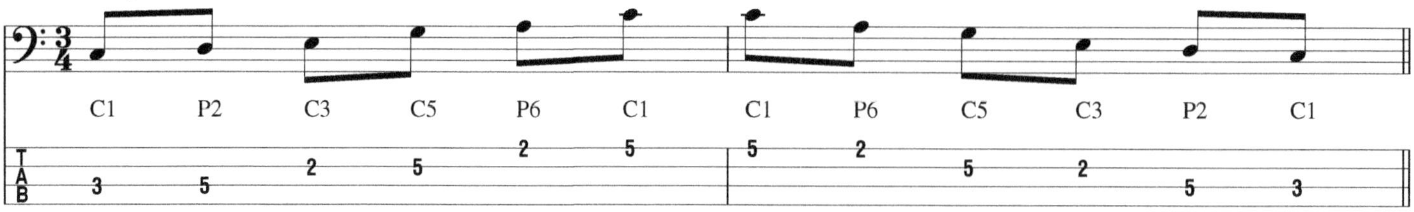

Minor Pentatonic

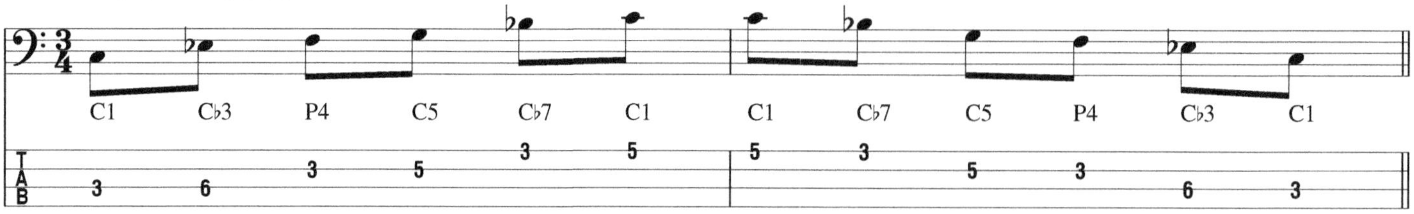

Major Blues

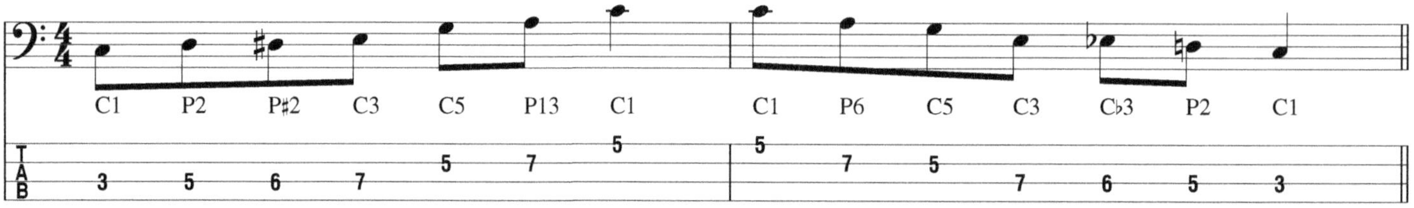

Minor Blues

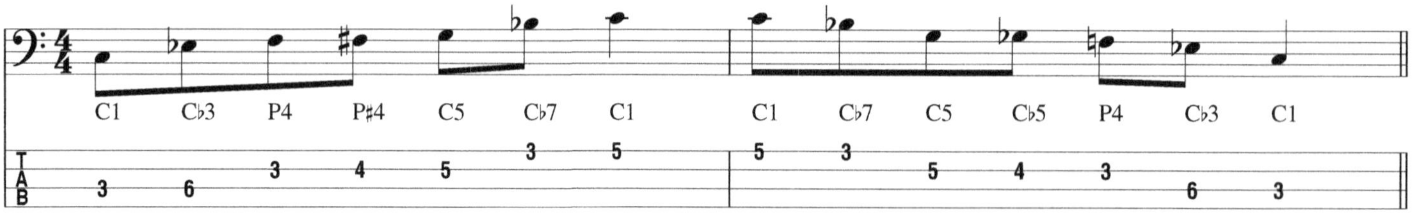

13 Arpeggio Glossary

This section shows all the seventh chord arpeggios and the theoretically possible scales that could go with them.

Chord | **Possible Scales**

Major Seventh — Ionian, Lydian, Major Pentatonic, Major Blues

Cma7

Major Seventh Flat Five — Lydian

Cma7(♭5)

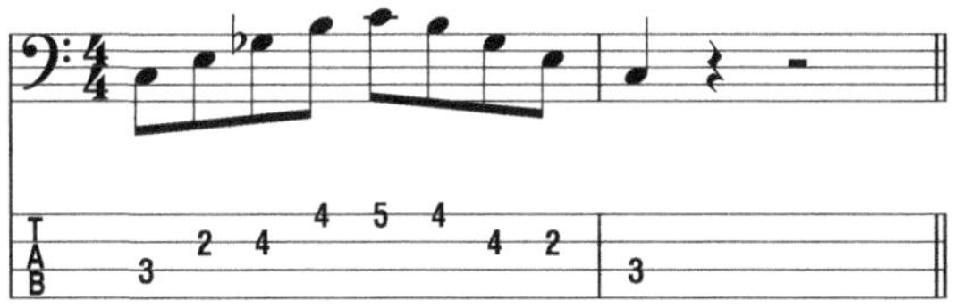

Major Seventh Sharp Five — Ionian♯5, Lydian♯5

Cma7(♯5)

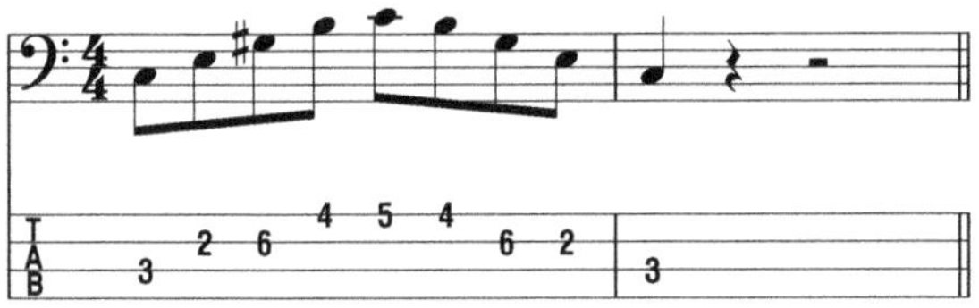

Major Sixth — Ionian, Lydian, Mixolydian, Major Pentatonic, Major Blues

C6

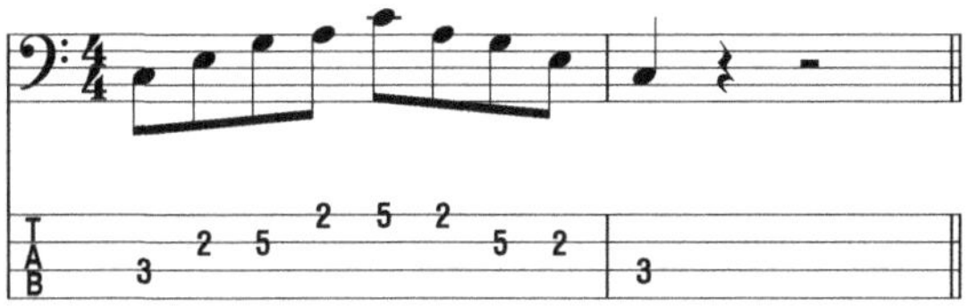

Dominant Seventh — Mixolydian, Phrygian♯3, Mixolydian♭13, Mixolydian♭9, Altered, Whole-Tone, Half-Whole Tone, Lydian♭7

C7

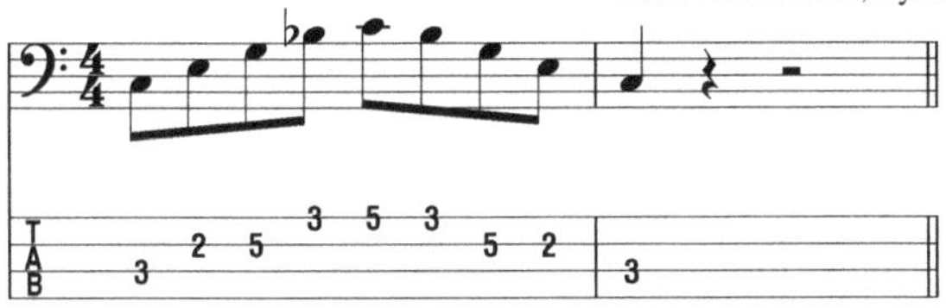

Dominant Seventh Sharp Five — Phrygian♯3, Mixolydian♭13, Altered, Whole-Tone

C7(♯5)

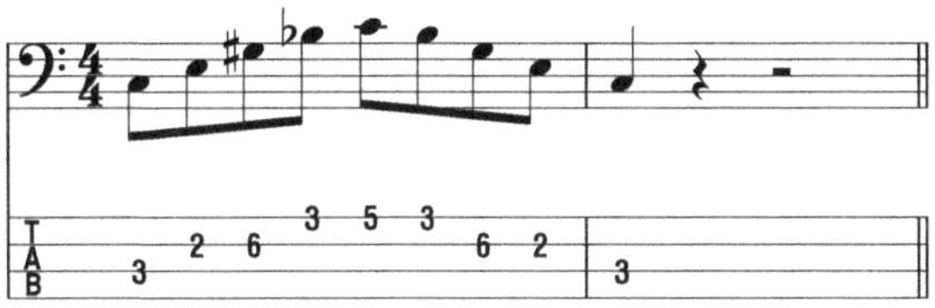

Dominant Seventh Flat Five — Altered, Whole-Tone, Half-Whole Tone, Lydian♭7

C7(♭5)

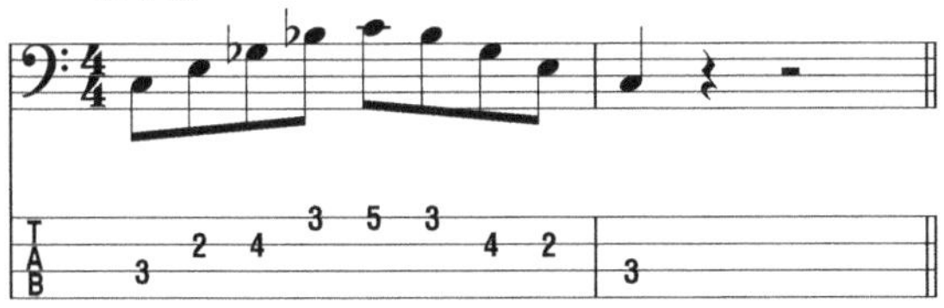

Minor Major Seventh — Melodic Minor, Harmonic Minor

Cmi(ma7)

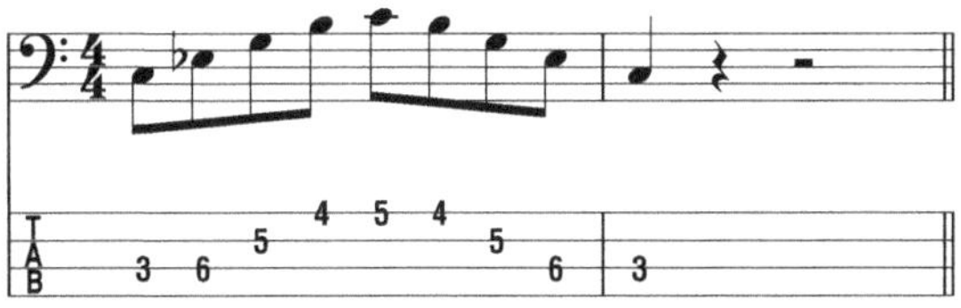

Minor Seventh — Aeolian, Dorian, Phrygian, Minor Pentatonic, Minor Blues

Cmi7

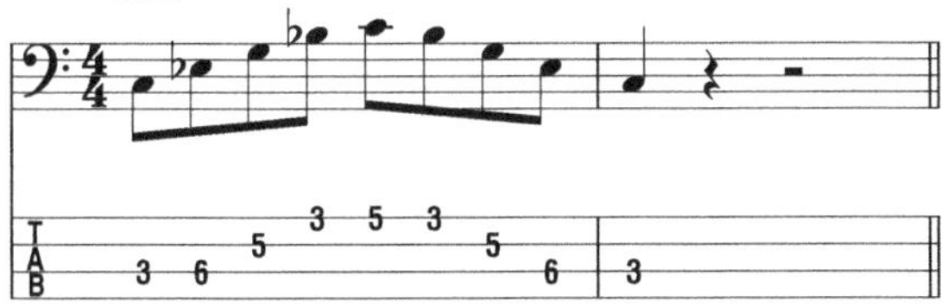

Minor Sixth — Dorian, Melodic Minor

Cmi6

Minor Seventh Flat Five — Locrian, Locrian♮2, Locrian♮6

Cmi7(♭5)

Diminished Seventh — Whole-Half Tone

C°7

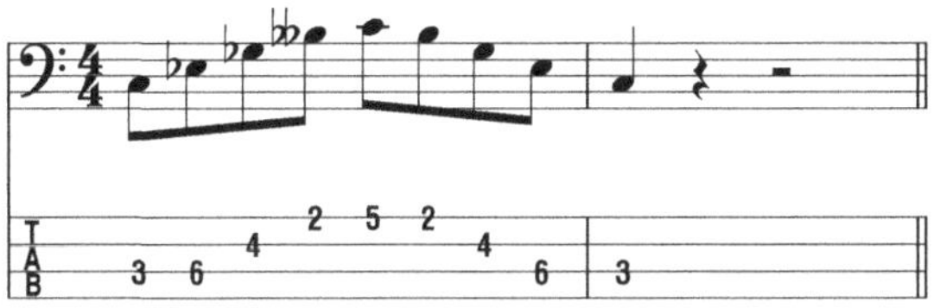

MUSICIANS INSTITUTE ™

MUSICIANS INSTITUTE PRESS is the official series of Southern California's renowned music school, Musicians Institute. MI instructors, some of the finest musicians in the world, share their vast knowledge and experience with you – no matter what your current level. For guitar, bass, drums, vocals, and keyboards, MI Press offers the finest music curriculum for higher learning through a variety of series:

ESSENTIAL CONCEPTS
Designed from MI core curriculum programs.

MASTER CLASS
Designed from MI elective courses.

PRIVATE LESSONS
Tackle a variety of topics "one-on one" with MI faculty instructors.

GUITAR

Acoustic Artistry
by Evan Hirschelman • **Private Lessons**
00695922 Book/Online Audio $19.99

Advanced Scale Concepts & Licks for Guitar
by Jean Marc Belkadi • **Private Lessons**
00695298 Book/CD Pack $16.95

Basic Blues Guitar
by Steve Trovato • **Private Lessons**
00695180 Book/CD Pack $15.99

Blues/Rock Soloing for Guitar
by Robert Calva • **Private Lessons**
00695680 Book/CD Pack $19.99

Blues Guitar Soloing
by Keith Wyatt • **Master Class**
00695132 Book/Online Audio $24.99

Blues Rhythm Guitar
by Keith Wyatt • **Master Class**
00695131 Book/Online Audio $19.95

Dean Brown
00696002 DVD $29.95

Chord Progressions for Guitar
by Tom Kolb • **Private Lessons**
00695664 Book/CD Pack $17.99

Chord Tone Soloing
by Barrett Tagliarino • **Private Lessons**
00695855 Book/CD Pack $24.99

Chord-Melody Guitar
by Bruce Buckingham • **Private Lessons**
00695646 Book/CD Pack $17.99

Classical & Fingerstyle Guitar Techniques
by David Oakes • **Master Class**
00695171 Book/CD Pack $17.99

Classical Themes for Electric Guitar
by Jean Marc Belkadi • **Private Lessons**
00695806 Book/CD Pack $15.99

Contemporary Acoustic Guitar
by Eric Paschal & Steve Trovato • **Master Class**
00695320 Book/CD Pack $16.95

Creative Chord Shapes
by Jamie Findlay • **Private Lessons**
00695172 Book/CD Pack $10.99

Diminished Scale for Guitar
by Jean Marc Belkadi • **Private Lessons**
00695227 Book/CD Pack $10.99

Essential Rhythm Guitar
by Steve Trovato • **Private Lessons**
00695181 Book/CD Pack $15.99

Ethnic Rhythms for Electric Guitar
by Jean Marc Belkadi • **Private Lessons**
00695873 Book/CD Pack $17.99

Exotic Scales & Licks for Electric Guitar
by Jean Marc Belkadi • **Private Lessons**
00695860 Book/CD Pack $16.95

Funk Guitar
by Ross Bolton • **Private Lessons**
00695419 Book/CD Pack $15.99

Guitar Basics
by Bruce Buckingham • **Private Lessons**
00695134 Book/CD Pack $17.99

Guitar Fretboard Workbook
by Barrett Tagliarino • **Essential Concepts**
00695712.............................. $19.99

Guitar Hanon
by Peter Deneff • **Private Lessons**
00695321.............................. $9.95

Guitar Lick•tionary
by Dave Hill • **Private Lessons**
00695482 Book/CD Pack $19.99

Guitar Soloing
by Dan Gilbert & Beth Marlis • **Essential Concepts**
00695190 Book/CD Pack $22.99
00695907 DVD $19.95

Harmonics
by Jamie Findlay • **Private Lessons**
00695169 Book/CD Pack $13.99

Introduction to Jazz Guitar Soloing
by Joe Elliott • **Master Class**
00695406 Book/CD Pack $19.95

Jazz Guitar Chord System
by Scott Henderson • **Private Lessons**
00695291.............................. $12.99

Jazz Guitar Improvisation
by Sid Jacobs • **Master Class**
00695128 Book/CD Pack $18.99
00695908 DVD $19.95
00695639 VHS Video $19.95

Jazz-Rock Triad Improvising
by Jean Marc Belkadi • **Private Lessons**
00695361 Book/CD Pack $15.99

Latin Guitar
by Bruce Buckingham • **Master Class**
00695379 Book/CD Pack $17.99

Liquid Legato
by Allen Hinds • **Private Lessons**
00696656 Book/CD Pack $14.99

Modern Approach to Jazz, Rock & Fusion Guitar
by Jean Marc Belkadi • **Private Lessons**
00695143 Book/CD Pack $15.99

Modern Jazz Concepts for Guitar
by Sid Jacobs • **Master Class**
00695711 Book/CD Pack $16.95

Modern Rock Rhythm Guitar
by Danny Gill • **Private Lessons**
00695682 Book/CD Pack $16.95

Modes for Guitar
by Tom Kolb • **Private Lessons**
00695555 Book/Online Audio $18.99

Music Reading for Guitar
by David Oakes • **Essential Concepts**
00695192.............................. $19.99

Outside Guitar Licks
by Jean Marc Belkadi • **Private Lessons**
00695697 Book/CD Pack $16.99

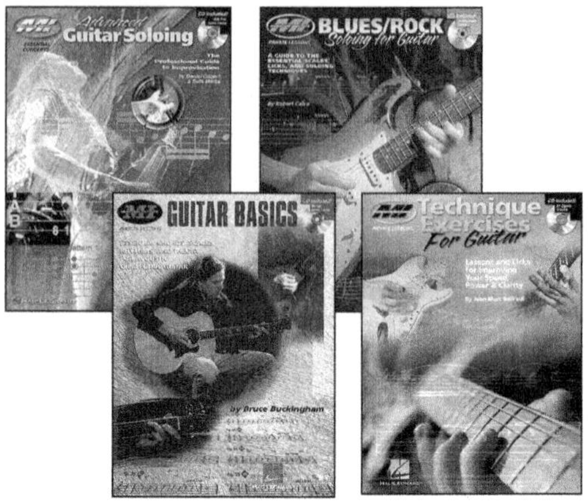

Power Plucking
by Dale Turner • **Private Lesson**
00695962.............................. $19.95

Progressive Tapping Licks
by Jean Marc Belkadi • **Private Lessons**
00695748 Book/CD Pack $15.95

Rhythm Guitar
by Bruce Buckingham & Eric Paschal • **Essential Concepts**
00695188 Book $17.95
00114559 Book/Online Audio $24.99
00695909 DVD $19.95

Rhythmic Lead Guitar
by Barrett Tagliarino • **Private Lessons**
00110263 Book/CD Pack $19.99

Rock Lead Basics
by Nick Nolan & Danny Gill • **Master Class**
00695144 Book/CD Pack $18.99
00695910 DVD $19.95

Rock Lead Performance
by Nick Nolan & Danny Gill • **Master Class**
00695278 Book/CD Pack $17.95

Rock Lead Techniques
by Nick Nolan & Danny Gill • **Master Class**
00695146 Book/CD Pack $16.99

Shred Guitar
by Greg Harrison • **Master Class**
00695977 Book/CD Pack $19.99

Slap & Pop Technique for Guitar
00695645 Book/CD Pack $14.99

Technique Exercises for Guitar
by Jean Marc Belkadi • **Private Lessons**
00695913.............................. $15.99

Texas Blues Guitar
by Robert Calva • **Private Lessons**
00695340 Book/CD Pack $17.95

Ultimate Guitar Technique
by Bill LaFleur • **Private Lessons**
00695863.............................. $22.99

Prices, contents, and availability subject to change without notice.

HAL•LEONARD CORPORATION
7777 W. BLUEMOUND RD. P.O. BOX 13819 MILWAUKEE, WI 53213
www.halleonard.com

0516